G000058939

Ideators

Ideators: Their Words and Voices

BY

PIERO FORMICA

Maynooth University, Ireland

United Kingdom – North America – Japan – India – Malaysia – China

Emerald Publishing Limited
Howard House, Wagon Lane, Bingley BD16 1WA, UK

First edition 2022

Copyright © 2022 Piero Formica. Published under exclusive licence by Emerald Publishing Limited.

Reprints and permissions service
Contact: permissions@emeraldinsight.com

No part of this book may be reproduced, stored in a retrieval system, transmitted in any form or by any means electronic, mechanical, photocopying, recording or otherwise without either the prior written permission of the publisher or a licence permitting restricted copying issued in the UK by The Copyright Licensing Agency and in the USA by The Copyright Clearance Center. Any opinions expressed in the chapters are those of the authors. Whilst Emerald makes every effort to ensure the quality and accuracy of its content, Emerald makes no representation implied or otherwise, as to the chapters' suitability and application and disclaims any warranties, express or implied, to their use.

British Library Cataloguing in Publication Data
A catalogue record for this book is available from the British Library

ISBN: 978-1-80262-830-2 (Print)
ISBN: 978-1-80262-829-6 (Online)
ISBN: 978-1-80262-831-9 (Epub)

Printed and bound by CPI Group (UK) Ltd, Croydon, CR0 4YY

ISOQAR certified
Management System,
awarded to Emerald
for adherence to
Environmental
standard
ISO 14001:2004.

Certificate Number 1985
ISO 14001

INVESTOR IN PEOPLE

*To the young ideators and knowledge nomads of Maynooth and Padova
Universities, who shape the future of their communities.*

Table of Contents

Biography

Professor Brian Donnellan is Vice President of Engagement and Innovation, and Professor of Management Information Systems at Maynooth University where he is responsible for Enterprise and Regional Engagement. His other activities include:

- Chairman of the All-Ireland Smart Cities Forum and a board member of the Irish Centre for Local and Regional Development (ICLRD).
- Co-Principal Investigator in the Irish Software Research Centre, 'LERO' and The Smart Cities Research Centre, 'ENABLE'.
- Funded Investigator in the Research Centre for Advanced Manufacturing, 'CONFIRM' and the Centre for Future Networks and Communications, 'CONNECT'.
- Academic Director of the Innovation Value Institute

Brian's research interests include Technology Adoption, Innovation Management and Data Governance.

He teaches in the areas on topics relating to IT-enabled innovation and Technology Management.

Prior to becoming an academic, he spent 19 years working in the ICT industry.

Piero Formica, a winner of the Innovation Luminary Award 2017, began his career in the early 1970s as an Economist in the Economic Prospects Division of the OECD. He is a Senior Research Fellow with the Innovation Value Institute of Maynooth University in Ireland and a Guest Professor at the Contamination Lab of the University of Padova and the Business School Esam in Paris. He is also an Advisor of the Cambridge Learning Gateway. Professor Formica serves on the Editorial Boards of *Industry and Higher Education*; the *International Journal of the Knowledge Economy*; the *International Journal of Social Ecology and Sustainable Development*; the *Journal of Global Entrepreneurship Research*; the *South Asian Journal of Management*; the *Journal of Comparative International Management,* and *Frontiers in Education*. He has extensively published in knowledge economics, entrepreneurship and innovation. With Emerald, Formica has published: *Grand Transformation towards an Entrepreneurial Economy: Exploring the Void*, 2015; *Exploring the Culture of Open Innovation: Towards an Altruistic Model of Economy*, 2018; *Innovation and the Arts: The Value of Humanities Studies for Business*, 2020; and *Econaissance: The Reimagined School and the Culture of Entrepreneurialism*, 2020.

Alan Barrell has worked in Health Care as a frontline Medical Scientist, in Medical Research, and more recently as Chairman and Chief Executive of large multi-national companies and smaller technology start-ups. His international experience includes the establishment and Chairmanship of a subsidiary in China of a British technology company. He teaches in Universities in the UK, Europe, North America and Asia with professorships in European and Chinese universities. He has raised and managed a venture capital fund, is a business angel investor and trustee of charities. He has been honoured with the Queen's Award for Enterprise Promotion in the UK and with membership as Knight First Class of the Order of the White Rose of Finland for services to Education. His current work is focussed on the commercialisation of research, technology start-ups, understanding Innovation Districts and Ecosystems with a focus on Science Parks and Innovation Centres, together with a special interest in the development of UK–China Education and Trade Relationships. Alan promotes the vision of 'A World Without Borders'. His career experience has prepared him well to be Executive Chairman at Cambridge Learning Gateway. Cambridge and its innovation ecosystem remains a principle pre-occupation.

Acknowledgements

The roots of this work lie in the soil of the knowledge economy, which I have cultivated by working with academic institutions in different countries. I have fond memories of the professors, researchers and students with whom I have shared thoughts and projects.

I express my gratitude to the University of Maynooth and my colleagues at the Innovation Value Institute for their unwavering support in allowing me to proceed along the research path.

My thanks also go to the Contamination Lab, University of Padua, and specifically to its Director, Professor Fabrizio Dughiero, for allowing me to carry out experiments at the Lab on ideation processes aimed at creating transformative enterprises.

To Professor Alan Barrell, founder of the Cambridge Learning Gateway, go my thanks for giving me access to the communities of scholars that enabled me to float the words and voices of innovation into the blue sky of research.

To the journal *Industry & Higher Education* and its Academic Editor, John Edmondson, I owe the opportunity to expound my thoughts in advance in the course of exploration.

Maynooth University, 23 June 2021

Foreword
Rage against the Machine

Brian Donnellan

Situating Humans at the Centre of Knowledge Creation

This short essay traces an intellectual thread relating to the role of the individual in Knowledge Creation from the roots of empiricism to current management theory. I identify schools of thought that promoted modes of thinking that subverted the prevailing orthodoxy of the time by placing the individual at the centre of knowledge creation. Starting with the classical definitions of knowledge, we see a train of thought that identifies human experience as the nexus for action, rather than other approaches that privilege artefact-driven systems solely based on codified information derived from reified forms of human understanding. Starting with the Aristotelian worldview, connections are made to a medieval mystical tradition centred on individual experience which, in turn, laid the foundations for the phenomenological movement of the nineteenth century. Some recent thinking on non-deterministic modes of thinking is then presented as an evolution from phenomenology. The focus is on praxiological methods that are rooted in situatedness and context rather than being encumbered with the inertia of doctrinaire methods based on codified historical information.

The creation of knowledge has been a basic human endeavour since the dawn of Western civilisation. Kelly (2016) pointed out that in Book VI of the *Nicomachean Ethics*, Aristotle identified five distinct ways in which human beings may reveal what is true. The first two of these, ἐπιστήμη (epistêmê) and τέχνη (techne), are typically translated as 'knowledge' and 'skill'. These are two different ways of knowing in the broadest sense, what we sometimes call scientific knowledge, on the one hand, and skill or know-how on the other. The German philosopher Martin Heidegger (1977) gives a helpful exploration of these terms: in their own way each of them means, he says, 'to be entirely at home in something, to understand and be expert in it'.

This bifurcation in the treatment of theoretical and practical knowledge persisted down through the Middle Ages. Early craft-based skills (τέχνη) were supported organisationally by the medieval guild network in Europe while theoretical knowledge (ἐπιστήμη) was supported by the nascent academic communities in Paris and Bologna in the eleventh century. There was little agreement between the approaches to topics requiring combinations of different academic subjects, especially science and the humanities. Wilson's (1998) concept of consilience would eventually address these challenges in the twentieth century but Muslim Andalusian polymath Abu Al-Walid Ahmed Mohammad Rushd (also known as Averroes in the West) devoted his scholarly life to connecting seemingly disparate streams of knowledge creation.

Averroes was born in Córdoba in 1126, and wrote about many subjects, including philosophy, theology, medicine, astronomy, physics, psychology, mathematics, Islamic jurisprudence and law, and linguistics. He spent much of his life studying the writings of Aristotle, whose ideas proved popular but controversial among the intelligentsia in the Muslim world at the time. Averroes identified physicians, and with them, surgeons and opticians, as exemplifying the necessary connection between theory and practice. In his *Generalities* (of medicine) or *Kulliyat* (1169), he viewed

> surgery which is learned through practice alone, and which is practiced without previous study, like surgery of peasants and of all illiterate folk, was a purely mechanical undertaking, and not truly theoretical, and was truly neither science nor an art. But, on the other hand, he specified that following theoretical studies the physician must avidly engage in practical exercises. Lessons and dissertations teach only small part of surgery and anatomy.
>
> (Gea, 2006)

He regarded medicine not only as a science dealing with diseases but also with the preservation of health, the predominance that he gave to personal observations, and the importance of understanding the causes (etiology) and mechanisms (pathogenesis) that lead to diseases. The seven volumes of the *Kulliyat* were adopted as study texts by the best medieval and Renaissance faculties of medicine, such as those in Montpellier, Oxford and Paris (Gea, 2006). Averroes' main influence on the Christian west was through his extensive commentaries on Aristotle (Bodetti, 2020).

After the fall of the Western Roman Empire, western Europe fell into a cultural decline that resulted in the loss of nearly all of the intellectual legacy of the Classical Greek scholars, including Aristotle. It is said that Averroes understood, and interpreted and analytically discussed Aristotle's philosophy more than any of his predecessors or contemporaries. Averroes maintained that the deepest truths must be approached by means of rational analysis and that philosophy could lead to the final truth (Tbakhi, 2008). He accepted revelation, and attempted to harmonize religion with philosophy without amalgamating them or eradicating their differences. Averroes has been described as the 'father of free thought and unbelief' (Guillaume, 1945), the 'Prince of Science' and an early advocate of unfettered modes of decision-making freed from the constraints of conventional thinking and institutional norms. Averroes was buried in Cordova, and it is said that his coffin 'was placed on one side of a mule, while on the other side were his books, which served as a counterweight' (Real Academia de la Historia, 2021).

We see resonances of the Averroes focus on the centrality of personal experience in the works of Meister Eckhart. Eckhart was born around 1260 in the little

Thuringian village of Tambach as the son of noble parents and joined the Dominican priory in Erfurt when he was about 15 years of age. He studied at the Studium Generale in Cologne and at the Sorbonne in Paris. In 1303, he was named provincial of the new Dominican province of Saxonia, and by 1311, he was magister of theology at the University of Paris. Eckhart has been described as the pre-Cartesian discoverer of subjectivity and infinity, harbinger of modernity, mystic preacher of loss of self, detachment, going out from oneself, innerness or intimacy, and living 'without the why', themes that continue to bring Eckhart into comparison with Eastern philosophy. Eckhart is also seen as having anticipated Descartes with his turn to subjectivity in an effort to counterbalance the more rigid prescriptions of the Neo-Thomist revival. The existentialist psychiatrist and philosopher Karl Jaspers presents Eckhart as overcoming the subject–object divide; others see him as developing a conception of the epistemological subject (Moran, 2013).

The Middle Ages witnessed an emerging train of sceptical and critical thinking as well as a growth in anti-intellectualism which originated with Duns Scotus, was fuelled by Averroism and the mysticism of Meister Eckhart and popularised by Cardinal Nicholas of Cusa. In 1449, Nicholas wrote *The Defense of Learned Ignorance* in his hometown of Kues, Germany, in which he states:

> The greatest danger against which the sages have warned us, is that which results from the communication of what is secret to minds enslaved by the authority of an inveterate habit, for so powerful is a long observance of authorities that most people prefer to give up life rather than their habits; we can see this regarding the persecutions inflicted on the Jews, the Saracens, and on other hardened heretics, who affirm their opinion as law, confirmed by the usage of time, which they place above their own lives.
>
> (Cusanus, 1440)

A keen devotee of Eckhart, after coming to Eckhart's defence when he was denounced by the institutional church in Rome, Nicholas concludes with this statement:

> There is absolutely no doubt that your speculation will triumph over all the philosophers' means of rationalizing... For it is only there that in a sort of divine pasture joyfully regain my strength, insofar as God allows me, using Learned Ignorance and endlessly aspiring to take pleasure in that life which for the moment I perceive only through distant images, but toward which I attempt each day to get a little closer.
>
> (Cusanus, 1440)

In the twentieth century, Nicholas's cautionary tales of 'minds enslaved by the authority of an inveterate habit' and his advocacy of Eckhartian mysticism proved influential in Heidegger's formative years. The philosophy of Heidegger explicitly drew on the tradition of mystical theology and especially Eckhartian *Gelassenheit*, translated as detachment or releasement to express a new attitude towards the technological world.

> We let technical devices enter our daily lives, and at the same time leave them outside as things that are dependent on something higher. I would call this comportment toward technology which expresses 'yes' and at the same time 'no', by an old word, releasement towards things.
>
> (Gelassenheit zu Dingen) (Heidegger, 1966)

This releasement from somewhat mechanical linear sequential forms of thinking was further developed by Spinosa, Flores, Fernado and Dreyfus (1997), who described how we need to be drawn out of instrumental perspectives of the world by new thinking modes that are immune to calculative manners of thinking as the only way of relating to the world. This critique was also developed by some of Heidegger's pupils such as Herbert Marcuse, whose book *One Dimensional Man* described a society in which growing productivity goes hand in hand with growing destruction, where demands for products that do not meet genuine human needs are artificially created and where the rationality of the technological society, which propels efficiency and growth, is itself actually deeply irrational. Marcuse put it thus:

> The more rational, productive, technical, and total the representative administration of society becomes, the more unimaginable the means by which the administered individuals might break their servitude and size their own liberation.
>
> (Marcuse, 1971)

In the late twentieth century, a number of influential thinkers in technology management emerged who could be seen as natural successors to Heidegger and Marcuse. Andrew Feenberg and Claudio Ciborra are especially noteworthy in this regard. Feenberg's (2005) point of departure is in the phenomenological tradition, but his Instrumentalization Theory of Technology is concerned with current societal challenges associated with the connectedness of the internet world and offers a platform for reconciling many apparently conflicting strands of reflection on technology. He builds on Heidegger's history of being, whereby the modern 'revealing' is biased by a tendency to take every object as a potential raw material for technical action. Objects enter our experience only in so far as we notice their usefulness in the technological system. Release from this form of experience may come from a new mode of revealing, but Feenberg contends that Heidegger's new mode of revealing had been hitherto under-developed. Like Marcuse, Feenberg relates technological revealing to the consequences of persisting divisions between classes and between rulers and ruled in technically mediated institutions of all types. However, he argues against any conceptualization of technological thinking as in a one-way direction of cause and effect.

Rather, he proposes an 'Instrumentalization Theory' that holds that technology must be analysed at two levels, the level of our original functional relation to reality and the level of design and implementation.

In a similar vein, Claudio Ciborra's work on organisation theory and information systems, emphasises the 'situated' context within which change and other developments take place as an alternative to the functional/positivist view of organisations and technologies. He traces the use of the situatedness concept from the American pragmatist research tradition, drawing on a concept that was originally developed by Husserl and Heidegger. In this context 'situated' is the translation of the German term 'befindlich', which refers to both the situational circumstances of action and the emotional disposition of how you feel in that context. Hence, the original term 'befindlich' not only refers to the circumstances one finds himself or herself in but also to his or her 'inner situation', disposition, mood, affectedness and emotion. Heidegger (1962) states that understanding (i.e. cognition) is always situated, meaning that 'it always has its mood'. In other words, situatedness refers in its original meaning to both the ongoing or emerging circumstances of the surrounding world and the inner situation of the actor. Ciborra argues that the emotional heart of the phenomenological definition had been lost and what is needed is an alternative to the somewhat doctrinaire, sterile approach to thinking about organisations and a return to 'the emotional heart of the phenomenological definition of context' (Ciborra, 2004). He drew from Heidegger's analysis of a 'situation' as having three senses – a sense of content; a sense of relation and a sense of actualisation or enactment. Critically, the sense of actualisation or enactment is linked to the happening and the situation as an action, and this key dimension guarantees a study of the situation as part of the stream of life and not as an objectifying desk exercise. Furthermore, the sense of enactment captures other fundamental dimensions of the situation and its temporality: a sense of history and a sense of embodiment.

Situatedness has also found a role to play in a relatively recent management theory that has been developed to explore the complexities of modern economies and uncertainties surrounding emerging phenomena. The theory has been called *chemin faisant* (path-making or road-making) and refers to a process of designing and implementing an organisational strategy where the strategy is adapted as it is implemented in order to take advantage of situations that emerge along the way (Avenier, 1997). This adaptation is based on progress assessments which deal with the feedback from the actions taken, the possibly unforeseen changes in the context and the relevance, or not, of maintaining the aims of the strategy in the new context as it has evolved. The concept was developed in 1996 and central to this approach is the idea of a 'liberated company', offering not a turnkey management model but a managerial philosophy based on principles of trust, autonomy, initiative, accountability, self-control and collective intelligence. The key to success lies in activating these principles at the level of the individual by keeping them in dialogical tension with antagonistic principles like control, governance and process-based thinking.

And so, it can be claimed that an appreciation of the importance of individual agency and the need for a reflexive approach to dealing with emergent technological phenomena has persisted down through the ages. Sheila Jasano (2020), in her recent essay on the risks of society being led by technocracy, reminds us that this is an era of unprecedented convergence across multiple fields, propelled by breakthroughs in nano-, bio-, information, and cognitive sciences and technologies (Roco & Bainbridge, 2003). She identifies three risks associated with what she sees as a current inclination towards technocracy-led thinking:

- *Technology leading society*: This belief encourages an unthinking and unreflective extension of the power of engineering. It assumes that the new is good in itself and disruption is the path of virtue.
- *The Mt. Everest syndrome*: This view assumes that if engineers can do something, then, as with climbing the highest mountain ('because it's there'), they should do it. This way of thinking may yield short-term benefits for some, but it does not ensure that innovation will serve the needs of the wider human community.
- *Value-free Engineering*: The third temptation is to insist that engineering design is value-free and merely a tool for solving problems. This conviction avoids reflection on how and why engineers choose the problems they wish to solve. It marches hand in hand with the perception that technological failures are due to misuse or abuse.

At the heart of Jasano's work is a cry for greater reflexivity on how technocracy is shaping our world, based on the Socratic maxim of 'know thyself', which would stimulate critical reflection on all aspects of research and practice.

This short essay has traced a lineage of thinking that 'situates' the Human Being at the centre of Knowledge Creation and challenges overly instrumental approaches to how we see the world. The essay starts with the roots of empiricism in the Aristotelian worldview which was foundational to the medieval human-centred experiential perspective espoused by the Rhineland mystics. It is then argued that Eckhartian mystical theology with its emphasis on human experience laid the platform for phenomenology's rejection of the subject–object divide. Then a link is established between Heidegger's history of being and recent technology management theory as exemplified by Feenberg and Ciborra. Finally, we see that today's emphasis on context and situatedness is reflected in 'chemin faisant' management theory and Jasano's pleas for greater reflexivity in how we respond to the challenges of technocracy-led thinking.

References

Avenier, M. J. (1997). *The "road-making" strategy*. Paris: Economica.

Bodetti, A. (2020). How Averroes bridged the east and the West. *Inside Arabia*, June 6.

Ciborra, C. U. (2004). Getting to the heart of the situation: The phenomenological roots of situatedness. Interaction Design Institute Ivrea, Symposium 2005.

Cusanus, N. (Nicholas of Cusa) (1440). *De Docta Ignorantia* [*On Learned Ignorance.*]. 12 February. Minneapolis, MN: The Arthur J. Banning Press, 1981.

Feenberg, A. (2005). Critical theory of technology: An overview. *Tailoring Biotechnologies*, *1*(1), 47–64. Winter.

Gea, J. (2006). Averroes, rationalism and systematization in medicine. *Open Respiratory Archives*. doi:10.1016/j.opresp.2020.06.002

Guillaume, A. (1945). *The legacy of Islam.* Oxford: Oxford University Press.

Heidegger, M. (1962). *Being and time* (p. 182). Oxford: Blackwell Publishing.

Heidegger, M. (1966). *Discourse on thinking* (p. 54). New York, NY: Harper & Row.

Heidegger, M. (1977). The question concerning technology. In *The question concerning technology and other essays*. Tr. W. Lovitt (p. 13). New York, NY: Harper & Row.

Jasano, S. (2020). Temptations of technocracy in the century of engineering. *The Bridge, National Academy of Engineering*, Vol. 50, No. S, Winter.

Kelly, S. D. (2016). *Technê, technology, and Truth from Aristotle to Foucault.* A public lecture, February 2, 2016. Dublin: Lochlann Quinn School of Business.

Marcuse, H. (1971). *One-dimensional man: Studies in the ideology of advanced industrial society* (pp. 1–18). Boston, MA: Beacon Press.

Moran, D. (2013). Meister Eckhart in 20th-century philosophy. In J. M. Hackett (Ed.), *A companion to Meister E. Ckhart. Brill's companions to the Christian tradition* (Vol. 36). Leiden: Brill.

Real Academia de la Historia. (2021). Retrieved from http://dbe.rah.es/biografias/7043/averroes. Accessed on March, 2021.

Roco, M. C., & Bainbridge, W. S. (Eds.). (2003). *Converging technologies for improving human performance.* New York, NY: Springer.

Spinosa, C., Flores, F., & Dreyfus, H. L. (1997). *Disclosing new worlds: Entrepreneurship, democratic action, and the cultivation of solidarity.* Cambridge, MA: The MIT Press.

Tbakhi, A. (2008). Amr Samir S., Rushd (Averroës): Prince of science. *Annals of Saudi Medicine*, *28*(2), 145–147.

Wilson, E. O. (1998). *Consilience: The unity of knowledge.* New York, NY: Knopf.

Part 1

Chapter 1

Ideators: The Revolutionaries of Knowledge in Action

Great minds discuss ideas; average minds discuss events; small minds discuss people.

(from Socrates to Eleanor Roosevelt)

Ideas are like rabbits. You get a couple and learn how to handle them, and pretty soon you have a dozen.

(John Steinbeck)

Up to the present, man has been, to a certain extent, the slave of machinery, and there is something tragic in the fact that as soon as a man had invented a machine to do his work he began to starve.

(Oscar Wilde, The Soul of Man Under Socialism)

Prologue: The Ideation Field

Enlarging the field of ideation and making it available to a multitude frees humanity from that greatest atrocity which is the inner nature of work in the industrial society. Without ideation, people could die, if not of starvation, of cognitive decline. There are many ways of conceiving. The classic economists, among whom Nicolas de Condorcet (1743–1794) stands out in this respect, urged the reading of novels as an intellectual vehicle for making important decisions, including engaging in the process of ideation. Regrettably, as argued by the philosopher and political activist Simon Weil (1909–1943) (Zaretsky, 2020), working conditions prevent workers from thinking. A reflection shared and taken up, as we shall see, by the poet Wislawa Szymborska (1923–2012) in her speech on the occasion of the award of the Nobel Prize for Literature in 1996.

At the beginning of the first industrial revolution, between 1760 and 1780, Adam Smith (1723–1790), the 'father of economics', was concerned about the condition of work that mortifies intellectual qualities:

Ideators, 3–23
Copyright © 2022 Piero Formica
Published under exclusive licence by Emerald Publishing Limited
doi:10.1108/978-1-80262-829-620221001

The man whose whole life is spent in performing a few simple operations, of which the effects, too, are perhaps always the same, or very nearly the same, has no occasion to exert his understanding, or to exercise his invention, in finding out expedients for removing difficulties which never occur. He naturally loses, therefore, the habit of such exertion, and generally becomes as stupid and ignorant as it is possible for a human creature to become. The torpor of his mind renders him not only incapable of relishing or bearing a part in any rational conversation, but of conceiving any generous, noble, or tender sentiment, and consequently of forming any just judgment concerning many even of the ordinary duties of private life.

(Smith, 1776)

Later, as machines progress, they assist or replace human muscles in their work, the Scottish historian and essayist Thomas Carlyle (1795–1881) wrote in 1829:

It is the age of machinery....; the age which.... teaches, and practices the great art of adapting means to ends. Nothing is now done directly or by hand; all is by rule and calculated contrivance.... On every hand, the living artisan is driven from his workshop to make room for a speedier, inanimate one. The shuttle drops from the fingers of the weaver and falls into iron fingers that ply it faster... There is no end to machinery... For all earthly, and for some unearthly, purposes, we have machines.

(*Lapham's Quarterly*, 2021)

In a tomorrow bereft of new ideas sprouting from the human brain, machines could ideate. That would be the case if human beings, concerned only with making machines germinate ideas, were no longer concerned with thinking. It will be the mind-expanding ideation of many ideators that will give impetus to the post-pandemic economy. This goal is reachable if fewer and fewer people occupy predetermined and fixed positions in companies. Ideation requires flying like butterflies from one side of the organisation to the other. It is the movements of people that will raise waves of disturbance, anticipating change, in the flat sea of the hierarchical organisation. Insights can be expected by looking at the industries that, according to Nobel Prize winner for Economics Michael Spence (2021),

seem poised for a period of extraordinarily rapid growth. Specifically, in sectors with a combination of technological possibilities, available capital, and high demand for creative new solutions, conditions will be highly favorable for investment and new company formation. Three leading candidates are the application of digital technologies across the entire economy, biomedical science (and its applications in health care and beyond), and technologies that address the various challenges to sustainability, especially those associated with climate change. Elevated growth in this context means not just sector growth, but high levels of entrepreneurial activity and innovation, a plethora of new fast-growing companies, and large inflows of capital carrying higher expected rates of return.

The research ground has been sown in these areas, and the entrepreneurial harvest can be plentiful if the ideators also act as knowledge entrepreneurs.

By moving from the economy of mass production to knowledge-driven entrepreneurship, value creation is embedded in the lifeblood of ideas in action (the 'ideation'), combined, shared with investors, disseminated territorially and adapted to the conditions of individual communities. Knowledge multiplies when it is shared. Its energy feeds the mental models that map knowledge. Collaborative efforts are incentives not to collude but to combine cooperation and competition to increase the forces working for the general interest of the knowledge society.

Knowledge clusters occupy the very centre of a society attentive to new ideas, findings and opportunities. Entrepreneurial ideators, embedded in knowledge clusters, devise commercially viable and growing knowledge-intensive businesses unbounded by geography and culture. Adept at tapping into the global talent pool, those ideators contribute to raising and crossing cultural integration and creative entrepreneurship. That is how knowledge clusters take shape as uniquely human twenty-first-century urban ecology driven by the culture of entrepreneurialism imbued with a passion for ideating (Formica, 2003).

The Double Track of the Ideation Process

Ideation is an adventure. In order to conceive, do we get on the train that runs along the data track? Or do we take the train on the track of subjective experience, of the sphere of thoughts that are alien to what Adam Smith called 'political arithmetic' that tinkers with numbers (Williams, 2020)? There are bare facts and data, supposed, apparent, accepted, expected, reported. There is, therefore, a polygamous love that forces us to proceed with setbacks and reversals. Our magic lamp to take the best route is curiosity, which challenges conventional wisdom.

From the window of the first train, we see what is: data and thoughts that descend from them. We are trying to map better, in more detail, the known territory. We started with hypotheses, then confirmed by data. In the end, we got measurements, Enrico Fermi would say. Travelling on the second train, we envision the panorama we would like to see. Our adventure does not involve mapping what exists, but in conjecturing and, if anything, discovering new territories: what we would like reality to be.

In *The Little Prince* (1943/1995), the French writer Antoine de Saint-Exupéry (1900–1944) pens: 'adults are obsessed with facts and figures and fail to understand the real meaning of things'. Facts that narrow the field of imagination can lead to confusing one thing for another: in the words of the Little Prince, to mistaken for a hat a boa snake that has swallowed an elephant. To not make such gross errors, reading helps us peel a book and discover the very precious part under the 'peel' (librum is the inner part of the tree bark). It is precious because it is white and can therefore be used for writing on. Those who do so annotate, comment in the margins, reproduce real or imagined things with marks. These are the marginalia that readers over the centuries have produced for sometimes personal, sometimes public purposes. In *Il libro altruista: Metodo per la generazione di un'opera annotata ad elevata fruibilità*, Vincenzo Naclerio (2020) opens the debate on the vast panorama of marginalia. The stories written by a humanist might entice a scientist to annotate new musings and vice versa. Beyond the boundaries drawn by the author, one enters the vast territories of the reader's imagination where extraordinary works of thought can manifest themselves. Einstein said that reading the Scottish philosopher David Hume's writings helped him formulate the theory of special relativity. In the oasis of reading and writing, one pauses quietly and thinks deeply, making ideas collide and then merge into unexpected combinations. A book is a vehicle for the transmission, the sharing of ideas and their constructive contrast.

Ideators, Those Who Sprout Ideas: The Case of the World's First Geographic Society

Ideators turn knowledge into action that yields in the marketplace innovation-based advantage. Ideators spontaneously gather in a community of practices, a constituency of many different characters. This community harnesses creativity and promotes the cross-fertilisation of ideas. A compromise between individuality and group harmony reduces personal antagonism induced by affective conflicts and facilitates confrontation through cognitive conflicts whose intellectual disagreement produces energy conveyed to the ideation process.

The seventeenth-century geographer, Father Vincenzo Coronelli (1650–1718) of the Order of Friars Minor in Venice, was the catalyst of a community of practice, the Cosmographic Academy of the Argonauts. Under various forms of participation, that community included princes, illustrious savants all over Europe, merchant-politicians and explorers who were the vanguard of European power. Thanks to geographic information obtained inside the community, Coronelli improved his cartographic and printing workshops in the Franciscan convent in Venice.

Traditions, beliefs, norms, values and artefacts: these are the seeds of the culture that cultivates the mind. When culture yearns to be the engine of evolution, it goes around new experiences, it runs 'all the orb of science', as the philosopher Giambattista Vico (1668–1744) would say. He recommended young people to compare all ideas 'because the variety of doctrines helps discoveries and advises the right choice' (Tommaseo, 1985).

The co-evolution of ideas (the content) and their historical, social, organisational and institutional forms (the context) have been the mainspring of progress throughout history. It is the stream of human activity, its flow of energy as described by Isabel Paterson (1886–1961) in *The God of the Machine* (1943/2003), her treatise on political philosophy, that makes possible the co-evolution featuring one civilisation from the next. Fifty years or so later, the time had come to reappraise that theme. In their celebrated book, *The Knowledge Creating Company*, Nonaka and Takeuchi (1995) portrayed the Paterson's flow of energy as a flow of knowledge.

The energy circuit of the sailing-ship era or that of the iron-hulled, ocean-going steamship age differs widely from today. The relentless technological changes and the ever-changing geopolitical and geo-economic maps are the results of the creativity of independent thinking, which, in turn, is prompted by the changes. Cognitive skills come into play, such as rethinking, unlearning and learning several skills at once, transferring the application of skills mastered in one domain to another. The game is played on several levels: collaborating to co-create; critiquing one's ideas as well as those of others in order to stimulate new thinking; comparing the problem under investigation with something else that has little or nothing in common in leading to new insights and results diverging from those expected; wandering with thought to seek inspiration. The players in the field are the ideators, people capable of generating ideas that turn into ventures, not just entrepreneurial ones. They are people who prioritise well-being, with themselves and with the community, in the sense of altruism, which Adam Smith expounded on in his famous essay *Theory of Moral Sentiments* (1759). The ideators replace the workers of past industrial revolutions. The current one is the revolution of knowledge in action, which requires people to conceive and move original ideas.

Renaissance Workshops

A breeding ground for new ideas, Renaissance workshops were mainly envisaged as an ideation field, in the sense that the ideas moved ahead up to cross the finish line of entrepreneurship. It is as if those workshops were equipped with a forge to make the ideas incandescent, and then worked until they turned into enterprises. Likewise, today's idea places should be equipped with an ideal furnace that heats insights, inspirations and mental representations, and then submit them to the entrepreneurial process. That is how in the Renaissance workshops innovative ventures in art, culture, science, and at their points of intersection were forged.

Family habit, societal norms and educational institutions accustom us to be exposed to in-depth teaching. We enter the well of knowledge and descend it to apprehend more and more in detail. At the bottom of the well, what has been learned to be true is a dogma to which we cling. Isabel Paterson (1943/2003) wrote:

> Theories, when they have gained credence, become vested interests. The prestige and livelihood of schools and teachers are bound up in them; they tend toward enclosed doctrine, not open to fresh information.

In the meantime, emerging evidence to the contrary has come into sight. To comprehend and assimilate it, we should go back up the well and come out to see the stars of change. Dogma, now turned into superstition, prevents us from doing so. We move only defensively to consolidate the fundamental tenets of formalised knowledge.

Dogmatism Lockdowns Novelties

Daring and subversive ideators escape the teaching that would confine them to the enclosure of defensive incrementalism and take the path of learning. Having reached the high peaks of ideation, they are the ones who discover the sources of a new knowledge river flowing through creative territories. During the navigation along a course that swerves from the route traced by today's knowledge, those inquisitive minds are impatient to grasp the reality that the 21st century is revealing – which requires intelligence and knowing how to make choices that diverge from the capacity to understand the past century reality. Downstream, the river navigation continues until it brings bunches of ideas to the bank dotted with gardens where the spirit of a new entrepreneurial renaissance is cultivated, with nurseries fed by the waters of that river. In the nurseries, ideas are welcomed by the opportunities that translate them into transformative actions. The events that unfold from ideation are characterised by complex relationships in a chaotic and teeming melting pot of cultures and provenances.

Prominent Advocates for Learning: David Hume, Giovanni Papini and Mahatma Gandhi

David Hume, in the eighteenth century, wrote:

> Learning has been as great a Loser by being shut up in Colleges and Cells, and secluded from the World and good Company.
> (Of Essay – Writing. https://davidhume.org/texts/empw/ew)

1919

The Italian intellectual Giovanni Papini published a pamphlet, *Chiudiamo le scuole* (*Let's shut down the schools*), arguing that schools should be transformed into experimental labs, where teachers and students can ask previously unconceivable questions and learn together from mistakes.

In Italy, we have to wait about 100 years to see the birth at the University of Padua of the Contamination Lab. This learning institution gives way to the personalisation of learning. The Lab bypasses the trap of memorisation, emphasises trans-disciplinary exploration, practises trans-disciplinary skills, cultivates divergent thinking, tests creative capacities and trains in empathic communication. Protagonists are the students who, among themselves, with mentors and companies, practice the experimentation of ideation processes.

1921

Mahatma Gandhi (1869–1948) claimed that schools must enable students to think with their head. He insisted on learning as a source of reasoning in the 1920s, accusing the teaching given in Indian schools by the English government to educate Indians to become clerks and interpreters. The world-renowned thinker and activist so argued in the weekly paper on *Young Indian*, 1 June 1921, a famous Indian magazine of that time, wrote:

> The worst thing that can happen to boys in school is to have to render blind obedience to everything the teacher says. On the contrary, if teachers are to stimulate the reasoning faculty of boys and girls under their care, they would continuously tax their reason and make them think for themselves....
>
> (Fisher, 1962)

Self-Portrait of the Ideator

Prosilient and Versatile

I am the Ideator, gifted with a prosilient and versatile character, trained to live in the certainty of uncertainty, devising the most varied scenarios and drawing actions to be put in place. I combine science and entrepreneurship, and both with nature, pursuing multiple and multi-faceted knowledge associated with the ability to get up high, seeing further and then jumping and leaping forward.

The Ideators are representative figures of the ages ranging from the Renaissance to the Enlightenment, the 'long eighteenth century' (1685–1815) – a time frame that has produced profound discontinuities. We are the polymaths of the twenty-first-century cognitive revolution, engaged in broad and different fields of study and work, applying mental models that link them. Like the three princes of Serendip (the ancient name of Sri Lanka), we make discoveries, by chance and sagacity, of things we were not looking for. To practice serendipity, we grow restless. Our desire is to keep moving because one cannot stumble into something unexpected by standing still. The heart of the new era beats to the rhythm of our avant-garde. As educators, scientists, artists, literati, innovators and entrepreneurs, we are the ultimate athletes of social progress fuelled by sustainable and environmentally friendly economic development in the current time of revolutionary changes.

While nature calls into question human beings' behaviour towards it, humans see their economic security threatened. The Ideators contrast the '+' of producing ideas to the '−' sign of job losses. These, first of all, come from inside us. I extract them as the Scottish philosopher David Hume (1711–1776) would do, tapping into the power of imagination, creativity, passion and wisdom. Unlike Meno (c. 423–c. 400 BC) – a young aristocrat, Socrates's interlocutor – I go in search of what is unknown, even though not knowing what I have to look for.

Storyteller

I am a storyteller of provisional truths that create disorder, leaving listeners speechless. Numbers and graphs come later because a bundle of facts and data is not knowledge, like a pile of stones is not a house: what I learned from the French mathematician Jules Henri Poincaré. It is the right part of the brain that I activate. For the left one, logic and rationality could be the computer performing better than humans do.

I move beyond the interaction of the two bits of intelligence, mine and the computer. The awareness of the community strength in defence of consolidated interests pushes me to dialogue with the collective brain of small teams, intimate groups able to influence the community's behaviour on a large scale. If new ideas are locked in a ghetto, their energy does not reach the general public. Those responsible for allocating resources in research and development would conform to the will of the majority. My intellectual exploration would not bring about the change imagined as the innovation stemmed from the original thoughts would remain at the starting blocks. Therefore, the needed investments in health, environment and education called for by the voice of nature, which I listen carefully, would not be implemented. Such an outcome would leave me very disappointed and prostrate since I intend to put my skills into practice for a specific purpose. The aim is to respond positively to nature's voice and act accordingly to achieve a value proposition in contrast to the current trend with a few producers who make fortunes, many low-paid workers, and the voice of nature unheard.

Conversationalist

The conversation of humans with nature demands ideators who shun the pedantry of experts. These spread their books and words everywhere, creating a vortex of exegesis of interpretations. The swarming of reciprocal comments, altercations, and excessive attachment to forms overwhelms and suffocates the listener. Otherwise, the ideators are conversationalists who enter cognitive territories distant from their own and collaborate to eliminate the background noises caused by ideas colliding with each other. The naturalist Charles Darwin rode the wave of the economist Thomas Malthus in elaborating the theory of evolution. In Darwin's words, as cited by Callum Williams (2020), 'I happened to read for amusement Malthus's *Population* [and] it at once trucked me that…favourable variations would tend to be preserved and unfavourable ones to be destroyed. The result of this would be the formation of a new species'.

During the conversation, signals are intercepted, pointing the way to the topic's solution under discussion. Thus, the transmission and expansion of knowledge in the conversation's course reinforce each other, leading to discoveries such as the DNA molecule structure that earned biologists Francis Crick and James Watson the Nobel Prize for medicine in 1962.

I Am the One Who Asks Questions

The worker answers the questions. As the British economist John Maynard Keynes used to say, I ask questions to escape from the old ideas, 'which ramify into every corner of our minds'. The former grows the expertise, taking advantage of the experience accumulated to innovate with the constraint of maintaining the existing structures. By strapping a pair of wings to those structures, some incremental innovators think they have built a plane, ironically observed Professor Clayton Christensen (1952–2020; 1997), the well-known author of *The innovator's dilemma*. I fear becoming a stupid expert when two twin revolutions, one of knowledge and the other of technology, lay bare the worker who does not know how to react to the challenges posed by those twins. They are the ideators who reinvent themselves by asking questions and then discovering original answers, which spawn work that the humans will do better than the algorithm.

Flying as High as Icarus

The industrial revolution has created jobs. With the knowledge revolution, I, the ideator, replace the worker. I transport thoughts from one mind to another. Great traveller on a par with the philosopher and scientist René Descartes (1596–1650), I open the great book of the world interacting with people of diverse temperaments and all walks of life. The mutual exchange makes them get new knowledge. The more knowledge is being gained, the more one is aware that much remains to be discovered. Progress reveals itself in my occupation. It is no longer the inhuman toil of which Cesare Pavese (1906–1950; 1968) poetised. Driven by talent, not just man-hours, I fly as high as Icarus. If the sun's rays were to melt the wax used to fix the wings, I would detect a design or manufacturing defect and search for a remedy.

Co-ideator

I am connected to buyers to co-ideate products and services – a whole different scenario from what the Fordist factory has designed, zeroing out the employee's entrepreneurial potential. With the digital revolution underway, not from the separation but the interweaving between the human mind and artificial intelligence, superior performance will be obtained, acquiring new knowledge that would otherwise not be obtainable. The society of managers and employees is retreating as the communities of those who do it themselves advance by leveraging the growing power of new technologies – the 'DIY (Do-It-Yourself)-ers' mentioned by Diamandis and Kotler (2011). The ideators' professions are activities of thought carried out in digital and hybrid form, merging the worlds of bytes and atoms.

Owner of ideas that turn into actions, each person can be an ideator engaged in the creation and experimentation of concepts to share and develop with others. Thus, we the ideators trigger fundamental innovation processes followed by plummeting product development costs. There is in embryo a high birth rate of entrepreneurial realities in life sciences, energy and the cleantech capable of bringing beneficial effects to the whole living world. So, I am engaged with many independent manufacturers willing to share ideas, finance and co-own new shops. As with manufacturing in the past, we have a marketplace outside the door: just taking short online walks around the world, surfing the Internet and acting like sea turtles, which explore faraway places and then lay their eggs (ideas and projects) at home.

Opening Up Unthinkable Possibilities

Ideators aspire to be successful people wandering in uncertainty and doubt by not clinging to reason supported by facts. This quality, which the British poet John Keats (1795–1821) called 'negative capacity', attributing it in the highest degree to William Shakespeare (1564–1616), is the hotbed of the cognitive revolution that follows the digital one. As happened in the Renaissance, our protagonists' intellectual impetus is a new way of creating; it makes us see the world with fresh eyes. The ideators' alternative viewpoints first conflict and then converge, through cognitive flexibility, on a scenario that opens up unthinkable possibilities.

The French scientist and man of letters Bernard Le Bovier de Fontenelle pushes us towards the time when the moderns (the ideators) will overtake the ancients (the workers), mending their ways. You can already glimpse the figures of the ideators who transfer thoughts from one mind to another through me. This strategy brings about the creation of a micro-ecosystem of ideators and their followers. They all are focussed on producing projects supported by a sense of possibility, which means motivation and intuition. Those projects mobilise intangible resources such as know-how, patents and trade-marks, images and fashions, roles, networks and new conceptions.

We, the Ideators, Contrast the Plutocrats of Ideas

The ideators play a role that transcends the boundaries of the economic arena. The most determined and fearful opponents of the plutocrats of ideas promote the free movement and evaluation of arguments. The plutocrats, holding a high financial position, exert a decisive influence on political and social life by being carriers of unobjectionable ideas, not subordinate to cognitive conflicts. Their voices' strength produces many exits, i.e. ideas that are kicked out once they enter the listening circuits, suffocated. Only those who amplify the voice of the plutocrat have a voice. The same voice repeated thousands of times. Hence, the enormous disparities in political and, therefore, decision-making influence. The plutocrat of ideas decides the well-living and the well-being of a multitude. The result is disparities measurable by the metres of wealth, income, schooling and many other facets of inequality. The phenomenon is devastating in communities with deep roots of feudal culture and in those where media gurus, also plutocrats as theatrical characters, rule the media stage, their echo chamber.

The Ideator Seen from the Outside

There Is a Profound Difference between Working and Ideating

By working, we draw on and exploit what nature allows us to take. Working is labour, hard work 'to make a way through the raw material, hollowing it out, transporting it, transforming it. And where there is no effort, there is no work' (Morselli, 1976).

By ideating, we create and perform an act of rebellion. We have electricity not because we have made continuous improvements to candles but because we have devised solutions outside the false identity between product (candle) and function (to make light, to illuminate). Ideate is a lumen, i.e. the source that illuminates, allowing us to distinguish the function from the product.

From the Winter of Our Discontent to the Shining Summer

In Shakespeare's Richard III footsteps, an offspring of ideators will change the winter of our discontent into the glorious summer. In the face of unexpected events of a great magnitude, discouragement comes from not knowing. In 1665, Cambridge University closed because of the plague. Isaac Newton was one of the students forced home. His family, among the wealthiest leaving the city, took refuge in the country estate. There Isaac spent the year of the plague, pulling out ideas for infinitesimal calculus and motion laws.

What we know is often a projection of the past. Not knowing is an opening to a future not defined by the past; it is, therefore, an encouragement. The past is not only what has been but also a presence. The past changes as we revisit it through the interpretation of experiences and undertaken experiments. Ideas are not born out of anything; they take shape by comparison and contrast with time. It is decisive not to stand still, for not moving one does not stumble over the bone of a new idea. Initially, the Renaissance fed on the discovered ancient texts. The Humanists who uncovered them used them as sources of inspiration for a formidable intellectual surge of revolutionary ideas.

Seeing through the Eyes of a Child

The ideas in people's heads are the driving force behind change. No amount of planning can keep them down. The ideators look at the world as if they were seeing it for the first time. Their visions – Vladimir Nabokov would say – 'are round as the universe or the eyes of a child at its first circus show' (Grishakova, 2012). To reiterate the words of Saint Exupery, the narrow minds of experienced grown-ups conclude from the accredited knowledge in the fashion industry that the object they are looking at is a hat. Whereas the intuitive mind of children sees what that object really is, namely a boa constrictor that has swallowed an elephant. When the ideators' experiments diverge from known laws-based expectations, their open-mindedness is utmost since something unexpected has been caught.

Human history is all about an attempt – the pursuit of aiming for the impossible and achieving it. There is no logic, for if human beings had chosen logic, they would still be cavemen and tied to the Earth.

Viral Ideas Precariously Balanced between Driving Forces and Restraining Forces

We value commerce that moves goods, capital and people. It is, however, the movement of ideas that is even more highly beneficial. Ideas, like a virus, spread, mutate and evolve, argued the evolutionary biologist Richard Dawkins, to whom we owe the word 'meme', in analogy with 'gene'. Ideators want their ideas to go viral.

The accelerator or the brake? Using one or the other depends on our behaviour. Ideators release the brake, but the establishment breaks, for it perceives a landscape different from the usual in new ideas. Not yet prepared for change, those in power reject novelties. The 'Semmelweis effect', named after the young doctor who suffered ostracism from the medical community in the wake of his idea of handwashing in maternity wards to reduce the incidence and mortality of childbirth fever dramatically, is fought with a culture of communication, reinforcing understanding of the idea with the effectiveness of clarity of the rationale on which it rests.

The Poet, the Scientist and the Producer

In the ideator, the poet who inspires the idea that comes from 'I don't know' coexists with the scientist who tests it and the producer of actions who puts the idea to work. Steve Jobs warned,

> Ideas without action aren't ideas. They're regrets. Every day, most people let hesitation and uncertainty stop them from acting on an idea. (Fear of the unknown and fear of failure are often what stop me, and they may be what stop you, too.)Think about a few of the ideas you've had, whether for a new business, a new career, or even just a part-time job.
>
> In retrospect, how many of your ideas could have turned out well, especially if you had given it your absolute best? Would a decent percentage have turned out well? My guess is, probably so – so start trusting your analysis, your judgment, and even your instincts a little more. You certainly won't get it right all the time, but if you do nothing and allow your ideas to become regrets, you will always get it wrong.

It would be best to nurture the idea and make it interplay and mature with others adjacent to it.

For a New Renaissance: The Calcutta Adda, a Meaningless Conversation, but Not without Purpose

It is equally vital that ideators submit to the rule of discussing and critiquing each other's ideas. The conversation must be carried out in a completely non-linear way, like a Calcutta Adda. 'An Adda is something like a book club, only instead of talking about a book, participants can talk about anything – the train journey they're about to take, the latest cricket game, politics' (Weiner, 2016).

Conversation groups come up with more and better ideas when invited to debate and disagree by developing competing ideas.

STEAM, the Knowledge Tree That Predicts the Future of Ideation

From kindergarten to tertiary education, learning environments are all the more attractive by investing in the integration of creativity, that is, in the alliance across Science, Technology, Engineering, Arts and Mathematics. That is the unprecedented steam engine (STEAM) of the twenty-first century, heralding ideation's future by moving ideas towards action. For some time now, choreographers in California have participated in Stanford University's mechanical engineering doctorate, making robots movements functional to human behaviour. STEAM portrays the knowledge tree with all its ramifications, including creative thinking, future designing, innovations and technological solutions.

What should be the knowledge tree to plant in the soil of education? The one whose name is STEM – Science, Technology, Engineering and Mathematics? 'Root' is synonymous with the word 'stem'. Thus, STEM would be associated with the roots of the tree of knowledge. As a verb, 'stem' means 'to contain', 'to stem'. We ought then to question what meaning attributed to STEM learning. Is it understood, as is often said and written, as restraining classical high school studies, first of all by inviting students not to linger on the shore of the humanities and encouraging them to ferry on the technical-scientific shore? If so, a Ptolemaic conception of the school revolving around STEM would prevail. It would be a matter of repairing the existing system. Otherwise, if STEM were a root, the tree's name would be STEAM, in homage to the E of the engineer Leonardo and the A of the arts.

Cognitive Conflicts

Ideators come up with ideas to meet the multiple needs of life – for example, education, nourishment, mobility, lighting. By moving beyond existing artefacts to meet those needs – for example, classrooms, the food refrigerator, the automobile, the light bulb – ideators redefine, redistribute and recombine resources. Moving beyond the status quo, they enter virgin territories. In addition to clashing with defenders of dominant objects, rules, patterns and relationships, constructive cognitive conflicts arise among the ideators themselves who, by rethinking and unthinking to connect seemingly disconnected phenomena, perceive the world in new ways. The intellectual disagreement that arises in a cognitive conflict feeds, stimulates and renews energies in new insights and knowledge produced by the collision of ideas. Cognitive conflict is comparable to a particle accelerator; colliding ideas generate new ones.

Followers of the Newtonian mechanistic conception of the world, the ideators, pursuing order and rationality, quenched the tradition of superstition and kindled the Age of Enlightenment. Thus, mathematical methods were affirmed. The assertion that they are helpful and true in absolute was rebutted by a mathematician, Karl Menger (1902–1985). He supported the literary and verbal method as a language to express economic ideas. In addition to pragmatic considerations presiding over a method's choice over another, the preference for that language resulted from Menger's propensity to universality. He held the polymath mindset that addresses the entire body of knowledge, embracing and taking inspiration from many disciplines. Karl Merger portrays the ideator as the expression of the universal man who transposes in the economy the literary themes of Romanticism developed at the beginning of 1800.

To remain in the realm of economics, the marginal revolution, the fuse of which was lit by the English economist William Stanley Jevons (1835–1882), who elaborated the concept of marginal utility, was a battleground between ideators. Among these, Carl Menger (1840–1921), father of Karl Menger, about whom we have already spoken, and founder in 1871 in Vienna of the Austrian School of Economics, was a leading figure. His subjectivist approach to the theory of value entered into a threefold cognitive conflict. One with the then predominant idea of data collection advocated by the influential German historical school. Another with the objectivist price theory of the classical English economists who theorised natural or long-run prices of all goods aligned only with production costs, particularly labour costs. A third conflict struck with the Marxist orthodoxy, which viewed the marginalist revolution as an ideological degeneration of the political economy. The marginalists claimed the opposite. For them, marginalism was the foundation of modern scientific economics, thus freeing political economy from political considerations.

From the 1930s to the present day, conflicts between proponents of projects for Unified Science and hyper-specialisation advocates have occurred. With his manifesto of 1929, the Austrian philosopher, sociologist and economist Otto Neurath (1882–1945) launched the project to unify the various scientific fields, leading to a revolution in education, and therefore, to a re-imagining of schools. Neurath's design lives again today in the dispute between those who remain firm in the STEM field and those who would like to give concrete form to what remains in many ways abstract – the STEAM realm. The former think that the intellectual gyms of Science, Technology, Engineering and Mathematics should be better and better equipped. For the latter, the rise of artificial intelligence and digital transformation dictates creatively combining four pieces of knowing (making, thinking, imagining and understanding). The pairing requires familiarity with the arts. STEM changes to STEAM that breaks with the tradition of incremental adjustments. STEAM ideators present themselves as innovators; STEM, as incrementalist (see the corresponding entry in Chapter 4). The outcome of this ongoing cognitive conflict in the various human communities will depend on how generations to come will be trained to be idea hunters to meet the future's multiple needs.

The constructiveness of cognitive conflicts hinges both on the propensity of ideators to consider ideation a contact sport and the environments in which conflicts occur. Ideators in dialogue with each other trigger a process of ideas accretion in quantity and quality.

Ideators are agents whose ideas give rise to events. One idea will leap from its ideator to another agent, who, in turn, will create another to be employed in a different field, sometimes adjacent to the first, in a complementary, competing, or hybrid mode. The resulting changes will have few consequences and will be exhausted quickly if the emerging ideas manifest themselves in environments impermeable to their transmission. In contrast, if ideas enter densely connected networks sensitive to change, the outcomes will persist and multiply.

Routes to the Future

From Continuity to Discontinuity

In the sign of continuity, there is no future without a past. The route will take the future is outlined and conditioned by the events that have already happened. The discontinuity reverses the sequence between what was and what will be. There is no past without a future. The future marks out and traces its path independently, taking past events appropriate for its construction. Renaissance, Reformation, Scientific Revolution, Enlightenment, Industrial Revolution, Capitalism in its various forms (corporate, molecular, family): these are stages of transformative social and productive structures brought about by discontinuity.

Path Finders and Path Creators

In the sign of continuity, there are the path finders. These people follow the knowledge maps, which the incumbents in education and other human activities have designed. Knowledge maps are a stronghold that does not allow disruptive ideas brought by extroverted ideators. Into the well of established knowledge, path finders track paths in those maps.

In the sign of discontinuity, there are the path creators, Renaissance ideators who discover the unknown unknowns that dance the can-can behind their back, as Mark Forsyth (2014) has pointed out. They perform ideation processes disregarding the knowledge maps designed by incumbents. There is no map to be looked up. By walking and walking, they chart a path. So, path creators travel lightly and are ignorant of rules and set ways to do things. They feel accessible to ideate without the risk of being labelled a failure even after failing. The

Renaissance way of thinking recognises failure as an experience to build upon rather than a sign to stop. Their disruptive ideas shake up the existing ecosystem. Unlikely Bologna 'La Dotta' ('The Learned'), Renaissance Florence had no decent university with an academic culture that stifles creativity. So, what I call 'creative ignorance' (Formica, 2015) gave birth to an otherwise non-existent world where there were no set rules, once for all, on how to breed scientific, artistic and entrepreneurial top talents.

Ultimately, path creators are ideators who explore virgin and unknown cognitive territories to create ideas and funnel them into novel channels of knowledge that they map out ex nihilo. Those ideas are rapidly scalable by moving along these paths, and their entrepreneurial transformation is accessible and inclusive. A new and better time and space open up on the horizon. Cognition, the search for a new perception, and conation, the passage to action, strengthen the human mind's power, which voluntarily builds its future by using mental gymnastics to manage uncertainties since what tomorrow will bring is unpredictable.

Nomadic Ideators

The ideators are nomads who, while travelling physically and virtually, have for a blanket the sky studded with dreams that they intend to turn into future realities and for a mattress the ground of knowledge. Along their wanderings, the highest obstacle they meet is not the lack of money. The barrier is raised by the many who persist in maintaining the formula that lets them extract value instead of creating it. Society, therefore, should continue to move along the same path as always. On the contrary, the nomadic ideators intend to measure themselves on all fronts, cultivating the desire to voluntarily put themselves on the line to become autonomous and nurture their self-esteem. Open borders, education without frontiers, new connections, travel to other places and disciplines: these are the ingredients of their mobility, which is not an escape but the circulation of people carrying ideas that enrich society and economy. As they navigate the routes of innovation, the nomadic ideators carry a message of optimism. Mobility practised in this way is an ascent to the plateaus where ideators discover the best unconventional ideas and transformative entrepreneurship articulated in knowledge-intensive businesses is nourished.

Nomadic ideators are pollinators of ideas that run around international circuits. Their nomadism has a long history behind it. As we will see in Part Two under the heading 'Brain Circulation', since the dawn of the industrial revolution, a renewed yearning for entrepreneurship was fostered by intellectual nomadism. In our present times, on the Grand Tour of the World, in which globalisation has – above all – accelerated the international movement of students and neo-entrepreneurs, value is created by the connections intertwined by globetrotting talents.

The nomadic creators meet together in an ideal meeting ground between the strength of imagination and the imaginative man's imperfection. In their encounters, one breathes that cultural pluralism needed for reconciling human artefacts with the work of nature, a precondition for acting for sustainable development.

Ideators: Pro-active Learners and Scholars-In-Residence

> How appalling is that ignorance which is the inevitable result of imparting opinions.
>
> (Oscar Wilde, The Critic as Artist)

Ideators think and act to unveil new ways of being in society, the economy and relationships with nature. To this end, they intervene on the three links that form the value chain of knowledge: discovery, the act of recognising what already exists but that no one has found before; invention, the process of creating something that did not exist previously; innovation, i.e. the processes, products and services that are the evolutionary results of invention.

In the background of this scenario lies education, which prepares for knowledge and infuses it. For the ideators, preparation and communication must occur through learning. As was the case in the Middle Ages, the ideators want to negotiate learning methods with teachers. It should be remembered that in the green years of medieval universities, students organised themselves into unions or guilds. The guilds paid professors' salaries, and each professor had to swear obedience to each guild's head. Students decided the curriculum and the amount of time to devote to each subject, and they could get rid of unpopular professors simply by boycotting their lectures. When, beginning with Frederick II (1194–1250), King of Sicily and Germany and Emperor of the Holy Roman Empire, universities were founded by sovereigns, it was teaching that took over from learning. The answers to be given to professors who lecture on the traces of known maps of knowledge are judged far more important than students' questions fuelled by doubt and curiosity outside those maps. What the ideators resolutely reject.

It is with the wings of 'I do not know' that ideators fly. In the lecture she delivered on the occasion of the Nobel Prize she received in 1996, the poet Wislawa Szymborska said that the 'I do not know'

> expands our lives to include the spaces within us as well as those outer expanses in which our tiny Earth hangs suspended. If Isaac Newton had never said to himself 'I don't know', the apples in his little orchard might have dropped to the ground like hailstones and at best he would have stooped to pick them up and gobble them with gusto. Had my compatriot Marie Sklodowska-Curie never said to herself 'I don't know', she probably would have wound up teaching chemistry at some private high school for young ladies from good families, and would have ended her days performing

this otherwise perfectly respectable job. But she kept on saying 'I don't know', and these words led her, not just once but twice, to Stockholm, where restless, questing spirits are occasionally rewarded with the Nobel Prize.

That is why the ideators rely on those who can support them in their journeys to discover the sources of knowledge. Theirs is a wide-ranging wandering since, as they argue at the Massachusetts Institute of Technology, the university is not the central source of knowledge. New knowledge and discoveries occur throughout society. The movement, never unidirectional, occurs in fluid networks of interconnected agents who perform specific activities and draw strength and vitality from each other. The network is an adaptive system whose agents change the rules of conduct as the system evolves. Hence, the ideators aim to broaden the universities' scope so much as to promote greater diversity. They act not only as proactive students defying convention. They claim to perform in the role of scholars-in-residence as well. In either capacity, we might call them 'Renaissance thinkers' who turn upside down today's edifice of education sustained by the herd-like behaviour of learners and faculty.

Ideators redesign the knowledge value chain by forging path-breaking relationships, born of a continuous 'I don't know', with the world of education and society at large. Their universities, in particular, revert to the medieval future, characterised by being wider communities of scholars, inclusive of students with their learning contracts. If this event should ever happen, we will begin to glimpse the dawn of society so estranged from what work is, even today and in a future without many ideators who have a voice, who are protagonists of change. Poet Szymborska, in her Nobel Prize speech, realistically described todays' society this way:

> Most of the earth's inhabitants work to get by. They work because they have to. They didn't pick this or that kind of job out of passion; the circumstances of their lives did the choosing for them. Loveless work, boring work, work valued only because others haven't got even that much, however loveless and boring – this is one of the harshest human miseries. And there's no sign that coming centuries will produce any changes for the better as far as this goes.

Ideators as Knowledge Entrepreneurs

Progressive, economically successful communities empower universalist values and reject the culture of medieval-style individual fiefdoms concerned only with their well-having. These communities rely on original, shared ideas whose positive spill-overs are reflected in higher productivity and quality growth. Multifaceted thinkers, polymaths familiar with different fields of study, and endowed open minds, ideators creatively resolve complex problems such as raising the quality of economic activity to balance economic values with environmental concerns and assessing the compliance of human initiatives with the conservation of nature.

Their will is to give birth to and flourish knowledge-intensive enterprises unbounded by geographical and cultural limits. Investment is focussed on high-quality projects to raise subjective well-being, symmetrical to eudemonism, i.e. happiness. Original cognitive maps leading towards a future defer quantity to the test of social and life-threatening costs in and on the planet. From this perspective, the usual accountant's measure of profit is worn out. Disobeying this measure is a symptom of a change in the way resources are organised and administered, would say John Maynard Keynes.

Named after the economist and sociologist Thorstein Bunde Veblen, the 'Veblen effect' ends up in a shadow cone. Veblen pointed out that individual demand for good increases as the price rises. The potential buyer assumes that a higher price purports better quality. Capturing that effect for their benefit are the few who capture the gains of quantitative economic growth. Since the early 1970s, decade after decade, while those snobs have increased their fortunes, more and more families have been left by the wayside or have seen their income fall in real terms. We have thereby presented an excerpt of this story resorting to fiction (Formica, 2013):

> The many Manufacturers who had made fortunes with the 'Made in' brand socialized with Mr Snob and Mr Veblen, inviting them to their homes. They learned from both how satisfying it was to own status-symbol material goods: in fact, they rejected anything that was not intended exclusively for the wealthy few. They loved to buy at prices high enough to assure themselves of the luxury and exclusivity of what they acquired. It was then that the prices they paid started to escalate: prestigious properties, luxury cars, yachts, fine art, precious carpets and the rest were acquired and ostentatiously put on a show.

The ideators as knowledge entrepreneurs in transformative action with a high degree of innovation do not have to bow to the pronouncement of experts who would judge them according to rules dictated by custom. On the contrary, in conformist communities prone to vested interests, only ideas that fit nicely into one of the economic domains are accepted. The golden rule set by the experts is that creators outside the sectoral perimetre are not listened to. Worse, they are to be prevented from acting with new ideas to adapt society to changing circumstances. It is then up to the ideators to fight hard to give themselves a voice to set up ventures outside the dominant cultural patterns.

In a nutshell, ideators gifted with the sixth sense – the intuition stimulated by saying to themselves, 'I don't know' – enter virgin territories of thought, not covered by the maps of knowledge, and from there go on to create transformative enterprises. They show a three-fold entrepreneurial trait: their organisation is entrepreneurial, relentlessly seeking new frontiers to explore; all organisation members seize entrepreneurial opportunities; hence, entrepreneurial patterns mould their reciprocal relations. More specifically, entrepreneurial ideators:

- Build trust.
- See the creativity of staff and the capacity of innovation as the primary production factors.
- Create informal networks of alliances. Knowledge entrepreneurs rarely act alone. Entrepreneurs are traditionally seen as individualists. Knowledge entrepreneurs usually emerge from a network of complementary ideas and people (Leadbeater, 2000).
- Forge and handle relationships that are sideways (i.e. where there is no authority and no orders).
- Tear down the human-made barriers (cultural, institutional and geographical) that prevent knowledge sharing.
- Build bridges to different communities and countries.

The creative energies of the ideators illuminate and feed the mind with novel ideas turner into entrepreneurial initiatives that address both product and conceptual markets, such as:

- Knowledge and information systems
- Customer knowledge and support
- Knowledge arbitrage and exchange
- Expert exchange
- E-learning exchange
- Intellectual property
- Economic and business intelligence.

References

Christensen, C. M. (1997). *The innovator's dilemma: When new technologies cause great firms to fall*. Brighton, MA: Harvard Business Review Press.

Diamandis, P. H., & Kotler, S. (2011). *Abundance. The Future is better than you think*. New York, NY: Free Press.

Fisher, L. (Ed.). (1962). *The essential Gandhi: An anthology of his writings on his life, work, and ideas*. New York, NY: Random House.

Formica, P. (2003). *Industry and knowledge clusters: Principles, practices, policy*. Tartu: Tartu University Press.

Formica, P. (2013). *Stories of innovation for the millennial generation. The Lynceus long view*. New York, NY: Palgrave Macmillan.

Formica, P. (2015). *The role of creative ignorance. Portraits of path finders and path creators*. New York, NY: Palgrave Macmillan.

Forsyth, M. (2014). *The Unknown Unknown. Bookshops and the delight of not getting what you wanted*. London: Icon Books.

Grishakova, M. (2012). *The models of space, time and vision in V. Nabokov's fiction: Narrative strategies and cultural frames*. Tartu: Tartu University Press.

Lapham's Quarterly. (2021). *Back matter: Thomas Carlyle considers the mechanical age.* May 2.

Leadbeater, C. (2000). *Living on thin air: The new economy.* London: Penguin Books.

Morselli, G. (1976). *Il Comunista.* Milano: Adelphi.

Naclerio, V. (2020). *Il libro altruista: Metodo per la generazione di un'opera annotata ad elevata fruibilità.* Verona: Edizioni Zerotre.

Nonaka, I., & Takeuchi, H. (1995). *The knowledge-creating company: How Japanese companies create the dynamics of innovation.* Oxford and New York, NY: Oxford University Press.

Paterson, I. (2003). *The god of the machine.* New Brunswick, NJ: Transaction Publishers. (Originally published in 1943 by G. P. Putman).

Pavese, C. (1968). Hard labor. In *The selected works of Cesare Pavese.* New York, NY: Farrar, Straus and Giroux. (Lavorare stanca, Firenze: Edizioni di Solaria, 1936).

de Saint Exupéry, A. (1943/1995). *The little prince* (English-language Wordsworth ed.). Ware: Wordsworth Editions.

Smith, A. (1759). *The theory of moral sentiments.* Printed for A. Millar, in the Strand; and A. Kincaid and J. Bell, in Edinburgh.

Smith, A. (1776). *An inquiry into the nature and causes of the wealth of nations.* London: W. Strahan and T. Cadell.

Spence, M. (2021). High growth sectors in the post-recovery decade. *Project Syndicate*, April 29.

Szymborska, W. (1996). *The poet and the world.* Stockholm: Nobel Lecture. December 7. Retrieved from https://www.nobelprize.org/prizes/literature/1996/szymborska/lecture/

Tommaseo, N. (1985). *Giovan Battista Vico e il suo secolo*, Palermo: Sellerio. Un saggio tratto dal volume di Tommaseo *Storia civile nella letteraria.* Torino: Loescher.

Weiner, E. (2016). *The geography of genius: Lesson from the world's most creative places.* New York, NY: Simon & Schuster.

Williams, C. (2020). *The classical school. The birth of economics in 20 enlightened lives.* London: Profile Books Ltd. And Public Affairs.

Zaretsky, R. (2020). *The subversive Simone Weil: A life in five ideas.* Chicago, IL: The University of Chicago Press.

Chapter 2

Ideators as Path Creators: Their Quest for the Holy Grail of Disruptive Innovation

Thoroughly conscious ignorance is the prelude to every real advance in science.

(James Clerk Maxwell, a Scottish scientist in the field of mathematical physics)

The Tree of Life is agriculture and the Tree of Knowledge is horticulture. We cultivate food, and when there is a surplus of it, producing wealth, we cultivate the spaces of contemplation, a garden of plants not necessary for physical survival. The awareness of that fact is what gives the garden its special, powerful place in our lives and our imaginations. The Tree of Knowledge holds unknown, and therefore dangerous possibilities.

(Jamaica Kincaid, an Antiguan-American novelist)

Prologue: Five Thoughts in Changing Times

Between light and greyness, we live in exciting times that are sources of creative thoughts.

On the one hand, the brightness of the cognitive revolution underway with recent technological advances, from synthetic biology to artificial intelligence (AI) and pervasive computing, on the other, a sort of Victorian memory 'smog age' due to geopolitical tensions, social and economic unrest and uncertainties (from anthropogenic climate change to epidemics). Most people are not comfortable with uncertainty (will the crowds of disruptive technologies crash down on jobs, wiping them out?), openness to the unknown, confident intuition and the freedom of the mind to wander.

With looming trade wars and the vast geographical spread of viruses, the greed market is still frightening.

In 1930, imprisoned in Yeravda prison, Gandhi (1932) wrote,

Ideators, 25–44
Copyright © 2022 Piero Formica
Published under exclusive licence by Emerald Publishing Limited
doi:10.1108/978-1-80262-829-620221002

If each retained possession of only what he needed, no one would
be in want and all would live in contentment.

Around the same period, Keynes' approach to economic analysis helped to
weave a link between greater equity and more robust growth. The more equitably
the economic cake is divided, the more cake there will be tomorrow for everyone.
Sharing is instrumental in multiplication. In the aftermath of World War II, the
echo of this message was heard in war-torn Europe. In 1946, Chester Bowles
(1901–1986), American ambassador to India from 1951 to 1953 and then from
1963 to 1969, published *Tomorrow Without Fear*, a pamphlet on the transition
from wartime to the peacetime economy. The American diplomat reiterated the
favour to be accorded to shared wealth. The logic of 'every man for himself'
would have yielded widespread stagnation.

*Whether caused by economic and financial causes (the Great Recession of
2007–2013), natural events (the Fukushima earthquake) or epidemics (the 2020
Coronavirus), global crises bring to light diseconomies in cost-based supply chains
from which just-in-time delivery ensues.*

These crises jeopardise globalisation, for they erroneously lead people to
believe that globalisation is the trigger. AI contributes to the construction of an
intelligent infrastructure that averts such a danger.

The AI evolution points to a mutation in how trade relations across national
borders are built and assessed. The cost will no longer be the decisive factor in the
design of supply chains. A set of digital technologies, including 3D printing that
makes it possible to create three-dimensional objects through additive production
starting from a digital model, has far-reaching implications.

According to the Ricardian principle of comparative advantage, the regional
specialisation of activities and the innovation potential even before the cost
advantage will take centre stage. By building upon one another's strength, we
all dance together, in a game that inextricably holds together cooperation and
competition in the free movement of people, goods and services. That is how
value is transmitted and multiplied. The world economy is no longer perceived
and valued as a zero-sum game, with the loss of one country gaining another.

*In the time of epidemic, entrepreneurship is in a transition mode, from productive
activities to thought activities – the spawn of restless spirits who leave the field of
knowledge scattered with many wells of fractionated, super specialised knowledge.*

Restless spirits place themselves at the crossroads between the Republic of
Letters and the Republic of Sciences, drawing on those golden resources that are
fresh insights and new understanding.

Thought activities have a profound cultural and economic impact. They are
the vanguard of a renewed age of arts and crafts that arise from initiatives based
on people's ability to improvise and create. Practices of completing an activity as
soon as possible, even at the cost of additional physical effort, fall into disuse. We
do not chase any more fast and easy successes and do not postpone long-term
tasks favouring instant and straightforward pleasures.

Social innovations play an equally critical role.

Among them is the reversal of the belief that a territorial community is a collection of individual workers and companies seeking their way in the direction of the markets. On the contrary, the community economy is a web of intricate knowledge relationships between workers and businesses, between these agents and citizens. The ensuing innovation is the emergence of producers, consumers, users and citizens who consciously carve out large collaborative and social spaces. That would be a sign that technology is not placed at the service of the few, thus fuelling inequalities. A policy favouring the participatory economy would reduce the tide of wealth that swells the coffers of a privileged minority. A reversal of the trend in generation and accumulation of wealth would expand the exercise of the right to entrepreneurship through the sharing of ideas, technologies and values.

On the Edge between Knowledge and Creative Ignorance

The path creator is a creative ignorant: a child who is not content to be taught to read knowledge maps; a flower that fades in a single day if placed in a knowledge vase as large as it is old. They aspire to be taught the freedom to draw maps of the desire to make one or more discoveries.

What is unknown is perceived as something that entails danger; it could inflict irreparable damage on our certainties. Woe, then, to be under the power of the unknown. Nevertheless, once out of our *hortus conclusus* (enclosed garden) of knowledge, the long journey into the unknown will make us discover how dangerous false knowledge is. Enlivened by the spirit of creative ignorance that comforts us in the thought that nothing noble is accomplished without danger, as the philosopher Michel de Montaigne argued, that journey will take us into a future marked by beating the hours of human history's rebirth. It is the time of the turning point towards a new Renaissance. In the words of the Italian poet Francesco Petrarca (1304–1374), a 'return' (*redeat, revertatur*), 'flourishing' (*reflorescat*), 'relive' (*reviviscat*), '*rebirth*' (*renascatur*) and 'resurrect' (*resurgat*). It is time to anticipate the revolt against regularity and order. Going back in time, Charles Perrault (1628–1703), member of the Académie Francaise, in his famous *Paralelle des Anciens et des Modernes* (1688–1696) foreshadowed the Age of Enlightenment and the essayist Bernard Le Bovier de Fontenelle with his *Digression sur les anciens et les modernes* (1688) advocated overtaking the ancients in knowledge.

In the search for freedom to innovate, the focus should be shifted from those who are strong in narrow subject areas to others who observe events, problems and opportunities from a broad perspective. Locked up in the cage of rigorous knowledge, we lack the freedom to look at things directly in a new way and end up treading known paths. In the house of our mind, we do not discover new rooms. It gives the freedom to step out of the cage the recognition that knowledge begets creative ignorance. The more the former grows, the more the latter increases. Creative ignorance goes hand in hand with serendipity. It is precisely on the two legs of creative ignorance and serendipity that path creators walk. They are creative ignorant who embrace ignorance and remain in it for an undefined period to fill it with new ideas. Therefore, they are not scared by ignorance and use it to probe new worlds from which they extract new knowledge. Exploration requires travelling light, without the existing conceptual baggage, and, therefore, being free to indulge in thinking differently, which is the essence of creativity.

Words and voices in economic discourse are too often centred on the existing. Forecasts bear the stamp of what is known. Little or no thought is given to what is not there: what is ignored. The cultural humus of creative ignorance is in short supply. When it manifests itself with the mark of the Schumpeterian creative destruction, the prerogative of innovations that present such a decisive cost or quality advantage as to threaten the very life of companies, that economic discourse is exposed to a bombardment, much more effective than breaking down a door – as the Austrian economist Joseph Schumpeter (1883–1950) would say.

The future of each one of us and of our community lies in the space between the gravity force of facts, which keeps us with our feet firmly on the ground, and the antigravity force of the imagination, which allows us to leap over the hedge *'che da tanta parte dell'ultimo orizzonte il guardo esclude'* (*'which cuts off the view of so much of the last horizon'*), described in his poem *L'Infinito* (*The Infinity*) by the Italian poet Giacomo Leopardi (1819). The neuroscientist Stuart Firestein in his TED Talk 2013 put it like this:

> The facts are important. You have to know a lot of stuff to be a scientist. That's true. But knowing a lot of stuff doesn't make you a scientist. You need to know a lot of stuff to be a lawyer or an accountant or an electrician or a carpenter. But in science, knowing a lot of stuff is not the point. Knowing a lot of stuff is there to help you get to more ignorance. So knowledge is a big subject, but I would say ignorance is a bigger one.

The hedge is as high as the knowledge learned and accumulated over time. Beyond, blocked from view by the hedge, is Lorenzo's *broncone* (stump) of laurel with the motto 'Le temps revient', recalling the passage of the Fourth Eclogue of Virgil (70 a.C–19 a.C) *'redeunt Saturnia regna...surget gens aurea Mundo'* (The reign of Saturn is returning...a golden race arises throughout the whole Earth)? Can we say that a new age of knowledge is the *viaticum*, our supply of provisions and money, for a journey towards the ideal golden age? Has the recent past been a darkening season with unresolved problems deemed insoluble but which, on the contrary, we can answer shortly? We ask ourselves such questions as we stand on the edge between knowledge and creative ignorance. In the bordering, we run the danger of falling into the trap of seeking to achieve incremental results today that prevent us from entering the space of creative ignorance to get superior results tomorrow.

One avoids the fall by adapting to uncertainty while exploring unknown and gloomy spaces. Besides the ability to recover from a fall, some persons add the willingness to cross the border of the original state to go beyond resilience, understood as a quick return to the initial state of a presumed golden age. Those personalities move into unknown territories crossing vast fields of thought where the most diverse disciplines meet and clash. They are the creative ignorant and emulators of the beetle's capacity to adapt, to enter the world that the Cuban writer Fernando Ortiz called 'transculturation', referring to a process of mutual influence that leads the protagonists of change to make their respective cultures interact.

Changes can occur as a combined product of external shock and endogenous phenomena. An external event we are involved in affects our behaviours and interactions within the network of relationships. In turn, our responses inform the outcomes of that event. The reverse process also applies. Changes in individual interactions in networks can shake up the external environment. Vienna, Drucker Forum 2019: *The Power of Ecosystems – Managing in a Networked World*. It was through this event that I met a group of young Nigerian students. With them, I started a conversation about creative ignorance, entertaining them on the essay *The Role of Creative Ignorance* (Formica, 2015). In the following weeks, that encounter triggered a chain of reactions among those students. One of them, Chibuzor Ndubisi, a student of Mechanical Engineering at the University of Nigeria, Nsukka, launched 'Formica's Series', a collection of articles in LinkedIn based on my writings and insights. That has headed to the *Maps of the Unknown*, a long intellectual journey to break the patterns and rules used to deal with problems, open the door to new ideas and give space to creativity. The journey is difficult and can only be tackled by shedding the mental habit of feeling secure in being a member of a community with which one shares layers of knowledge built up over time, and the values and behaviours that flow from it.

In that group of youngsters, I sensed a desire to cross the business case studies' teaching boundary. They are explorers aspiring to open up new paths with revolutionary effects on the market, founding enterprises that exploit the knowledge economy culture. Such an attitude reflects well on an Italian student's fictional story in the third millennium who leaves his country. The protagonist says,

> This is how my generation was trained: looking in the rear mirror – observing and analysing things that had already happened. We learned what we knew we did not know, but this approach ignores what lies ahead and the uncertainty in exploring unknown, dark spaces. There was no thought of creating, for example, business laboratories to simulate and experiment with new entrepreneurial ideas, to balance the emphasis on case studies. So, as you will understand, I had no choice but to flee.
>
> (Formica, 2013)

The young designers of *Maps of the Unknown* have decided to leave for *terrae incognitae* (unknown lands), sailing into the uncharted waters of 'unknown unknowns', 'things that move', 'unexpected events', 'volatility' and 'black swans' – to mirror Nassim Taleb's view in *The Black Swan* (2007). In a voyage of discovery, they have chosen to go down the road of creative ignorance, which, according to tradition, leads nowhere. No one among the knowledgists has ever gone to see if this is true. Our wayfarers have done so with sagacity, serendipity and mobility. The first requires training to be ready in intuition. The second asks the heart to beat fast. The third requires one to set out on a journey into the unknown. They have also treasured other words that harmonise with creative ignorance – words suggested here by the writer Jennifer Ann Gordon Perea, and evoking Friedrich Schiller's thought, the poet and playwright who sees in those who play the fully human being.

BABYBRILLIANT: The quality of being present and completely engaged; curious.

BILLBOARDBRAIN: Concise and engaging storytelling so that people travelling at 75 m.p.h. + can understand your idea in 3 seconds, aka graffiti of your innovation's soul.

INTERPLAYGROUND: A safe place where people can play with ideas, let down their guards and be themselves without fear of repercussion or negativism; an invitation to play; responsiveness to one another; a place that encourages spontaneity and fun; learning through play; a collaborative laboratory.

LISTEN-LISTEN-LISTEN: To listen without judgement; to become very quiet inside so that one can receive new ideas; to become deeply aware of the environment; to listen more than one talks; to perceive things which before were invisible; to intuit.

PLORK (rhymes with work): Work that is play and play that is work. The equation: Work = Play.

QUESTIONANSWER: The right question that leads to and/or contains innovative answers.

WORDWINDOWS: Words carefully chosen to let in light and fresh air, and to reveal the landscape of possibilities.

The journey has led our wanderers to make discoveries, hunting and gathering ideas in advance of numbers and graphs, and made us aware of the urgency of deviating from traditional teaching patterns. Learning the language of the extremes, of the extraordinary, large deviations make the difference. Events supposed not happening, happen. Deviations could be texts, essays, articles and courses focussed on ignorance, which enrich both the literature and learning practices. They come into conflict with knowledge maps and mental structures so far mastered.

As for the literature to be integrated into the students' learning baggage, by way of illustration we cite Michael Smithson (1989), Stuart J Firestein (2012), Mark Forsyth (2014), the present author (2015), Gross and McGoey (2015), and

Holmes (2015). Concerning learning practices, there are courses designed by the surgeon Marlys H Witte, the sociologist Michael Smithson, the neuroscientist Stuart J Firestein and the present author. At Columbia University, Firestein, Chair of the Department of Biological Sciences, is an explorer. He claims that overcoming the limits of the known requires an ability to remain in the realms of the unknown. In his own words,

> I began to sense that the students must have had the impression that pretty much everything is known in neuroscience. This couldn't be more wrong. I had, by teaching this course diligently, given these students the idea that science is an accumulation of facts. Also not true. When I sit down with colleagues over a beer in meetings, we do not go over the facts, we do not talk about what's known; we talk about what we'd like to figure out, about what needs to be done.
>
> (Firestein, 2012)

The Contamination Lab at the University of Padua is equipped with an experimental business laboratory where the learning process takes over the teaching process to cultivate abstruse questions that reveal unusual paths to go. Learning prepares the mind to understand ignorance as something normal rather than deviating from the norm. Learners exploring ignorance take pleasure in not finding what they were looking for, and they are not afraid to confront the uncertainty that comes from the 'unknown unknowns'. That is how the facts classified as immutable, fixed once and for all, are challenged and proven wrong.

Towards Transformative Entrepreneurship

In the long run, productivity drives the standard of living, and its performance depends heavily on investment in digital technologies. If, as some of the world's best-known economists believe, the large firms invest and the small ones lag far behind, productivity gains will accrue to the giants, whose growing strength will act as a Goliath, choking off competition and reducing the pressure to innovate. Challenging Goliath will require a large number of Davids to create businesses by innovating. Will Goliath be able to bar the entrance to innovators or stop them in their tracks? It was not an isolated case that entrepreneur Preston Tucker (1903–1956) clashed and lost to the automotive giants when in 1948, he produced the first samples of the Tucker Torpedo T, a model with revolutionary solutions for that time, including the active and passive safety of the vehicle.

Today, the Davids are buzzing. According to a recent international survey by JA Worldwide (Junior Achievement), which prepares young people for work and entrepreneurship, 53% of those born between 1997 and 2007 (Generation Z) hope to start their own business within the next 10 years. This percentage rises to 65%

for those who have already entered the workforce (http://jaeurope.org/about/ja-worldwide.html). While the traditional route to employment and subsequent career progression is viewed with pessimism by these young people, the falling costs of starting their own business and the desire to master their destiny expose Generation Z to entrepreneurship.

The point is that the ongoing digital and cognitive revolution opens up new entrepreneurial perspectives that go far beyond sustaining and regenerating existing business models. It is a renaissance that heralds an intellectual surge, a paradigm shift, the transformation of entrepreneurship, as the examples below illustrate.

Cloud computing, e-commerce, the mobile Internet, the Internet of Things, AI, machine learning, genomics, nanotechnology and the scientific method are challenging entrepreneurship.

Technology is also available at a low cost. What is high is the cultural risk when enterprise and other institutions have old and perished roots, while new roots are not there or shallow.

- Digital doctors monitoring our health and helping us to prevent diseases.
- Digital companions for the elderly, thanks to robots powered by AI.
- Drought-resistant plants that feed the planet.
- Moisture sensing devices for wheat farmers at very affordable prices compared to current solutions.
- A new generation of solar and storage technologies to make energy accessible and available to all.
- Inchworm-size biohybrid robots.
- Robots made of polymers and muscle tissue.
- Robots and machines that use biological materials to move and sense their environment; get them more robust when they need to and heal when they get damaged.
- Big data to diversify personal education and career development portfolios.
- Internet of Things to improve product functionality.
- 3D printers to build 100-foot-tall rockets.
- Augmented art and other new artistic languages.

Once they reach the boundaries of entrepreneurial lands, exploration can no longer rely on familiar knowledge maps. Beyond, there are unknown lands. To move into them, we have to invent another kind of creativity. Since we do not know how it will work, we cannot instruct the learning machines. All that remains, then, is experimentation to be done without relying on those machines. Transformative entrepreneurship is a target that new technologies allow us to glimpse, and we strive to achieve by experimenting along with an elusive rather than a precise path. New cognitive skills will accompany us on the journey to move from a culture of 'us against them – we win, they lose' to one of interdependence, of 'we all win together – we humans and all other living species'. 'Winning against' may bring short-term productivity gains to the winner, but that victory will in the long run cause fragility, lack of vitality. The balance of damage is even graver if we add the unintended consequences of extracting nature's resources faster than they can regenerate. Believing that a collapse of the whole of human civilisation is unimaginable by predicting only local damage is an old-fashioned and dangerous credo.

The scene of change promises to be blindingly bright with the dawn of three-dimensions quantum computing and the sunset and the effects of Moore's empirical law of two-dimensions digital computers running out of steam. The logic and computational languages that presided over the exponential clustering of transistors on a silicon wafer, as predicted by Intel co-founder Gordon Moore, no longer apply to quantum computers. There are more things in three dimensions, including new entrepreneurial and scientific skills to approach the quantum world in unexpected forms (Fuchs, 2010).

As with Go's Japanese game referred to in Yasunari Kawabata's (1899–1972) novel *The Master of Go* (1972), for a long time now, the games of entrepreneurship have been played according to a set of quibbling rules. They have made the game lose its artistic sense, spontaneity and neglected the value of the players' human qualities and mutual esteem. A return to the old way of Go is desirable for entrepreneurship if we want to grasp the entrepreneurial transformations promised by the double revolution. To believe that the spontaneity of surprise on the journey into the new digital world can be designed according to specific rules is tantamount to losing serendipity, the art of chance discovery whose sensations and emotions foster the imagination needed to solve the problems posed by the transformation. Think of the gravitational force exerted by existing capabilities, such as old technologies and employed staff. Rather than ignoring them, the question is how to use them to turn what would otherwise be an opposing force into an assist. In particular, the attitudes of employees are at stake. Anguished by the uncertainty of their future, they are questioning the transformation, fearing that the conceptual age may lead to the brain's automation in the same way that the first industrial revolution automated the muscles.

With a detective's eye, it is up to the evangelists of transformational entrepreneurship to open up uncertainty paths and get the people involved in change accustomed to following them. They are guided by Socrates's thought, taken up by Petros Markaris (2012). The Greek-Armenian writer of crime novels writes:

> 'Truth is found in uncertainty', Socrates had said. The problem with certainties is that they sometimes corroborate illusions and lead to only apparent truth. Conversely, uncertainty drives us to seek the truth of facts. However, it is also possible that it leads us towards another conviction: that, to put it bluntly, truth is liquid and changeable and that, therefore, its search is an endless one, doomed to repeat itself each time in different circumstances. Incompleteness has much in common with uncertainty. If

uncertainty opens, according to Socrates, the road to truth, incompleteness is the mechanism that sets the imagination in motion.

After all, the imagination must be called upon when the uphill path of specialisation curves and then descends. If one remains entrenched within the silos of acquired knowledge, the loss of vitality is inevitable. It is time to abandon reproductive thinking according to learned technical skills that narrow the horizon of knowledge. It is time to embrace the productive thinking of transversal skills that lead to imagining unconventional self-renewal ways and then taking the path of transformation.

What will happen is shrouded in uncertainty. As we travel into the future, however fast the time goes, let us hasten slowly. While we explore the landscape of transformational entrepreneurship in-depth, the speed of action must be accompanied by the slowness of careful reflection.

Conformists and Freethinkers, Experts and Non-Experts

Conformists resort to laws to guard against innovation. Everyone must remain in their place. Certain professions are hereditary by law or custom, including that of the entrepreneur within the entrepreneurial family. Remaining in one's place, wrote the French historian Jacques Le Goff (1924–2014; 1964), creates 'a society of 'manenti', from *manere*, 'to remain'. A society stratified by horizontal behaviour'. By standing still, conformists limit themselves to satisfying material needs. It is alien to their thinking that the greatest danger for most of us lies not in setting our goal too high and falling short, but setting our aim too low and achieving our mark, as Michelangelo Buonarroti argued.

Europe's biggest economies (France, Germany, Italy, Spain and United Kingdom) are the conformist's vivid expression who feels fulfilled. In order not to run the risk of falling, they have restrained their aspirations. By hesitating and stalling, over the last 30 years, decade after decade, productivity growth has lagged. In the United Kingdom and Italy, countries that have invested the least in the future and thus in innovation, the fall has been disastrous. Suppose one survives by defying death rather than living to change one's own life for the better along with the lives of others. In that case, one fumbles the vital signals emanating from creativity and innovation. Uncertainty, digression, interpretation, discussion, imaginative investment and, ultimately, imagination are not encouraged. Conformists, 'doctors of memory', lose the importance of being open to the unknown and trusting intuition.

The COVID-19 epidemic has made the journey to the infinite field of knowledge even more daunting for the learners who are random wayfarers and freethinkers, wearing the robe sewn by creative ignorance. Freethinkers have to face the hostility of groupthink – the dominant thought – devised by the grim conformists. The latter argue that the opponents' freedom of expression, those who express opinions contrary to the dominant conformist thinking, should be banned as error-bearing. They do not acknowledge the value of disagreement, which is to invite a re-examination of their certainties. It is not recognised that, if they were ever wrong, non-conformist views would have the merit of reinforcing what is believed to be the truth. Nevertheless, whether they are considered mad or lunatic, non-conformists have in many cases opened up views that have gone from being considered fanciful and misleading to being considered thoughtful and correct.

Macroeconomics is an illustrative case of the conflict between conservative conformists and revolutionary freethinkers. During the Great Recession and now in the pandemic, it has been noticed how resistant to change the standard mental model can be in the macroeconomic discourse. In the dominant macroeconomic theory, which has so much influence on the unfolding of the above events, economies are cyclically stable. There is a single equilibrium around which the economy fluctuates. Conformists are anchored to this Ptolemaic conception, claiming to be in a position to repair the standard model once shocks have occurred, but stubbornly refusing to recognise 'multiple equilibria, i.e. that the economy can jump from a good to a bad state or vice versa' (Sandbu, 2021). That would be tantamount to triggering what would appear a sort of Copernican revolution. The narrative about people's beliefs and collective imagination would be set to become a key term in the economic discourse alongside accounts of the volatility of economic phenomena in the context of inconsistent trends, irrational exuberance, erratic behaviours, fads, persistent poverty and many other anomalies. Those stories highlight the value of trust. Economic states do vary in response to the changing expectations of cooperative behaviour within a community. Coordination and shared decision-making enable more desirable balances to be achieved. Conversely, a fall in trust entails undesirable equilibria, as does the underemployment equilibrium.

Conflicts between preservation and innovation of even greater magnitude can be found in education. In this respect, based on a true story, the film *Lessons of a dream* is an instructive tale. Here, the contrarian is a German teacher who returns home to Braunschweig in Imperial Germany to teach English at a school with pupils from different social backgrounds. Konrad Kock, the teacher's name, does not just impart the use of English. He wants to mould a group of young people who value trust, friendship, solidarity and fair play, breaking down fences raised by prejudice and social differences. Our maverick achieves this by getting young people to play football. This completely new sport for Braunschweig's community is a big stone thrown into the pond of the preservation of hierarchy with its rigid rules governing human relations. Administrators, teachers, parents of students and local authorities are united in cornering Kock with his unusual and liberal teaching method, which puts everyone, students and teachers alike, on an equal footing. The culture that subverts the established order is false, dangerous and, therefore, to be banned.

A third example of clashing with the dullness and retrogressive attitudes of conformists comes from the corporate world. The dominant thinking supporters have only one, albeit big, idea in mind: to accomplish the business plan's goals. To this end, they present a document, an artefact in the form of a definitive collection of facts, based on bizarre data, about the enterprise's functioning and market. 'The business plan says so' is a sacred formula repeated countless times. The contrarian intends to go beyond the business plan's limits whose cash flow projections have little or no basis in reality. Instead of insisting on that static document that does not survive the first contact with customers, nonconformists like entrepreneur Steve Blank suggest conducting iterative experiments instead of linear projections and simulating new concepts that describe how the company creates and delivers and captures value. Experiments and simulations transform the way new products are built and launched. The unconventional movement has taken the name 'lean star-up'.

On the journey in search of knowledge, we can then fall into the trap set by socio-economic experts. A trap that non-experts are determined to dodge. Experts aim to gain our esteem, to be rewarded and flattered for their beliefs, for the opinions they express. Sociologists and economists operate in society and the economy, which are not the twins of science. In science, the process of falsification separates the wheat (the true, the excellent element) from the chaff (the false, the harmful element). The scientific explanation of natural phenomena is subject to the iron law of nature, which is indifferent to the theories put forward by scientists. If a specific phenomenon predicted by a model conceived by scientists does not occur, that model is false. High barricades were raised against Einstein's scientific imagination, but these collapsed in the face of the evidence of nature's facts.

In contrast, society and the economy are affected by sociologists and economists' theories and predictive models. Power struggles arise between groups of different schools of thought, disguised behind the ostensible neutrality of academic peer review and intergovernmental organisations. Their outcome will determine which theory and model will be accepted. The ensuing persuasion process on the part of the triumphant experts makes people favour the winning theories' policies. Here is where the non-experts come in. They do not question why favouring the winner. The intention is to ask how those policies might work in practice. Non-experts can do this by being equipped to rethink and even unlearn what those experts advocate. Should they decide to reject the choice presented to them, they may find other solutions, even those not sought.

The Creative Ignorant: Unconstrained Path Creators

In the gymnasium of thought followed by action, encounters and clashes between conservatives and freethinkers, between experts and non-experts reveal another character, the creative ignorant, who deserve to be seen up close.

If we thought we understood everything, our imagination would shrink. We would end up falling into a lazy routine. In order not to stiffen knowledge so as to make it dogmatic, the creative ignorant detache themselves from experience by experimenting with how to make mental leaps. These are the tenets of experimentation:

- Not adapting to existing knowledge to not be forced into the Procrustean bed prevents one from making those leaps.
- Making assumptions using analogies and associations of ideas that are the offspring of the imagination.

It is the power of knowledge (first and foremost if absolute and coupled with precise measurement) that leads some, the path finders, to discover paths as yet untrodden. Others, the creative ignorant, however, take a new stance and embark on unknown paths. They are the path creators. Path creation occurs through a learning process of creative performance that is at odds with knowing. Discarding the known, path creators go beyond the limits of reason, to penetrate the not-knowing space. Where path finders face and manage risk when they decide to set out in search of a path within their maps, path creators live with and embrace the uncertainty and unpredictability of creating a new path from nothing. They do not resort to knowledge practices, rules and handbooks.

Path creation generates a new source of knowledge, a deviation from the usual route and with no pre-existing market space into which to move. Visionary persons escape the 'locked-in success' syndrome and explore uncharted waters beyond the horizons of existing technologies, societal and business models. In the process of exploration, they are keen to uncover facts and data that disprove assumptions derived from acquired knowledge. As Enrico Fermi argued, if you carry out an experiment and 'the result is contrary to the hypothesis, then you've made a discovery'. Therefore, those who create paths do not invest in a strong hypothesis that confines them to experiments which are likely to prove it. We must not forget that *experiri* (to try) was the key with which Galileo Galilei's alleged declaration of *Eppur si muove* ('and yet it moves'), regarding the movement of the Earth around the Sun, which opened the door to the future of science.

Path creators are Galilean characters. Like astronauts contemplating the rotating earth from the moon, they see that the knowledge map is in perpetual motion and rotates around the sun of insights unlimited by the knowledge of why something cannot be done. This different perspective is the factor that pushes them to create new paths off the map rather than find paths within its boundaries. In economic science terms, path creators are followers of Jean-Baptiste Say (1767–1832) for they feed the supply side of a dynamic economy by proposing innovations that involve revolutionary changes in industry, business and the markets, bringing consumers substantial benefits over the products and services that are currently available. The supply of such innovations creates its own demand, because consumers are inclined to spend rather than save in the presence of novel and exciting products and services.

Following the ideas of Karl Popper (1902–1994), according to whom 'future knowledge is not possible in the present' (Popper, 1957), path creators, armed with the strength of uncertainty, head towards the horizon of doubt. Far-seeing pioneers who create innovative entrepreneurship through discovery and rebellion against conformity in business, they appear well equipped to take a leap into the dark of the unknown.

Path creators are like soldier–explorers with a wide range of vision, who proceed barefoot (that is, with no or little monetary and relationship capital), rejecting current understanding and past experience, along a course that swerves away from the route traced by today's knowledge. This *clinamen* exhibits the double characteristic of being unpredictable and of undermining those who work within the horizon of certainty. The paths they create map new trends that dramatically change the direction of an industry: consider the case of path creators such as Apple and Google that have reoriented technology spending towards the end-consumer, leaving path finders like BlackBerry struggling to keep pace.

Path creators and trade routes flourish together. Path creators generate fresh business ideas that stand out from the crowd and travel easily along new trade routes which, in turn, thrive on those ideas as they are converted into smart companies. In China, during the Han dynasty, the Silk Road and the invention and production of paper flourished together. Later, under the Mongols in the 13th and 14th centuries, Samarkand, with its central position on the Silk Road, was the cradle of an early papermaking establishment whose production, spread by trade along that route, supplanted other writing materials. Stimulated by the invention of paper, it was also on the Silk Road that path creators devised printing technology. Centuries later, the combination of a primary trade connection through Europe, the Rhine, and a technical genius with a visionary entrepreneurial mindset, Johannes Gutenberg, gave birth to the printing revolution – the development of printing using moveable type.

Creative, Learned and Purposeful Ignorance

Ignoring is a mindset that has deep roots in the centuries-old history of humanity. Consider this: it is 6 July 371 BC, we are on the Orchestra of Ares Plain, during the Battle of Leuctra. Epaminondas and Pelopidas, the Theban army commanders, ignore the traditional deployment of troops and, with ingenuity and courage, prepare an unconventional strategy. Tradition has dictated that the most skilled warriors should be located on the right flank of the deployment of troops, for the left flank is thought to bring bad luck. In this way the best troops of the two sides never clash directly. Epaminondas and Pelopidas overturn tradition by deploying the most skilled warriors on the left wing. Their battleplan creates surprise and panic among the Spartans and their allies, who are defeated (Scott, 2009).

There is a lack of awareness of creative ignorance – the ignorance which contains a good dose of unreasonableness and comes after knowledge, not before it. Creative ignorance unlocks otherwise unthinkable paths of economic growth and social development, and is potentially revolutionary. As humanity struggles supposedly to eradicate ignorance, those who lobby for knowledge and expert groups push creative ignorance into a corner. It was not so in the ancient world whose scholars and sages pioneered the idea of creative ignorance. In today's world, we need more than ever *Homines Novi*, New Men, who enable us to exploit the strengths of creative ignorance and overcome the weakness of accrued knowledge.

According to the German polymath Nicholas of Cusa's doctrine of learned ignorance,

> ..ignorance and knowledge are not wholly distinct epistemic phenomena, but combine and overlap in interesting ways...The more [a wise person] knows that he is unknowing, the more learned he will be. In other words, learned ignorance is not altogether ignorance, but a kind of knowledge or wisdom.
>
> (cited by Verdoux, 2009)

By purposeful ignorance we mean that attitude of open mindedness which challenges what, according to current thinking, appears to be an irrefutable truth. From this perspective, purposeful ignorance is 'knowledgeable, perceptive, insightful' (Firestein, 2012) – a learning process for cultivating a fertile land of ideas seeded with unexpected questions that reveal unanticipated solutions. So, path creation is the fruit of learned ignorance. The creation begins in the space of unknown questions. To create a new path requires an emptying of the mind of survivor's/winner's bias, past experiences and the perspectives of current experts (Tjan, 2010). Purposeful ignorance is comparable to the echo sounder used for exploration of the seas and oceans, to seize the innermost needs of people (Formica, 2020).

The Pleasant Path and the Beauty of Creative Ignorance

Ignorance is not an exotic plant; it is present everywhere. Just when we think we have eradicated it, it flourishes again. I don't know that I don't know: this is the unawareness that makes ignorance normal. Not being exceptional, ignorance urges us to admit the imperfection of our knowledge. Viewpoints and prejudices that reinforce personal beliefs drive out doubts. We end up, then, fearing new ideas rather than old ones.

Perfectionists commit themselves with the same passion and great skill attributed by the Argentine essayist Jorge Luis Borges to the geographers of Popinga, protagonists of one of his stories (1999). Big Data can rise to essential elements of their reasoning to design a future map by adapting to the signals transmitted from the outside world and received, precisely, from those data. The drawing of that map is equivalent to the exercise of skating on a thin plate of ice – what John Maynard Keynes said about mathematics applied to economics. Nevertheless, if creative ignorance is used as a food of the mind to fuel intuition, it will be possible to avoid ruinous falls by skating on ice.

Knowledge gained enables suitable ways to find an approach to incremental innovation. The smart path to take looks like *The Philosopher's Path* in the northern part of Kyoto's Higashiyama district – a pleasant path besides a canal that connects Ginkakuji (Silver Pavilion) with the vicinity of Nanzenji. This is the path of meditation, with flowering cherry trees in springtime. Kitarō Nishida

(1870–1945), a prominent Japanese philosopher, practiced meditation while walking this safe and enjoyable route. After the blossom comes the harvest. The incremental approach to innovation prompts meditation to find methods that lead to blossom and better harvests. Ultimately, it is one and the same topic: cherry trees along The Philosopher's Path. Incremental repetitions reinforce the rules and the recurring motif cushions the blows of the first surprise.

Let us change our perspective to immerse ourselves in the beauty of the immensity offered by the panorama of creative ignorance. We find our young creatives, some in one garden, some in another. From and between these places, dialogues are woven from which ideas born that are not so minute as dust fragments. The air of conversation is clean and blows in the direction of areas not yet explored. During the exploration, in view of the ensuing cultivation, those young people in the guise of gardeners are respectful of threads woven by nature: those between the tree and the forest, the fish and the water, the mineral and its veins, as the Italian philosopher Emanuele Severino (1929–2020) would say (2021). Likewise, they configure an economic system that counters the forces intent on using labour as if it were a thing, severing the link between workers and their families. By reasoning around creative ignorance to navigate the river of thoughts, the young creatives dispense with the knowledge maps that keep human groups apart from nature groups, with the former in the latter's role of exploiters.

One remains bound for life to mental, conceptual and argumentative maps mastered and to which an absolute character of truth is attributed. New thoughts that clash with the totem are rejected as dangerous; they are made inaccessible. The resolute innovators like Galileo prepared and resolved to act by breaking away from those maps are repudiated. Favour is granted to those in love with their image reflected in the mirror of received knowledge maps. In trying not to end up like Narcissus who fell into the river where he was reflected, creative ignorance gives the mind the freedom to wander. It will give birth to an ugly duckling – an innovation that, at its inception, appears useless and even harmful – which can then morph into a beautiful swan.

Creative ignorance is, therefore, an attractive as well as dangerous point of reference. Each innovator who traces new paths should then ponder these words of Voltaire (1924):

> Our wretched species is so made that those who walk on the well-trodden path always throw stones at those who are showing a new road.

Those who love to venture into the unknown, it is a life lesson to pay heed to the masters who were once pioneers of knowledge. In his memoirs dated 1895–1899, Guglielmo Marconi to whom we owe the development of the radio-telegraph, recounts that he had never attended Professor Augusto Righi's (1850–1920) lessons, a pioneer of electromagnetism. When Marconi told him his idea of wireless telegraphy, Righi replied that it was not feasible. Since then, Marconi never spoke with him about that subject (Falciasecca, 2020). At the top of their field, renowned and revered, yesterday's pioneers remained in place, losing the mental agility to jump from known space to an unknown one.

When the masters' knowledge spreads and becomes a popular belief, both the mockery and the rejection of novelty are heightened. The vicissitudes of the adoption of the heliocentric system are definitive proof of this. The Greek astronomer and mathematician Aristarchus of Samos (c. 310–c. 230 BC) designed the first known heliocentric model with the Sun at the centre of the universe and the Earth revolving around it. His astronomical ideas broke against the concrete wall erected by Aristotle and Ptolemy's geocentric theories and supported by people's belief that there was the Earth at the centre of the universe. Later some Islamic astronomers, among them the Egyptian Ibn Yunus (c. 950–1009), found flaws in Ptolemy's calculations that cast doubt on the geocentric model. In the tenth century, people still believed in the central position of the Earth in the universe. Henceforth, the investigations of those astronomers were relegated to conjecture. When in the sixteenth century Nicholas Copernicus (1473–1543) burst on the scene of astronomical studies, about eighteen centuries had passed since the enunciations of Aristarchus of Samos. It was between 1510 and 1514 that the astronomer and Catholic canon introduced his new idea. Whether his heliocentric model was built independently from Aristarchus or relying on the latter's body of work is doubtful. What is certain is that in those years Copernicus wrote an essay about it, which he transmitted in manuscript copies to his closest acquaintances. This is because he did not want to incur the contempt of many who would have come to know that Earth circle the sun. Only in 1543, under the intense pressure exerted by Georg Joachim Rheticus (1514–1574), a mathematician of Wittenberg, he will publish in Nuremberg *De revolutionibus orbium coelestium*, a work that he had mostly completed in 1532. Such and many other pieces of evidence show the tenacity of the authors of knowledge maps in defending them from what they define as subversive attacks launched only for the sake of novelty. Nothing but an absurdity, nonsense, such as that of moving the Earth and stopping the Sun, as the German Lutheran reformer Philip Melanchthon (1497–1560) had to say.

Accredited with containing truth, the baggage of knowledge available at a given time shields people from the intrusion of mind-blowing discoveries that would upset their beliefs. By challenging what is accepted as true and without the weight of that baggage, path creators unveil *terrae incognitae* of knowing. By defeating truth, knowledge advances.

Epilogue: To Be a Path Finder or a Path Creator? That Is the Question

Knowing is not a blessing forever. The overconfidence given to it does not allow for doubt and prevents one from seeing problems differently. The significance of a path creator's move precedes the moment it occurs. The expert connoisseurs, who do not grasp the significance, only admit defeat after the event manifests itself. That is true in business as well as in science. It ranges from small but symptomatic episodes to shocking realities. The Satchel Company, a British company that produces handbags and other leather goods, was founded in 2008, in Cambridge, England, by Julie Deane and her mother Freda Thomas to pay private school fees for Deane's children. Julie states: 'I never imagined I would start a factory without any manufacturing knowledge'. The view of the Universe changes as it passes from Newton's laws to Einstein's theory of relativity.

Not knowing is the engine that drives the exploration process aimed at path creation. Its probability of success relies not so much on objective analysis as on a feeling, an estimation or a belief of path creators who have clever legs and a foolish brain, enabling them to be flexible and responsive to opportunities. Their ideas are shaped by walking into the void of knowledge without predetermined destinations. They enjoy competitive pastimes, discover subtle analogies and, by sagacity and accident, exceed the boundaries set by knowledge maps to open up new, unprecedented routes and connect them. In changing trajectories, path creators reveal latent, unexpressed consumers' needs, who will replace their traditional wants with new, revolutionary ones brought forth from seemingly nothing.

Innovators must decide which path to walk. To be a path finder or a path creator? To make forecasts for the future with the tools of knowledge and then, as Joi Ito, the former director of the MIT Media Lab, says in his TED Talk, stay on hold until you have proof that your idea conforms to expectations? Or choose to replace forecasts and expectations for immediate action, 'being open and alert to what's going on around you right now? In short, to be a "now-ist" path creator'?

The genesis of a new era has the imprint of the path creators. With novel ideas path creators disrupt the legacy accumulated by the rulers of the bygone era. Path finders cannot sense a threat on their visible horizon. Wang Laboratories remained committed to the word processor when IBM launched its first personal computer; BlackBerry considered the iPhone that Apple introduced in 2007 to be no more than a simple toy. Those who generate paths look at the far away horizon which, from the path finder's location, is obscured by the trees of consolidated knowledge and the 'mountains' of longstanding prejudices. The locked-in syndrome hurts them in two ways. On the one hand, the grip of tradition is strong enough to hold them back: they remain in the role of path finders, confined to the range of investigation circumscribed by the visible horizon. On the other hand, the locked-in syndrome causes a loss of instinct, intuition and insight. These essential attributes are plentiful among the outsiders – those fresh talents who, by creating new and more productive paths, go beyond the visible horizon.

Path creators pay no attention to or consciously reject trends plotted with knowledge maps. They shift their behavioural trajectories from a knowledge-burdened to a clean-sheet mode of exploration. Like explorers setting out on voyages across uncharted waters, path generators create new paths by cultivating imaginative visions and moving randomly. For them innovation is, in fact, disobedience. They intentionally diverge from the road already well-travelled, cease modulating their visions and perspectives through the judgements of others, and are untroubled by questions from others as to why they open unanticipated doors and pursue alternatives to well-trodden paths.

Thus, non-compliant innovators do not inhabit knowledge zones densely populated by past data. The lenses they wear do not reveal a future that is a projection of the past: their way of seeing enhances the imagination. The future is no longer a place identified by logical exercises and anchored in the past. With imagination, the future is based on uncertainties that are not quantifiable in manageable risks calculated from existing knowledge maps. An acceptance of 'ignorance' and a willingness to venture into the unknown are critical elements in radically creative innovation.

References

Borges, J. L. (1999). On exactitude in science. In *Collected fictions*. London: Penguin Books.

Bowles, C. (1946). *Tomorrow without fear*. New York, NY: Simon & Schuster.

Falciasecca, G. (Ed.). (2020). *Guglielmo Marconi. Memorie 1895–1899*. Bologna: Pendragon.

Firestein, S. (2012). *Ignorance: How it drives science*. Oxford: Oxford University Press.

Firestein, S. (2013). The pursuit of ignorance. TED 2013. Retrieved from http://www.ted.com/talks/stuart_firestein_the_pursuit_of_ignorance/transcript?language=en

Formica, P. (2013). An Italian millennial fleeing his country. In P. Formica (Ed.), *Stories of innovation for the millennial generation*. New York, NY: Palgrave Macmillan.

Formica, P. (2015). *The role of creative ignorance: Portraits of path finders and path creators*. New York, NY: Palgrave Macmillan.

Formica, P. (2020). *Econaissance: The reimagined education and the culture of entrepreneurialism*. Bingley: Emerald Group Publishing. forthcoming.

Forsyth, M. (2014). *The Unknown Unknown. Bookshops and the delight of not getting what you wanted*. London: Icon Books.

Fuchs, C. A. (2010). QBism, the perimeter of quantum Bayesianism. Retrieved from http://arxiv.org/pdf/1003.5209 v1.pdf. Accessed on August 28, 2014.

Gandhi, M. K. (1932). *From Yeravda Mandir, Navajivan Mudranalaya*. Ahemadabad: Jitendra T. Desai Publishing House.

Gross, M., & McGoey, L. (2015). *Routledge international handbook of ignorance studies*. London: Routledge.

Holmes, J. (2015). The case for teaching ignorance. *New York Times*, August 24.

Kawabata, Y. (1972). *The master of go*. New York, NY: Alfred A. Knopf Sr.

Le Goff, J. (1964). *La civilisation de l'Occident medieval*. Paris: Arthaud. [Medieval Civilization 400–1500, Hoboken (Hoboken, NJ: Wiley-Blackwell, 1991)].

Leopardi, G. (1819). *L'infinito*. Retrieved from http://www.textetc.com/workshop/wt-leopardi-1.html (Tales).

Markaris, P. (2012). Smarriti fra troppe certezze. *Il Sole 24 Ore*, July 8.

Popper, K. (1957). *The poverty of historicism*. London: Routledge.

Sandbu, M. (2021). The revolutions under way in macroeconomics. *Financial Times*, January 28.

Scott, M. (2009). *From democrats to kings: The brutal dawn of a new world from the downfall of Athens to the rise of alexander the great*. London: Icon Books.

Severino, E. (2021). *Il dito e la luna* (p. 34). Milano: Corriere della Sera.

Smithson, M. (1989). *Ignorance and uncertainty. Emerging paradigms.* New York, NY: Springer.

Taleb, N. N. (2007). *The black swan: The impact of the highly improbable.* New York, NY: Random House.

Tjan, A. K. (2010). *The power of ignorance.* HBR Blog Network, August 9.

Verdoux, P. (2009). *Towards a theory of ignorance.* Philosophical Fallibilism Blog, March 20. Retrieved from http://philosophicalfallibilism.blogspot.co.uk

Voltaire. (1924). Men of letters. In *The philosophical dictionary.* New York, NY: Knopf. Retrieved from https://history.hanover.edu/texts/voltaire/volmenol.html

Part 2

Chapter 3

The Big Picture

> Innovation is the specific instrument of entrepreneurship. The act
> that endows resources with a new capacity to create wealth.
>
> (Peter Drucker, economist and essayist)

Travelling through the lands of innovation, one encounters a changing reality
that mixes with narrative fiction. Words and symbols, voices and gestures, which
in the first part were reiterated with ever unconventional nuances, interwoven and
reformulated, are on display. Each word is a sound emitted by a voice and a
character transcribed on a device. Says Humpty Dumpty, the big anthro-
pomorphised egg: 'When I use a word, it means exactly what I choose it to mean –
neither more nor less', and if Alice replying argues that so many meanings can
have the words, Humpty, in turn, replies: 'When I make a word do a lot of work
like that, 'I always pay it extra.' Two other contrasting personalities are the
hedgehog and the fox. The first one captures only one, albeit big, word of
innovation. The second, on the contrary, captures the many facets of innovation
to know many expressions. The volume of her voice rises when she pronounces
'emptiness' and 'unreasonableness', two words that we will find again.

The present is already old. The time has come to move towards tomorrow.
Humpty Dumpty and Alice's controversy helps us understand the tough challenge
we face navigating through the waters of the strait between mental closure and
openness to change. The former tends to follow the regular rhythm of the time of
improvement in the sign of continuity. The latter entails, on the contrary,
speeding up the race of time and directs it towards discontinuity (see the corresponding entry in Chapter 4). In the course of navigation, it happens to come
across words that are more or less true and false at the same time. In short, 'A' coexists with its opposite 'non-A'. The sailor is asked to be a bit of a Buddhist,
accepting nuances and blurs.

Tracing an innovative path is a process of learning creative performance in
contrast to the knowledge received. It is about crossing the visible horizon with
the lenses of knowledge to penetrate the space of not knowing. Those who find a
path in their cognitive map accept to face and manage the risk when they
propose to build something new. Whoever, without a map, creates a path from
nothing embraces the uncertainty and unpredictability of finding *sui generis*
solutions. They do not resort to best practices, rules and manuals. Innovation is
disobedience.

Ideators, 47–53
Copyright © 2022 Piero Formica
Published under exclusive licence by Emerald Publishing Limited
doi:10.1108/978-1-80262-829-620221003

Is research or the creation of pathways more promising? As early as the 1960s, celebrated as the father of management, Peter Drucker warned managers that the most urgent problems to be tackled in the application of technology were not technical but human. If we want progress fuelled by technology, we should understand how to help human beings use it to open up new territories, not just to map out the terrain we know in increasing detail. Both are possible, for example, with big data. Path seekers appreciate them for their power to illustrate knowledge maps with as much detail as possible, allowing them to identify the most reliable routes to beat and the number of steps to take.

On the contrary, for trail creators, the attraction of extensive data lies in the possibility of finding models that disprove the assumptions of the received knowledge. The data allowed Galileo Galilei to uncover, contrary to all the wisdom he received, that the Earth moves around the Sun. 'And yet it moves', the concise reply attributed to him even when he was forced to retract his discovery, could be the battle cry of all the creators of paths.

Who, then, will chart the paths of innovation and innovative entrepreneurship in the years to come? How much weight will be given to the creative freedom of those (very often small minorities) whose words and voices express the significant changes? The positive response is weighed down by the great feudal lords' influence between the last two decades of the 1900s and the years closest to us. The pioneers and early followers of the digital age have accumulated fortunes that break down states, geographical, linguistic, cultural and economic barriers. What paths will their fortunes take? As in the Middle Ages, will their ambitions dictate the rules of the game? Or, as in the Renaissance, will a new generation feel motivated to encourage the social mobility of classes and individuals to the point of breaking the feudal hierarchy of the Digital Lords?

The 'cloud', e-commerce, mobile Internet, Internet of things, artificial intelligence and machines that learn how human beings act trigger changes in business models and blur the boundaries of industries. Genomics, nanotechnology and robotics challenge the scientific method. Such major upheavals subject the human beings in their dual profile as a person who does and thinks. To artificial intelligence, they must couple increased human intelligence to not again incur slavery from machines. In the early 1930s, the height of the Machine Age, Albert Einstein denounced that servitude in his speech to the California Institute of Technology students.

Dreaming, exploring and discovering are three distinctive features of that cultural movement that takes the name of 'innovative entrepreneurship'. A movement sparked off by a virulent epidemic of innovation: precisely the one that was so widespread during the Renaissance as well as during the Song Dynasty in China (960–1279), the Dutch Golden Age (1568–1648) and in Great Britain (1651–1851) – to mention three ages that experienced magical moments of the accelerated pace of innovation.

The words and voices of innovation leave the station of prejudice, experience and the arrogance of success already acquired by following the rule of 'doing everything at home' and get on the train of open-mindedness, epiphany and passion. Cultural changes and new technological discoveries make doable the idea that knowledge is something that anyone can acquire. As the British historian Theodore Zeldin writes in *An Intimate History of Humanity* (London: Sinclair-Stevenson, 1994),

> For a long time, knowledge has been something rare and secret, and this esoteric legacy, with its dream of superiority and mystery, lives on in the jargon with which every profession tends to protect itself.

With the advance of the Internet, a long tail of words has formed, hereafter briefly outlined. These have been followed by others which opened up a cultural front of innovation – the object of our exploration.

The Age of Knowledge

Era of access – The era in which connectivity drives access for everyone to everyone, everything to everything and everything to everyone.

Bionomy – The fusion of economic and biological theory. In its most metaphorical sense, the fusion of the world of fact and the world of born.

Building communities – People invest in sharing content and sending messages to each other.

Coevolution – Mutual evolutionary change. Coevolution pushes competitors to obligatory cooperation.

Communication – The basis of culture, which is a process of communication between individuals and groups.

Connectivity – The result of the fusion of computer use and communication.

Content – The artefact of the ability to communicate.

Cyberspace – Cyberspace is the way to network culture. Cyberspace is by nature anti-hierarchical. The identity of our cyberspace is our email signature.

Infoeconomy – An environment where atoms (products) and proprietary products have been replaced by bits (information) and information sharing. The faster the transmission of information, the higher the value.

Knowledge landscape – An irregular landscape of unknown interrupted by hills of knowledge and creative ignorance.

Metering – Thanks to a knowledge metre, everyone can buy whatever they want to drink instead of drowning in an ocean of information. Metering converts information into utility.

Net – A virtual environment for high-quality resolutions in mutual communication. The Net tends to grow organically – that is, not according to a specific project of a given person – it is by its nature a set of individuals that contribute to its growth.

Netmarket – On the Net, the market is not divided into cities and regions, but into affinity groups or invisible networks between colleagues that emerge from a high propensity for sociality. Non-commercial transactions are developed on the Net to promote community spirit.

Netted intelligence – Human intelligence augmented in networks of relationships built with social capital and supported by technology, such as interactive multimedia and so-called information highways.

Network – A workshop for information. When the value of the product increases via the amount of knowledge invested in it, the networks that create knowledge increase in value.

Source: Brockman, J., *Digerati: Encounters with the cyber elite*, London: Orion Business Books, 1997; Kelly, K., *Out of control: The new biology of machines*, Boston, MA: Addison Wesley Inc., 1994; Tapscott, D., *The Digital Economy: Promise and peril in the age of networked intelligence*, New York, NY: McGraw-Hill, 1995; Taylor, J. and Wacker, W., Speak the future, *Wired*, June 1997.

There are words and voices at the centre of knowledge inhabited by those who know and, precisely because they have the knowledge, hold power. Others are to be found in the suburbs. Here are the time-wasters who, having given up the habit of learning received, undertake the path of ignorance along unusual paths in search of revolutionary knowledge. We leave it to the individual reader's judgement to choose which words and voices to attribute to the existing knowledge that presides over the centre and which others abide in the periphery where unconventional ideas emit strange noises that disturb the inhabitants barricaded within the walls of the stronghold of acquired and accumulated knowledge.

Words whose common denominator is the physicality of factories, and market squares meet and collide with those of the virtuality of networks interwoven with personalised ideas and viral market spaces where knowledge, information and symbolic analysts co-exist. In the hybrid world, between physicality and virtuality, there is a bitter cognitive conflict between the incremental innovators tied to their entrepreneurial vocations established during past industrial revolutions and the disruptive innovators. These visionaries revolutionise consumption models and lifestyles. Unlike the former, for the latter, the most beautiful harmonies are built out of dissonance, as the French playwright Romain Rolland (1866–1944) apparently said.

The words of innovation are written in the language of the culture that invented them. English, in its various forms, has become a significant part of the vocabulary of the world. The love for Latin and then for Italian has given way to a predilection for English in the current age, which is variously defined: digital, of knowledge, of unreasonableness. Nevertheless, the revival of Latin was noted by *The Economist* on 27 July 2013: 'A dead language is alive and kicking online and on the airwaves'. Where does the former universal language derive new vitality from? There is imagination among the different forces at play in favour of this new 'Latin Lover'. The confrontation with Latin or other dead languages triggers a cultural process that takes us back to the origins of civilisation. Symbols and figurative expressions that are the baggage of our tacit knowledge thus come to light in our memory. From here, the imagination draws lifeblood, broadening its horizons to be induced to interact with others who are bearers of other cultures.

Today's words tell us about the things we are doing. Tomorrow's words are words to be invented by erasing the traces left by the past. 'Possibilist' (see the corresponding entry in Chapter 4) is a word that breaks with the tradition that the possibilist wants to adapt to circumstances. As we will see in the corresponding voice, she shows a diverse profile in the unfolding of innovation.

Words are ideas – so wrote Ernst Schumacher, German statistician and economist, in his 1973 essay *Small Is Beautiful: A Study of Economics as if People Mattered*, (London: Blond & Briggs, 1973), which made him famous. Words are ideas that make it possible to converse to discover new things. In his maxims and moral reflections on society and conversation, Jean de La Bruyère, a teacher and royal tutor, stated that,

> The true spirit of conversation consists more in bringing out the cleverness of others than in showing a great deal of it yourself; he who goes away pleased with himself and his own wit is also greatly pleased with you.... The most exquisite pleasure is giving pleasure to others.
> (Jean de La Bruyère, *The 'Characters'*, Good Press, 2019; originally published: 1687)

Words are ideas that require action. Fear, not trusting our judgement and instinct hinder action.

The words of innovation are energy agents of the ecosystem. It is in the crucible of experimentation that the words of innovation are born and transformed. The visionary experimenter masters the art of seeing things invisible. Experts live in a niche that narrows their field of vision. Their possibilities are limited, as they are locked in the fence of the received knowledge, which precludes them from entering into revolutionary, innovative thinking. By advocating experimentation in the field of applied sciences, Robert Recorde, a Scottish physician and mathematician, will pave the way for the impenetrable consequences of scientific discoveries. James Watt was the first to practice experimentation applied to industry to create the complex mechanism of his steam engine, the forerunner of capitalist production, which would affirm itself during the first industrial revolution.

The words of innovation point the finger at self-referentiality, immobility, order, predictability, and the walls raised to protect themselves from gusts of novelty. Those words are born and intersect in space-time. The protagonists of revolutionary changes give birth to them and accelerate their diffusion.

The words run, wrote the poet and singer-songwriter, James Douglas Morrison. Is it enough to run with a little breath, like Alice? Or should we rely on the Queen's words:

> A slow sort of country! Now, here, you see, it takes all the running you can do, to keep in the same place. If you want to get somewhere else, you must run at least twice as fast as that!
> (Lewis Caroll, *Through the Looking-Glass, and What Alice Found There*, Chapter 2)

There is, however, a third solution: making haste slowly ('Festina lente', one of our entries).

The words of innovation run in the collaborative space of the web where everyone can communicate through the exchange and sharing of information – noted Tim Berners-Lee, the inventor of the World Wide Web. The economy of sharing has set in motion a process of dematerialisation of consumption and production. An increasing number of consumers share goods and services with other members of the community with which they are associated. In addition to practising them, talented people invent the words of sharing and do so by engaging in altruistic behaviour. The result is new expressions, such as 'reform of the heart'.

The words of innovation are a karstic river flowing at a profound level, beneath the surface layer of the cultural fashions of the moment. Going down into the depths, one discovers that the Manichean vision of innovation, its clear division into the two opposite principles of closing and opening up the innovator, whether an individual or a team, to the outside world, does not stand the test of fact. As early as the 1980s, both in Sweden and Finland, technology programmes were carried out through collaboration between companies, universities and public authorities. In the absence of cultural openness, open innovation looks like an old wine put into new barrels.

There are words overshadowed by others. Thus, learning is commonly seen as the Cinderella of teaching. Some words cause shame, so for ignorance. However, there are opportunities to observe ignorance from other perspectives. In his programme *On Ignorance*, BBC journalist Mark Tully invited listeners to accept ignorance as to the first step on a journey of discovery, taking his lead from Socrates's well-known thought: 'The only true wisdom is in knowing you know nothing'.

The innovation of and in the school is denoted by the word 'revolution', a scary word. It is enough to read what Luigi Einaudi wrote as early as the early twentieth century about the University that did not practice the 'method of freedom'. Are universities called to act as an intellectual flywheel, selecting the best brains and investing in human capital to generate innovative competencies motivated to scientific entrepreneurship (but not only), or as a bureaucratic machine for the production of qualifications? The first option is the quest for talent in the most advanced economies and emerging countries, as well as their comings and goings (not emigration) that make them cross paths and navigate in the opposite direction. For some time now, young Chinese, Indian, Korean and, in general, Asian people have mixed with Europeans and Americans in the West. These latter ones are doing the same, moving eastwards.

The words of the University hover in the air, flying in the blue sky of research. 'That sky belongs to us': the universities that have their roots firmly planted in the culture that has developed during the unfolding of the second millennium gladly claim. In the third millennium we have just entered, the links between the organisational forms of science, innovation and entrepreneurship create new words. Universities are in danger of extinction. From the ivory tower in which they are locked up, they can see the flocks of words in their blue sky but cannot grasp them. To do it are those universities that intertwine scientific and entrepreneurial talents to translate the clothes in science into high expectations and a high potential for sustainable growth.

We enter the 'Kingdom of Intelligence', the theatre with the performance of innovation on its billboard. Among the characters' words put in the mouths of the actors, those expressed by the protagonists' voices stand out; first of all, by the 'Curiosity' that leads the audience on new paths. We will listen to them, knowing that while we dwell on a word, we learn enough to want to deepen its meaning as we detach ourselves from it.

Chapter 4

Words and Voices

Academic Enterprise

The academic enterprise is born out of research and is its commercial arm. Research staff promote its creation, participate in its foundation and support its take-off.

Academic enterprises demonstrate the ability of universities to master the entire knowledge chain: from creation to dissemination, conversion and entrepreneurial exploitation of learning, scientific discoveries and technical breakthroughs.

By investing in academic enterprises, universities promote entrepreneurial innovation with new knowledge and participate in ventures for acquiring companies whose products or services have a high market potential that entrepreneurs at their helm do not fully or adequately exploit.

In medieval Bologna, its university triggered an intellectual movement that sowed the seeds of the entrepreneurial soil from which the modern liberal professions sprouted. As in those days, university communities should strive for a change of phase, succeeding in channelling their students and knowledge workers along the most promising paths of innovation leading to the creation of academic enterprises.

Whether in the fields of food, medicine, healthcare, energy, the environment, construction techniques, clothing, furniture and much more, the entrepreneurial imprint of scientific research is visible. Material science, chemistry, biology and earth sciences are just a few of the categories in which new scientists blaze the trail for brilliant entrepreneurial insights.

By moving towards entrepreneurship built on science, the number of intellectual capitalists in the entrepreneurial knowledge economy would grow among the university population.

'Ago Ergo Erigo'

The Cartesian expression 'Cogito ergo sum' ('I think therefore I am') pairs with that proposed by Edward de Bono, the father of lateral thought – 'Ago ergo erigo' ('I act, and therefore I build').

By generating interaction between mental algorithms and their translation into production processes, both physical and in the domain of virtual reality, the action of doing enhances thought.

A representative figure of knowledge in action is that of the scientist who draws entrepreneurial inspiration from his discoveries to found a science-driven enterprise.

Ideators, 55–179
Copyright © 2022 Piero Formica
Published under exclusive licence by Emerald Publishing Limited
doi:10.1108/978-1-80262-829-620221004

Algorithm

In the years to come, with the accelerated progress of artificial intelligence, will the Algorithm be – 'a process or set of rules to be followed in calculations or other problem-solving operations, especially by a computer' (https://www.lexico.com/definition/algorithm) – be the new deity, replacing human creativity in the most varied forms of art and entrepreneurship? Will that 'superpower' determine the ways and means of the golden encounter? Or, on the contrary, will human beings enhance their freedom leveraging technology?

It is worth reflecting on the words of Zia Chishti, Managing Director of Afiniti (https://www.afiniti.com/team/zia-chishti/), a leading company in applied artificial intelligence:

> We have not moved a byte forward in understanding human intelligence. We have much faster computers, thanks to Moore's law, but the underlying algorithms are mostly identical to those that powered machines 40 years ago. Instead, we have creatively rebranded those algorithms. Good old-fashioned 'data' has suddenly become 'big'.
>
> (Artificial Intelligence: winter is coming.
> Today's AI is not much better at solving real world problems than its ancestors, *Financial Times*, 17 October 2018)

Altruism

If the invisible hand of the competition represented by Adam Smith in his work *The Wealth of Nations* (*An Inquiry into the Nature and Causes of the Wealth of Nations*, London: W. Strahan and T. Cadell, 1776) could induce selfish behaviour, the author himself in his *Theory of Moral Sentiments* (printed for Andrew Millar, in the Strand; and Alexander Kincaid and J. Bell, in Edinburgh, 1759) suggests that human beings, as social creatures, tend to shake hands to regulate their relationships better.

Being and counting more together with others is the pre-condition for innovating and having more. Human beings and innovation do not attract one another directly. At heart, there is the culture that both change and they are in turn influenced by it. Between selfishness and altruism, the range of cultural values is wide. Concerning the circumstances, selfish accent or altruistic intonation will be setting the scene. Egoism and selflessness chase each other in the cultural space.

Following selfish lifestyles, innovation takes shape through 'the astounding belief' – to borrow words attributed to the British economist John Maynard Keynes – that the wickedest of men will do the wickedest of things for the greatest good of everyone'. In contrast, in an open environment, innovation is shaped by people and organisations whose nature is altruistic and who are therefore biased towards cooperation, less selfish and more likely to share. According to David Sloan Wilson (*Does Altruism Exist? Culture, Genes, and the Welfare of Others*, New Haven, CT: Yale University Press, 2015), an evolutionary biologist, in communities in which selflessness is firmly woven into the social fabric, the altruistic groups get the better of selfish groups over time.

Experimenting with co-operative behaviour codes, where material motivations (money that bestows status) and intrinsic satisfaction coexist, can produce a balance between what each of us gives to the community and what we expect to receive in return. A propensity to altruism depends on maintaining a proper equilibrium between the two demands. It is worth noting that the type of altruism that is not disinterested being entirely linked to reciprocity (when and how much you will receive in return) plays its part in tilting the balance towards selfishness.

Anti-Discipline

The anti-discipline is a method that breaks down the barriers that separate disciplines and specialisations. In Europe, at the beginning of the nineteenth century, St Patrick's College in Maynooth – the National Catholic Seminary of Ireland founded in 1795, triggered an educational process aimed at embracing this method. Each student, without exception, encompassed a wide range of studies that included, in addition to Theology: Humanities, Rhetoric, Belles Lettres, Logic, Mathematics, and Physics.

Harvard biologist Edward O. Wilson (*On Human Nature*, Cambridge, MA: Harvard University Press, 1978) understands anti-discipline as an 'adversary relation that often exists when fields of study at adjacent levels first begin to interact' and generate creative tensions. With the aim of breaking down barriers that separate disciplines – which prevents the solution of problems increasingly difficult to deal with – Joichi Ito, the former director of MIT Media Lab (Massachusetts Institute of Technology in Boston), founded by Nicholas Negroponte, fights to ensure that 'more people [can] work in the wide-open white space between disciplines – the anti-disciplinary space'.

Broadening the perspective one can see, in the economy of ideas, the significance and continuing growth of the contribution of convergence – defined by Tom Siegfried (*A Beautiful Math. John Nash, Game Theory, and the Modern Quest for a Code of Nature*, Washington, DC: Joseph Henry Press, 2006) as 'merger fever' – between scientific (mathematics and the physical and natural sciences) and humanities subjects, and how open innovation, whose richness lies in the cultural diversity of participants, can accelerate that trend.

Art, Business and Innovation

According to the *Online Etymology Dictionary*, since the late Middle Ages throughout the Renaissance, the words Art, Business and Innovation come to light in the chronological order shown in Fig. 1. Preceded by Art and then

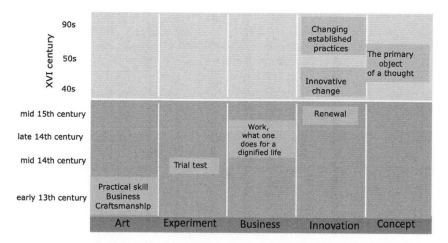

Fig. 1. Art, Business and Innovation Chronology of Birth and Development of the Three Words. *Source:* Online Etimology Dictionary.

Business, Innovation also has the word 'experiment' behind it; the word 'concept' follows it.

To gain an understanding of the world of interaction between Art (A), Business (B) and Innovation (I), one must enter into the order of ideas that A, B and I are not things that remain so, at least in appearance, but events that happen and change. Whoever has familiarity with humanistic culture will be better equipped to learn the meaning of that complex process that is the encounter between entrepreneurial and artistic movements from which descend innovations that break with tradition. Those who, from another perspective, dwell on Art that coexists with craftsmanship see in the encounter with entrepreneurship a return to Renaissance humanism, after mass production had reduced human beings to act like machines and since artificial intelligence 'humanising' machines challenges their acting.

The tension that translates into the bifurcation between Art and Business, between Art and Innovation, is an artefact that rests on vertical rather than transversal learning processes. That is alien to human nature. Among many, Samuel Morse was also a portrait painter, inventor and innovator. In our times, musicians who, for example, have drawn on Berlin's rock spirit since the 1980s, interacting with digital technology experts, have then found fertile cultural and entrepreneurial fields.

'When bankers get together for dinner, they discuss Art. When artists get together for dinner, they discuss Money'. Attributed to Oscar Wilde, this reflection gives a glimpse of the thread that links art to business.

Art and Business are not opposite poles. Business has a lot to learn from the arts, and management is more art than is commonly thought. Innovation is what creates the plot.

The ancient art of plotting regular, elegant and ornate writing meets with the automated machine that performs mathematical calculations and processes data. Attending the course of the Trappist monk Robert Palladino, Steve Jobs seizes the opportunity to combine the art of calligraphy with the style of typefaces that has made his Mac stand out.

The digital craftsmen of the twenty-first century take us back to the all-around and influential personalities of the Florentine Renaissance. Filippo Brunelleschi is the prominent name, whose famous dome of the Duomo of Florence is the result of the fusion of art, science and design. In today's Italy, in the footsteps of that time, the new craftsmen proceed, whose artistic flair in designing and producing glasses, lamps and many other Made in Italy products finds in 3D printers the tool that combines technological intensity with aesthetic beauty. In Trento, a small province in the North East of Italy, with strong aspirations and commitments to innovation, the technological craftsman Ignazio Pomini contributes to the creation of brands in eyewear (.bijouets) and lighting (.exnovo). As in the time of the Renaissance workshops, in the laboratory of Pomini, the contamination of different skills and knowledge transforms a feather into a lamp that is a real artistic object.

Art and Technology

Amid new technologies, we have to learn that technology alone is not enough and that alone we can do little. As Steve Jobs wanted, we will then be ready to start along the path of interaction between technologists and humanists.

In the nineteenth century, art contributed a great deal to arousing interest among ordinary people in steam technology. In the early decades of that century, James Bard was the best-known portraitist of the first steamboats. Compared to those of the first industrial revolution, the technologies now emerging are not rendered as scenes of work and images of everyday life with such a sharp visual impression. Rather than representing reality, artists are challenged to capture the emotions aroused by the pervasiveness of technologies that remain invisible to our eyes.

On the other hand, technology has always been a source of artistic creativity. Writes artist Rama Allen (*AI will be the art movement of the twenty-first century*, Quartz, 5 March 2018),

> The precision of flint knives (the high technology of the Stone Age) allowed humans to sculpt the first pieces of figurative art out of mammoth ivory.

Today, artificial intelligence technology ushers in a new artistic language that Allen calls 'augmented art'.

There are exhibitions on scientific abstractionism. In Bologna, at the September 2018 exhibition *Art at the Nano Scale*, 12 images created using a scanning electron microscope were exhibited together with another four works transferred directly onto a tile using the *Caravaggio Drawing Machine*, which allows the lines of any drawing to be reproduced in ink.

Beautification and Knowledgification

Beautification is the name of the current of beauty that throws light on the aesthetic values of those towns and villages, enhancing their knowledge.

Organised by the entrepreneurs of beauty, expeditions to the many parts that make up the living organism that is beauty bring together scientists and humanists to write stories about beauty and artists whose representations are visual replicas of those written narratives. The joint work of these protagonists is made available to citizens, presented in schools, made an object of study and reflection to immerse ourselves in the beauty which is the splendour of truth, as Plato seems to have said.

Gene Meieran, senior Intel Fellow (retired), coined the term knowledgification, the 21st century equivalent of the combination of electricity and mass manufacturing, which transformed the 20th century. Knowledgification is the name we shall give to the flow of knowledge that arouses love for beauty. The two currents together promote a harmonious social and aesthetical order that enhances the quality of living. Policymakers and civil society have a responsibility to keep intact the beauty of the Italian cultural heritage and its landscapes, relentlessly pursuing the objective of providing power to these two currents.

Big Data

Big Data are extensive collections of data sets that cannot be handled with traditional databases. In addition to large volumes, they stand out for their speed (they flow and must be managed in real time) and variety of sources and nature. According to the Gartner Group, the world leader in the analysis of information technology, Big Data provide a glimpse of valuable opportunities that can be exploited by the manufacturing industry. Experiments can be carried out by designing almost perfect maps in all particulars, drawing on millions of interactions.

Big Data are the lifeblood flowing through the body of the automated factory. Companies that are familiar with the manufacture of high-quality objects will have to stand up to the data giant (Google) and a dozen or so world leaders in the Internet of Things.

At the MIT (Massachusetts Institute of Technology) Media Lab in Boston, Big Data pioneer Sandy Pentland saw the dawn of what could be called the econo-physics of elementary particles. These are millions of small transactions bouncing between millions of individuals, measured and processed in their details in real time.

In the wake of the Big Data, society reinvents itself, inducing individuals to rethink their daily practices of life and work, and governments to redefine national economic accounting whose architecture was designed by economist Simon Kuznets in the 1930s.

Big Data anticipate improvements of around 100 billion euros in the efficiency of public administration in the developed countries of Europe, net of sharp increases in tax collection and substantial reductions in fraud and corruption.

Big Data can generate dependency and social obesity. The more you feel the need to have more data to discover something, the more you will never have enough. On the other hand, 'Not everything that can be counted counts and not everything that counts can be counted', a quote attributed to Albert Einstein.

Black Sheep

They are the employees whose unconventional ideas are driven out of the white sheep fence, those who live comfortably in the shade of the tree of custom, of 'that's the way it's always been done in the company'. By encouraging dissent and thus providing space for the creativity of the black sheep, companies can navigate the ocean of innovation without running the risk of the unsinkable Titanic.

A champion of the animated film like Brad Bird of the American Pixar could teach a lot about this. In an interview, he remarked,

> Give us the black sheep. I want artists who are frustrated. I want the ones who have another way of doing things that nobody's listening to. Give us all the guys who are probably headed out the door. A lot of them were malcontents because they saw different ways of doing things, but there was little opportunity to try them, since the established way was working very, very well. We gave the black sheep a chance to prove their theories, and we changed the way a number of things are done here.
>
> ("Innovation Lessons from Pixar: An Interview with Oscar-Winning Director Brad Bird", *McKinsey Quarterly*, 1 April 2008)

Black sheep are banned by those who, with only a hammer, make all problems look like nails. Innovation is slowed down by the nails of the 'grab-and-go business' that acts as a metronome for investment decisions.

The short-term mindset discourages leadership for change, keeps investment in human capital low and encourages a kind of financial gymnastics at the expense of the industrial body of the company and its good governance.

Brain Circulation

It is thanks to brain circulation that knowledge-intensive, borderless enterprises are born. Globetrotter talents and their entrepreneurial initiatives shape the nascent knowledge zones populated by new creative professionals.

Both the Phoenicians scholars and students of the Middle Ages have shown how the culture of transnationality produces flexible citizenship that induces people to respond in a fluid and opportunistic way to the changing conditions. The ensuing mobility and intellectual exchanges anticipated processes of cultural integration, knowledge creation and results-oriented innovation. The university cities of the Middle Age used to harbour for a while students from other communities. Each of them played to his or her strengths, rather than ape the host university city. Along the route the *clerici vagantes* (see the corresponding entry in Chapter 4) sowed new ideas and projects that made the university cities wealthy.

In the Renaissance age, brain circulation – notably, the ideators' mobility – triggered nine inventions: watches, gunpowder and artillery, spectacles, printing machines, flushing toilets, microscopes, telescopes, submarines, and matches. In turn, these inventions begat economic values. The Dutch philosopher Desiderius Erasmus spent some time in Venice as a proofreader for the technologist and publisher Aldus Pius Manutius. The intertwining of different personalities, including the humanist Pietro Bembo, led to the pocketbook's ideation that can be read anywhere and not only in libraries and classrooms.

In the eighteenth century, Naples was a crossroads of European cultural currents and was an obligatory destination on the Grand Tour for the talented and wealthy individuals. Ferdinando Galiani, an Italian economist and a leading Italian figure of the Enlightenment, said that value consisted of relationships between people. He had in mind economic value, and more: no less important are the ethical, moral and social values fostered through those relationships.

At the dawn of the industrial revolution, intellectual nomadism much helped to regenerate the entrepreneurial spirit. The academic Giovanni Aldini, professor of Experimental Philosophy at the University of Bologna and nephew of the physicist Luigi Galvani (1737–1798), known for discovering animal electricity, undertook a study trip to Europe between 1818 and 1819. Aldini investigated the transformations that the current industrial revolution was producing in the economic and social fabric of the then avant-garde countries. In this way, he learned about the best practices of the new technical education and training on offer in Europe. The fruit of the journey was the incubation followed around 1844 by the foundation of a technical school named after him and the economist Luigi Valeriani, professor at the same university and scholar of modern forms of technical education. They advocated a mix of in-company learning by doing training and formal training and offered new mechanical qualifications. In Bologna, the Aldini-Valeriani School thus acted as the incubator of several new firms, with a good number of students who were subsequently choosing to start their own companies – a propensity for entrepreneurial creations self-sustaining over time.

In our present times, globalization hastens brain circulation. The Grand Tour of the World has intensified connections woven by globetrotting talents or 'New Argonauts', as termed by AnnaLee Saxenian (*The New Argonauts: Regional Advantage in a Global Economy*, Cambridge, MA: Harvard University Press, 2007). The Knowledge Grand Tour winds its way through Beijing, Shanghai, Tokyo, Bangalore, London, Boston and San Francisco. It is attended by those who share a solid predisposition to grasp the cultures of others, accumulate experience abroad, engage in scientific and humanistic studies in order to be part of a new Renaissance. It is a caravan colourful by age, social status, ethnicity, religion, culture, studies, lifestyle. It is a caravan of knowledge nomads who jog the memory along with the camel and pack-pony caravans set off from Loyang in the north of China, crossing the arid high plains of central Asia towards Iran, Southern Russia and the Middle East. That was one of the Silk Routes. Thanks to multiple visas for different destinations, virtual mobility in the meanders of the web and physical mobility encourages borderless travel. Global trade currents and talent flows frequently intersect.

In the wake of Erasmus, a good step forward is to get more and more students from all over the world on what is now the Erasmus vehicle, the European Union's student mobility program. By boosting the investment in the other's knowledge, the various traditions and cultures prepare young minds to think and carry out initiatives springing from peers' physical and virtual presence from other countries and continents. Extraordinary will be the energy of young talents, nomads of knowledge, who, breaking down geographical borders, will give life to global enterprises driven by discoveries and their countless technological applications.

Digital innovation frontrunner Estonia passed a law offering one-year visas to freelancers who spend part of that time working from the Baltic state. 'Through our e-residency programme, we can give them a corporate entity which they can run from a distance as they travel around the world', says Siim Sikkut, Estonia's chief information officer.

In Italy, the *Manifesto of digital nomads* summarises the ideators' core values that we have tried to expose here. The *Manifesto* reads:

> We are mobile, creative, independent. Thanks to the Net, we are free to travel and work anywhere, redesigning our lives according to our real passions and interests. We support everything that represents innovation, provided that its path is developed through sharing and collaboration with others and not through exasperated competition. We believe that true wealth is not about accumulating assets and property but about having more time to follow our aspirations.

Business Agents and Civic Agents

Business agents strive to achieve results for their own benefit; their efforts may (but will not necessarily) have a positive external effect on the society as a whole, while the civic agents, the citizen-contributors to the pursuit of a civil society, act in the general interest of the body of individuals who constitute the city.

Civic agents are groups of citizens engaged in developing projects that aim to make the city better. The plans give shape to the so-called 'participatory budget', which translates into allocating shares of the municipal budget to the direct management of citizens gathered around a given project. The participatory budget triggers a dialogue between the citizens' plans and the choices made by local administrators. From ties between the two emerges innovation in the form of common goods – non-rival resources and therefore of mutual interest, shared among all participants.

As do water molecules when heated in a microwave oven, business and civic agents collide and mingle by moving from one team to another. In the process of mingling, teams change their configuration. This produces a disorder which creates interactions that fuel intellectual energy and give rise to very variable events. Innovation emerges from the disorder of events.

Business Angels

Many projects remain forever confined to research. Commercially promising technologies often get stuck at an early stage. Many growth-oriented companies fail because they cannot cross the so-called 'death valley' without enough financial resources and the right approach to the market.

Business angels invest in enterprising people for a variety of reasons ranging from fun to interest in mentoring promising start-ups and return on investment. In addition to providing funds, they give new entrepreneurs advice and contacts.

They build a bridge between the lower bank of the river 'Business Creation', where they collect their own money and that of their family and friends, and the upper bank of institutional venture capital. Thanks to the cash capital provided by the business angels and enriched by their knowledge of the entrepreneurial terrain, the aspiring business creator will be able to proceed along the path of testing the new entrepreneurial idea. With an action that imparts movement to the aspiring entrepreneur's vehicle, business angels facilitate access to institutional capital that supports the ambitions and growth potential of the new enterprise.

The typical investment of business angels is between 50,000 and 500,000 dollars. This amount fills a critical niche in the private equity market. Obtaining financing between 100,000 and two to three million dollars is quite tricky. These sums are often too small to attract the interest of venture capital companies, and too large to be generated through family, friends and other personal contacts. Therefore, angels play a critical role in promoting entrepreneurship.

In addition to money, the angels' experience brings several benefits to start-ups. These include:

- Backing potential entrepreneurs in developing market analysis, feasibility studies, financial planning, business contacts, recruitment of new managers.
- Providing advice and support to bring new products or product prototypes to market.
- Involving professionals and business people abroad so that they can act as a spearhead for new companies to enter international markets.
- Bringing the business idea into a phase where it will be an interesting argument for investment by a venture capital organization.

All in all, business angels contribute to transforming a workforce- and wage-based economy into an entrepreneurial economy. They also contribute to the wealth effect generated by new, fast-growing businesses that drive up consumption.

Organised groups of angels have become a key component in private capital markets. By reducing risk exposure, they encourage more people to consider investing in start-ups.

Already the intellectual centre of the academic celebrities, since the mid-seventies of the last century Cambridge (UK) added the title of city of innovative start-ups because of the contribution made to new entrepreneurship with a high economic impact by its business angels. They invested in the start-ups for three primary purposes. In their own words, having made a fortune in Cambridge, we are first of all obliged to be generous with our community: it is therefore out of solidarity that we invest in incubation and cradle entrepreneurship. Second, growing start-ups strengthen the local economy for the benefit of all. Thirdly, it is likely that the money invested will give us an economic return. Notice that the statue of entrepreneurial solidarity, not the return on invested capital, was placed on the pedestal.

Call to Innovation

The call to innovation is a consequence of the gravitational force exerted on us by the unravelling of history and the unfolding of personal life. The call is a window that opens onto a future that cannot be accurately predicted. Determinism and causality are put to the test. Whoever configures innovation as a science-based building that rests on the solid foundations of the classical Newtonian world has to measure herself against probability and uncertainty. The tools of experimentation and intentional construction of innovation stand in contrast to the tools of experience and prediction.

The call to innovation shows different facets of time: the time of the decision to innovate, having chosen in a crowd of ideas the one on which to act; the moment in which the action starts; the length of its temporal development; the instant in which the innovation manifests itself; the timing, i.e. its appearance at the most opportune moment. Hastening to innovate or lingering are mental attitudes that present themselves in all these meanings of time.

Cargo Cult Science

This is the expression used by Nobel Prize winner for physics Richard P. Feynman, the father of nanotechnology, to describe the behaviour of islanders in the South Seas after World War II. Writes Feynman,

> During the war they saw airplanes land with lots of good materials, and they want the same thing to happen now. So they have arranged to make things like runways, to make a wooden hut for a man to sit in, with two wooden pieces on his head like headphones and bars of bamboo sticking out like antennas – he is the controller – and they wait for the airplanes to land. They are doing everything right. The form is perfect. It looks exactly the way it looked before. But it does not work. No airplanes land. So I call these things Cargo Cult Science, because they follow all the apparent precepts and forms of scientific investigation, but they are missing something essential, because the planes do not land.
> (*The Pleasure of Finding Things Out*. The best short works of Feynman, R. P., London: Penguin Books, 1999).

Child

A child is a revolutionary innovator who goes beyond the visible horizon rich in information to aim for distant, unperceivable goals. The rules dictated by experience are no longer valid once such a journey of exploration begins. With her charge of naivety, she discovers and also invents a new world. The child causes permanent damage to the world that underlies the experience.

A close observation of that child allows one to recognize in oneself that swell kid so vividly represented by the American writer J. D. Salinger in his novel *The Catcher in the Rye* (New York, NY: Little and Brown, 1951),

> The kid was swell. He was walking in the street, instead of on the sidewalk, but right next to the curb. He was making out like he was walking a very straight line, the way kids do, and the whole time he kept singing and humming. I got up closer so I could hear what he was singing. He was singing that song, 'If a body catch a body coming through the rye'. He had a pretty little voice, too. He was just singing for the hell of it, you could tell. The cars zoomed by, brakes screeched all over the place, his parents paid no attention to him, and he kept on walking next to the curb and singing 'If a body catch a body coming through the rye'. It made me feel better. It made me feel not so depressed any more.

China

China is the hare leaping out of its hole, with a jump that has brought it into the group of the top 20 innovative economies, according to the Global Innovation Index. China is also the magnet of the East. The long march towards the new 'Middle Kingdom' began with low labour costs in that country and, in general, in the entire Asian basin.

Along the way, entrepreneurial teams have located their manufacturing activities in China. The major multinationals then established laboratories and research centres enriched with substantial venture capital, drawing on the Chinese culture and know-how. This process has primarily benefited Western multinationals themselves and, subordinately, local companies powered by an accelerated technology transfer mechanism.

We are immersed in the time that sees in the physical, digital (the virtual mobility that benefits from new open space technologies) and social mobility of people the emergence of transnational business communities. The knowledge of others will help West and East to recognise and dance together, using each other's specificities as a springboard for change. Innovation serves as a magnet that attracts each other. At the same time, the interweaving of knowledge and its organisation into entrepreneurial and social networks that span geographical, cultural, religious and ethnic boundaries helps to focus on how to exploit diversity and create benefits for all.

Clerici Vagantes (Wandering Students)

Founded in 1088, the Alma Mater Studiorum, the University of Bologna, had the mission of bringing knowledge and culture outside the monasteries.

Mother of the universities of the second millennium, the Alma Mater was the favourite destination and the centre of gravity of the students who travelled along the paths of knowledge.

The wandering students were pollinators of new ideas and projects that made university towns rich.

Today's talented young people who move internationally are the wandering students of the twenty-first century. They give birth to 'glocal' communities, where the local dimension changes into one that is both local and global. They are the ones who create and participate in borderless networks along the value-added stream of collaborative advantages, those who link the source of research to downstream commercial exploitation through the creation of companies involved in new knowledge markets.

The free international flow of talent allows for the development of globally designed, knowledge-intensive start-ups. The talents and the companies they found draw up emerging areas of knowledge that are very dynamic and populated by new creative professionals.

Young students from India and Asia enrich their cultural heritage in Western universities, primarily in the United States. Afterwards, they return to their countries to start their career in the industrial research laboratories of globally integrated companies.

Coevolution

The coevolution of ideas (the content) and their historical, social, organisational and institutional manifestations (the context) is the primary source of economic growth throughout history. We are shown the way to that source by men and women whose vision is so far-reaching that they can see beyond the walls of everyday routine. In the era of Greek mythology, Lynceus, one of the Argonauts, was the man with a penetrating sight. In the age of cartoons, it is Superman who can look through walls.

In Italy, in the last decade of the nineteenth century, we find the very young Camillo Olivetti who, while attending Stanford University, was able to climb on the shoulders of the giants of science and industry of the time to look further and further away. From those heights Olivetti was able to embrace a vast panorama, and so began a long journey in the land of innovation that led to the achievement, between 1962 and 1964, of the Olivetti Program 101, considered the first Personal Computer in history.

Cognition and Conation

Cognition, the search for a new perception, and conation, the passage to action, strengthen the power of the human mind which voluntarily builds its future by using mental gymnastics to manage uncertainties, not being able to predict what tomorrow will bring.

With his art of inventing stories that contributed so much to the education of so many children, the Italian writer Gianni Rodari showed how much children can acquire perceptions from images, ideas and words that lead them to create new things; what does not happen when they are not exposed to this learning but compelled to fill their minds with notions imparted by teachers.

Cognitive and Emotional Conflict

Some words recall those of physics. A case in point is the cognitive conflict, the great collider of ideas subject to the force of strong thought (the hadrons of innovation, borrowing the name given to the compound subatomic particles, subject to the strong nuclear force). From the clash of ideas and different points of view springs cooperation in order to achieve a creative result. Whoever enters into a cognitive conflict does not see in the adversary the problem (if so, the conflict would be affective, aka personal), but rather the opportunity to solve a problem together. The cognitive conflict is, therefore, constructive.

As written in the *Constitution of Prince Shōtoku*, also known as the *Seventeen-Article Constitution* (*Japan: Selected Readings*, compiled by Hyman Kublin. Boston, MA: Houghton Mifflin Company, 31–34, 1968),

> Let us control ourselves and not be resentful when others disagree with us, for all men have hearts and each heart has its own leanings. The right of others is our wrong, and our right is their wrong. We are not unquestionably sages, nor are they unquestionably fools. Both of us are simply ordinary men. How can anyone lay down a rule by which to distinguish right from wrong? For we are all wise sometimes and foolish at others. Therefore, though others give way to anger, let us on the contrary dread our own faults, and though we may think we alone are in the right, let us follow the majority and act like them.

Wearing the mental dress of cognitive prejudices, one becomes accustomed to filing information based on one's own experience and knowledge. In using it, other possible solutions are ignored. In other words, we make use of information that strengthens our ideas and avoids those that do not confirm them. In order to get out in the open field, that dress has to be discarded. We have to get out of the silo mentality in which we are locked up.

Inclined to feel bumped when the interlocutor expresses points of view opposed to ours, we have fallen prey of an affective conflict that is emotional and destructive. On the contrary, the prejudice-free mind reads the conflict between ideas as an enrichment – the conflict changes from affective to cognitive. In the course of the confrontation ignited by the cognitive conflict, the ideas colliding with each other generate new ideas. The process of collision of ideas characterises innovation-centred experiments.

The field of cognitive conflict between incrementalists (see the corresponding entry in Chapter 4) and visionary innovators is wide. In the half field of the former, there are acquired knowledge, deep-rooted beliefs, mechanical learning, causality, and risk calculation. Among the unintentional consequences, the perseverance to continuously improve things that will later prove obsolete, as in the case of analogue photography swept away by digital photos and then attempted with Kodak to return to fashion on the wave of vintage. Then there are complicated problems, nodes to be untied by following rules dictated by the hierarchical structure that commands and controls employees.

In the other half of the field, there are:

The uncertainty in facing complex problems with many unknowns and too many interrelated implications to submit them to rules.
The imagination of nonconformist people.
Thoughts in disagreement with accepted theories and norms.
The simultaneously processing and keeping two or more opposing thoughts in one's mind.

George Orwell in *1984* (London: Secker & Warburg, 1949), his dystopian science fiction book, identifies doublethink with the will to always be within the fence of orthodoxy preached by totalitarian society. For visionary innovators, double- and multi-thinking is a way to escape from the time of incrementalist (see the corresponding entry in Chapter 4) orthodoxy and act in sync with time that shows the changing faces of innovation.

Collaboration

It is an enduring process of learning how to manage relationships. In the sense of people's ability to work together to achieve common goals, social capital is the 'gene' that dictates the evolution of a network as complex and adaptable as collaboration.

Collaboration not constrained within geographical boundaries and not prevented by cultural and financial barriers is a critical success factor. It allows both to find skills wherever they are in the world, diversify research activities, and increase the likelihood of transforming new knowledge into innovative products and services for global markets.

Collaboratory

The collaborative research form of knowledge transfer aims at promoting a context where academic researchers work alongside company employees to create, developing and testing a prototype based on their reciprocal ideas.

Collaborative research can be carried out in a 'collaboratory' – an appropriate lab type infrastructure that links teams of people from university and companies with disparate cultures, different cognitive systems and skills. In a 'collaboratory', research is focused on specific company problems, and scientific research is carried out through the interactions between academic-trained corporate researchers and university researchers willing to apply their experimental results to practical use.

Collective Autocatalytic System

This is a system in which molecules accelerate the reactions by which they are formed. In practice, A catalyses B and B does the same with C, which, in turn, catalyses A. Now imagine a whole network of these continuous, self-propelling cycles. Given a supply of molecules that feed the cycle, the network will continue to recreate itself by expanding. Innovation is precisely a set of networks of autocatalytic, self-sustaining and self-propelling activities.

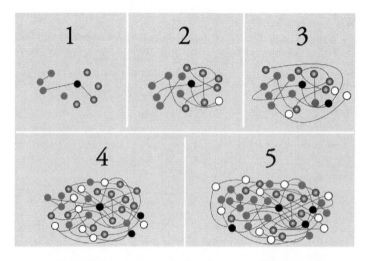

Autocatalytic Network Model: The Bologna Packaging Cluster.

In the image above, craftsmen, technicians, enterprises and educational institutions are the key players. Black dots are catalysts (people, enterprises, institutions); grey dots are growth nodes as attractors and drivers of new ideas; shaded dots represent circulating talents; white dots are spin-offs. The dots are randomly connected by an increasing number of lines (relational threads).

In the wake of Stuart Kauffman's study (*At Home in the Universe: The Search for Laws of Self-Organisation and Complexity*, Oxford: Oxford University Press, 1995), when there are very few threads compared to the number of dots, most of them will be disconnected. For a large number of points, a phase transition takes place. Once connected, a large skein suddenly takes shape. For example, the packaging industry in Bologna has long since passed the transition phase and is now a giant spider, whose growth rate slows down as the number of still-isolated dots decreases. Therefore, automatic machine manufacturers are being pushed to all-out innovation to accelerate growth by selling a system of which the packaging machine is only a part.

Communication

When addressed to incremental changes in products and services available in the market, communication faces consumers who have already experienced those products and services. By interacting with experienced consumers, the communication will have to use technical language.

Different is the case of the trajectory that flows into a cluster of innovations that for simplicity we call radical because (1) they change the rules of the game, (2) they are real technological leaps, (3) they offer consumers values different from the existing ones. If the idea to communicate transforms markets so profoundly that it has a radical impact on people's behaviour, then metaphorical, figurative language is helpful.

Think of Henry Ford who had no intention whatsoever of complying with the wishes of people who demanded carriages and coaches. Rather than submitting to the demands of customers and attempting the impossible task of breeding horses capable of pulling gigs, carriages and coaches at 60 miles per hour, he reflected on the meaning of transport. At that time, the road network connecting villages, towns and cities was designed to be used by horses and carriages, with paved, rutted roads. There were blacksmiths' workshops, post houses and hotels for weary travellers and exhausted horses. The 'how' that occupied his mind was a vehicle so innovative that it would require a new road network, fundamentally different from that developed for the coach and horses. So, it was – some might find it surprising – that our man started to look carefully at spider's webs. Of the various forms, these took – spiral, funnel-shaped, tubular and leaf-shaped – it was the tangled ones that attracted his attention most. It was the tangle of interests that Ford was questioning in his project to find a solution to his problem. This project revolutionised the concept of 'with what': no longer horse-drawn carriages, but the car for a multitude of people. Ford communicates his innovation figuratively:

> I will build a car for the great multitude. It will be large enough for the family, but small enough for the individual to run and care for. It will be constructed of the best materials, by the best men to be hired, after the simplest designs that modern engineering can devise. But it will be so low in price that no man making a good salary will be unable to own one – - and enjoy with his family the blessing of hours of pleasure in God's great open spaces.
> (Ford, Henry; Crowther, Samuel (1922), My Life and Work, Garden City, New York, USA: Garden City Publishing Company, 1922)

Communication is under stress in the presence of upheavals in the languages and techniques of information creation and dissemination.

Communities of Knowledge Practice

Xerox's John Seely Brown and Etienne Wenger ('Space for the chattering classes', *The Times Higher Education Supplement*, 10 May 1996) called the knowledge practice communities as

> ...groups of people who've worked together over a period of time...
> not a team, not a task force, not necessarily an authorised or
> identified group...They are peers in the execution of 'real work'.
> What holds them together is a common sense of purpose, a real
> need to know what the other knows... a shared passion for
> something that they know how to do and to interact regularly to
> learn how to do it better.

Knowledge practice communities attract all sorts of characters, unlike practice communities of practice that tie membership firmly to the job description (e.g. industrial machinery maintenance communities). Among the best-known knowledge practice communities, the Innovation Value Institute (http://www.ivi.ie) at Maynooth University contributes to structural change in the way businesses and governments gain value from information and communication technologies. The IVI brings together business and academic leaders from different countries and continents who pool their knowledge, having to solve problems that are not within reach of individual companies and want to create value for the community as a whole.

Competitiveness and Productivity

Competitiveness is an elusive word. More pregnant with meaning is productivity, which finds one of its most essential features in the encounter between Technology, Tolerance and Talent (see the corresponding entry in Chapter 4).

Competitiveness is the European Commission's mantra, and it has become commonplace to say that we must innovate to be more competitive.

Laura D'Andrea Tyson, President of the Council of Eco-Consultants at the time of the Clinton administration, defined competitiveness as

> ...our ability to produce goods and services that meet the test of
> international competition while our citizens enjoy a standard of
> living that is both rising and sustainable.

In a paper (*Competitiveness: A Dangerous Obsession*) dating back to March 1994 and published in the prestigious *Foreign Affairs* journal, Paul Krugman, Nobel Prize winner for Economics, claimed that competitiveness is a dangerous obsession. It is because one is led to think, mistakenly, that an economy is comparable to a large company competing in the global market. Krugman argues:

> When we say that a corporation is uncompetitive, we mean that its
> market position is unsustainable – that unless it improves its
> performance, it will cease to exist. Countries, on the other hand,
> do not go out of business. They may be happy or unhappy with
> their economic performance, but they have no well-defined bottom
> line. As a result, the concept of national competitiveness is elusive.

There is also a need to reflect on the relationship between innovation and productivity (one measure is the added value per hour worked). The latter is dependent on many factors, among which social capital stands out in its components of trust, cooperation and altruism that are becoming established in a community. The work done by productivity, its energy, produces ideas that give rise to innovations, vital sparks of all improvement, change and human progress.

Climbing the highlands of productivity and then ascending to the pinnacle of innovation is an effort accomplished by nurturing investment in education, research and transformative entrepreneurship.

Connected Cities

The book of history tells of cities crossed by currents that generate connectivity and, therefore, relationships between them. The encounters between cities are harbingers of commonality between peoples of different cultures.

For two centuries, *Sydney* has increasingly become a magnet for migration and brain circulation (see the corresponding entry in Chapter 4). With over 200 languages spoken by its multi-ethnic inhabitants, the city is shifting its economic narrative towards the Asia-Pacific region and the interdependence of its inhabitants with their cultures, creativity and collaborative connections.

Cultural interaction is the strength of *Bangalore's* industrialists and scientists. Talents arrive and depart from the capital of the state of Karnataka, one of the world's major hubs for the information technology industry.

In *Tel Aviv*, Israel's leading economic centre and recognised international community of innovative start-ups, Renaissance is the way of thinking. The intersection of artistic, scientific and commercial ideas translates into a creative process initiated by transdisciplinary research programmes aimed at creating global start-ups.

In *Milan*, from self-entrepreneurship to the solidarity economy of sharing, residents rediscovered the pleasure of living together and being part of a community. This attitude was a response to transformations, on a global level, of how work is produced (the boom in freelance work that has triggered the development of new poles of aggregation, such as spaces for collaboration). The academic world has also contributed to the entrepreneurial rebirth. PoliHub, the Polytechnic University's start-up incubator, ranked fifth in the ranking of the best university incubators in the world.

Stockholm is a city that draws vitality from intangible values, such as the flow of knowledge that intersects with the international mobility of intellectual capital. The latter contributes 72.5% to Swedish GDP, more than in the US (70.3%) and the EU (51.6%), and well above the world average (45%).

The geographical location of *Bournemouth*, a seaside resort in the Dorset on the south coast of England, is an attractive factor for a young cosmopolitan entrepreneurial population looking for a more engaging way of living life in terms of both business and leisure.

In *Dublin*, the presence of international research laboratories, such as Intel's, and the world's digital champions, attracts aspiring entrepreneurs from all over the world. Universities also contribute with their strong transdisciplinary imprint to the virtuous circle between the physical sciences, humanities and innovative entrepreneurship. Discoveries, inventions and innovations have flourished in hybrid contexts such as St Patrick's College where an invisible thread has linked together theology, philosophy, art and science. It was there that Father Nicholas Joseph Callan, professor of natural philosophy, demonstrated the transmission and reception of electricity without wires. Professor Callan is known for his research on the induction coil and for making the largest electric battery of his time. Callan's work has contributed to the fertility of innovative entrepreneurship during the industrial revolution. A legacy that the University of Maynooth has renewed and enriched with new content.

Conservative and Innovative Leaders

Conservative leaders play champions of the profit-maximising faith that they believe is the inevitable result of competition. They also suffer from technological determinism and underestimate cultural factors. Namely, the culture of the hunter-gatherer society, as portrayed by Ronald Wright (*A Short History of Progress*, Toronto, ON: House of Anansi Press, 2004), is alien to their thinking:

> In hunter-gatherer societies (barring a few special cases) the social structure was more or less egalitarian, with only slight differences in wealth and power between greatest and least. Leadership was either diffuse, a matter of consensus, or something earned by merit and example. Farmers whose effort and skill made them wealthier had an obligation to share with the needy, to whom they were bound by kinship.

Innovative leaders demand the freedom to innovate in the pursuit of quality. They derive their thoughts from movements characterised by promoting a culture of freedom and human values. They attach importance to the cultural relevance of creativity. It is the creative people who are put in charge because creativity cannot be bought. On the contrary, conservative leaders show a remarkable lapse of morality by being myopically focused on the bottom line of profit, leading them to dispense with creatives.

Conversation

Voltaire, pseudonym of François Marie Arouet le June, a guest at Cirey, the meeting place of the Enlightenment thinkers, of the scholar and scientist Madame de Châtelet who attended the literary and political salons of the French capital with him, wrote in his work *Memnon*, dated 1747 and later re-titled *Zadig* (*Zadig or the Book of Fate*), about the conversation that

...a young Man, a Native of Babylon, by name Zadig,...
notwithstanding he had such a Fund of Wit, he never insulted;
nay, never so much as rallied any of his Companions, for that
Tittle Tattle, which was so vague and empty, so noisy and confus'd;
for those rash Reflections, those illiterate Conclusions, and those
insipid Jokes; and, in short, for that Flow of unmeaning Words,
which was call'd polite Conversation in Babylon.

However, that was not the case in the intellectual salons (see the corresponding
entry in Chapter 4) of the Enlightenment.

The conversation is a dance performed by turning over a topic with partners. A
willingness and ability to change demonstrate the conversationalists' versatility.
The conversation thus becomes a collaboration, and those who have learned to
collaborate and improvise prevail, as Charles Darwin famously argued in his
theory of evolution of which he solves the puzzle by entering into disciplinary
territory far removed from his own, such as Thomas Malthus's *Essay on the
Principle of Population* (London: J. Johnson Publisher, 1798). Collaboration
eliminates the background noise that occurs when ideas collide with each other,
and in so doing, it recognises the signals that indicate the means of solving the issue
discussed.

The Dutch Renaissance humanist Desiderius Erasmus considered that the
development of understanding through students' conversations with each other
and with their teachers was far more critical than the process of memorising
required at many religious schools of the Middle Ages. In the wake of Erasmus,
the Moravian educator John Amos Comenius suggested teachers should exploit
the sensitivity, and therefore the feeling, of students rather than merely accepting
their ability to memorise. Equally, according to the English philosopher and
physician John Locke, learning through conversation had to be at the centre of
the school curriculum. One trades and innovates by conversing, said Ferdinando
Galiani in the eighteenth century.

At the root of the present forms of open innovation, the culture of conversation
had its cradle in Paris between the seventeenth and eighteenth centuries. The
Enlightenment's philosophies exalted the art of conversation as a culture of imagination, exploration, experimentation and creation, in a dynamic balance between
introspection and open-mindedness, which touches the most sensitive strings of
human inventiveness projected towards future events.

The age of conversation at the crossroads between the Scientific Revolution
with its two great agitators, Galileo and Newton, and the Enlightenment, sym-
bolised by the Encyclopédie under the direction of Diderot and D'Alembert, is
not the exclusive prerogative of Europe, with France and England contending for
the supremacy.

On the other shore of the Atlantic, members of the generation following the
Pilgrim Fathers, the first settlers in North America, committed to ploughing the
fertile ground of conversation that would have contributed to the formation of
the United States of America. In the foreground, there was Benjamin Franklin,
American polymath and one of the Founding Fathers of the American nation and

corresponding member of the Lunar Society of Birmingham, a club of personalities across science and practical affairs at the dawn of the first industrial
revolution.

Triggering the conversation to change together: this is the purpose that –
according to the 'nation builder' Franklin in his *Autobiography* – can be pursued
bearing in mind that 'the chief ends of conversation are to inform or to be
informed, to please or to persuade by adopting the Socratic method of the 'humble
inquirer and doubter', and, therefore, drop(ping) abrupt contradiction and positive
argumentation'.

Mutual improvement through conversation was Franklin's aim. In 1727, at
age 21, he formed a discussion group, the Junto Club, pursuing the ideals of
knowledge and freedom that distinguished the most famous Parisian salons of
that time. Learning by conversing involved a dozen friends, who met on Friday
evenings. As to the team spirit and shared goals of mutual collaboration within
the group, Franklin wrote:

> The rules that I drew up required that every member, in his turn,
> should produce one or more queries on any point of Morals,
> Politics, or Natural Philosophy, to be discussed by the company;
> and once in three months produce and read an essay of his own
> writing, on any subject he pleased. Our debates were to be under
> the direction of a president, and to be conducted in the sincere
> spirit of inquiry after truth, without fondness for dispute, or desire
> of victory; and, to prevent warmth, all expressions of positiveness
> in opinions, or direct contradiction, were after some time made
> contraband, and prohibited under small pecuniary penalties.
>
> (*The Autobiography of Benjamin Franklin*. New Delhi:
> Ocean Books. Original work published as Memoires de la vie
> priveé de Benjamin Franklin, 1791)

Informal and improvised conversations in the most disparate places, for example,
in a cafe, a pub, on the train or the river, are channels of knowledge transmission
that can lead to disruptive discoveries and innovations. Preferring open conversation
to isolation, biologist James Watson and neuroscientist Francis Crick identified the
DNA molecule structure that earned the two scientists the Nobel Prize for Medicine
in 1962. 'Linus Pauling – writes Alan Stewart – who had done extensive work on
the same project, had nobody to converse with (reportedly, by choice) and missed
out on this major discovery' ('The Conversing Company: Its culture, power and
potential', paper presented at the 'first World Conference for Systematic Management', Vienna, May 2001). It is inscribed in the history of humankind – said
Charles Darwin – that to prevail are those who learn to collaborate and improvise
effectively.

In Asia, two scholars (Yin, D., and Lin, J., 'Sharing tacit knowledge in Asia',
KM Review, 5(3), July–August 2002) observed that knowledge communities of
practice place much emphasis on the conscious conversation, which is 'a transformational change technique that incorporates deep dialogue skills of reflecting,

deep listening, interacting and connecting. It intends to foster common sense, build trust and understanding, and create positive and harmonious relationships among community members'.

Whether companies, institutions, trade associations, voluntary organisations or clubs, the time of easy conversation by keeping each person in a fixed position has passed for organisations. In his essay on *The post-capitalist society* Peter Drucker writes that in a baseball team-like organisation, each player receives the information appropriate to the task at hand and obtains it independently of the information reaching his teammates. Here the conversation is simple. Each tells the other what he does without having to receive anything in return. On the other hand, in the organisations resembling a symphony orchestra or football team, each musician or footballer receives from the conductor or coach most of the information he or she is called upon to share. They converse in such a way as to co-ordinate with all the others. The conversation is articulated, but understanding is not always immediate. If the organisation is that of a jazz ensemble or a tennis doubles team, the absence of fixed positions means that everyone has to adapt to the strengths and weaknesses of their teammates. It is, therefore, necessary to learn how to converse by receiving information from each other, without intermediaries such as a director or a coach. The transition from hardware to software pushes organisations towards this third stage of evolution. The managerial levels are skipped, entrepreneurial skills come into the picture, and there is to train in the gymnasium of complex conversation.

From the Past to the Present

Three Key Components of the Peer-to-Peer Conversation in an Open Innovation Mode with the Purpose to Expand Humanity's Knowledge.

§ Bringing out the cleverness of others (Jean de La Bruyère, 1645–1696).

§ Humble inquiry – 'asking instead of telling' (Benjamin Franklin).

§ Fully fledged serendipity process (The EU's Open Innovation Strategy and Policy Group, 2007).

§ Forcing curiosity into a field that could use more progression (The Thinkers Forums, 2017).

Controlled Sloppiness

The words of the research are challenging: controlled sloppiness, distraction, oversight. One thinks of the sloppiness of the Scottish scientist and Nobel Prize winner for Medicine Alexander Fleming, who neglected cleanliness and order in his laboratory; from one of his mould-contaminated cultures, Fleming would go on to discover penicillin.

Advocated by the microbiologist and Nobel Prize winner Salvador Luria, controlled sloppiness leads to improvisation, contradiction, combining logic and intuition, and exploiting inexperience. All these are mental attitudes that are oblique. Furthermore, this serpentine path leads to creating entirely new things rather than merely improving on the existing ones. Obliquity, which interested so many Renaissance writers and artists, was identified by them with the myth-ological figure of Hermes, the Olympian god who plays different roles while simultaneously travelling in different directions. Later, the oblique approach was a favourite subject of Francis Bacon, the multifaceted English intellectual and scientist, and, in our times, of the English economist John Kay in his 'oblique thinking' (*Obliquity: Why Our Goals Are Best Achieved Indirectly*, London: Profile Books, 2011), to regenerate the art of politics that is skewed towards the narrow linear path of planned evolution.

When research is institutionalised, philosopher Geoffrey E. R. Lloyd has put it (*The Ambitions of Curiosity: Understanding the World in Ancient Greece and China*, Cambridge: Cambridge University Press, 2002),

> ... less room the individual may have for genuinely innovative ideas. The more the programme of research enjoys the blessing of approval of the authorities, the greater the pressure to conform to it. The obvious danger is that ...individuals [finds] it extremely difficult to introduce new ideas, let alone to suggest new direction for the programme itself.

Cooperation

'If you have a candle, the light won't glow any dimmer if I light yours off of mine'. From this quote attributed to the musician Steve Tyler, it follows that coopera-tion is a form of collaboration that allows parties to maximise the joint product of their relationships rather than individual outcomes.

Ferrari and Battista 'Pinin' Farina (later Battista Pininfarina, 1893–1966) have had the world's best-known and most influential association between an auto-motive manufacturer and a car designer. Battista 'Pinin' Farina has been the creator of the Italian style in the architecture of the automobile. In the 1930s, he founded 'Carrozzeria Pinin Farina'. He planned to build unique car bodies.

Though Enzo Ferrari and Battista Pininfarina yearned to work with each other in the early 1950s, the road to real collaboration was hesitant to start. 'Ferrari was a man of very strong character', Sergio Pininfarina recalls. 'Therefore, Mr Ferrari was not coming to Farina in Turin, and my father was not going to visit him in Modena, which was approximately 120–130 miles away. So, they met halfway in Tortona'.

That fateful rendezvous would alter the world's automotive playing field. 'Everything became extremely easy once they sat down at the table' – Pininfarina continues. 'They never spoke about any type of price. I will give you one chassis, and you will make one car' – Battista Pininfarina would have said. The first steps were tentative, much like two outstanding dancers being paired for the first time. The initial effort yielded a handsome perfectly proportioned 212 Inter cabriolet that had its official public debut at 1952's Paris Auto Show.

The handshake between the two protagonists ushered in the golden age of Italian-made sports cars.

Coopetition

Innovating to compete can mean improving what you already do well, or changing the rules of the game to do new things in new ways. In the second case, one needs to familiarise oneself with the word 'coopetition'.

Competition is a finite game, with a winner and a loser. Those who bite win. It is not for nothing that the Asians depict it as a poisonous snake.

Cooperation, on the other hand, by creating new opportunities to the advantage of all players, is an endless game that evolves spontaneously towards coopetition in which cooperative and competitive behaviour coexists among the parties in the field.

The principles and practices of coopetition have been attributed to Harvard and Yale professors Adam M. Brandenburger and Barry J. Nalebuff. In their book *Co-opetition* (London: Harper Collins Business, 1996: 4–5), they expound on their thinking as follows:

> [There] is cooperation when it comes to creating a pie and competition when it comes to dividing it up. In other words, [there] is War and Peace. But it's not Tolstoy – endless cycles of war followed by peace followed by war. It's simultaneously war and peace... You have to compete and cooperate at the same time. The combination [that is, "coopetition"] makes for a more dynamic relationship than the words competition and cooperation suggest individually. [In the coopetition game] your success doesn't require others to fail – there can be multiple winners.

Hampden-Turner and Trompenaars (*Mastering the Infinite Game. How East Asian Values Are Transforming Business Practices*, Oxford: Capstone, 1997) argue that various combinations of competition and cooperation correspond to different games of coopetition.

Coopetition, which prompts actors to knot bonds of trust outside their historical groups, is a nudge that manages to move large boulders. With an image à la Aesop, we could say it is not the gust of the Northwind that removes the traveller's cloak, but the persuasive behaviour of the Sun's rays.

In Far Eastern culture, the coopetition game is represented by an inverted eight, the symbol of infinity.

To reconcile cooperation and competition, Asians have become masters of the practice of coopetition.

Coordination

The primitive form of collaboration is defined as 'coordination'. Coordination enhances the process of 'simultaneous adoption of identical or complementary strategies by independent agents' (John Kay, *Foundations of Corporate Success*, Oxford: Oxford University Press, 1995) whose relationships are informal and implicit, based on unwritten rules and unwritten codes of behaviour.

Distinctive features of the relationships prevailing in the coordination environment are the following:

- Arm's-length and kinship/family ties.
- Informal, opportunistic and short-term relations.
- Spontaneous dissemination of implicit knowledge.
- Joint problem-solving.

Coworking

An innovative workspace, coworking aims to foster mutual learning so that participants can turn their insights into entrepreneurial initiatives.

The coexistence of and collision among diverse talents help make the workshops lively places where dialogue allowed conflicts to flourish in a constructive way. The clash and confrontation of opposing views remove cognitive boundaries, mitigate errors, and help artists question truths taken for granted.

Coworking spaces are on the rise, from Google's Campus in London to NextSpace in California. Much has been made of these shared workspaces as a brand-new idea, one that barely existed 10 years ago. The way they function reminds a very old idea: the Renaissance bottega (workshop) of fifteenth century Florence.

The Renaissance put knowledge at the heart of value creation, which took place in the workshops of these artisans, craftsmen and artists. There they met and worked with painters, sculptors and other artists; architects, mathematicians, engineers, anatomists, and other scientists; and wealthy merchants who were patrons. All of them gave form and life to Renaissance communities, generating aesthetic and expressive as well as social and economic values. The result was entrepreneurship that conceived revolutionary ways of working, of designing and delivering products and services, and even of seeing the world.

Craftsmen, 'Merchants of Light'

Equipped with excellent entrepreneurial skills, the merchants of light see horizons so far away that they are imperceptible to the majority. They are detached from the context of systematic scientific research and proceed by trial and error, opening up unusual and unexplored paths. The boredom of taking the same roads every day fades. The fun of going on to new routes takes over. In the melting pot of science and technology, their entrepreneurship is brought to high temperatures.

They are the craftsmen who have anticipated the development of science. In his *Dialogue Concerning the Two Chief World Systems*, Galileo makes Giovanni Francesco Sagredo, experimenter and maker of scientific instruments, say that he had learned a great deal from the craftsmen of the Venice Arsenal, at that time a rich source of innovation for the shipbuilding industry. In Bologna, it was the artisans of the silk mills who pioneered the silk factories at the time of the first industrial revolution.

In the first period of the Renaissance, Johannes Gutenberg's invention of movable type printing represented a real epoch-making turning point. The German printer and other technological craftsmen with a profound knowledge of mechanics – 'the ingenuity of the makers of the machines', in the words of Adam Smith – managed to anticipate the advancements of science. In the eighteenth century, it was the author of *The Wealth of Nations*, the first modern work of economics, who highlighted the original and primary role of common workers and artisans in developing technologies followed by revolutionary scientific discoveries. In Book I, Chapter I of his *magnum opus* that Smith wrote,

> A great part of the machines made use of in those manufactures ...
> were originally the inventions of common workmen.

The craftsmen's imagination, intuition and artistic flair can benefit from the intensity and pervasiveness of digital technology. The many coworking spaces are the workshops where artisans experiment with the critical elements of design and development of digital products and services, how these can be configured and developed, and how the results should be managed.

Creative Ignorance

It is that which is learned, which is genuine, which is conscious, intentional and determined. In short, it is creative.

There is a long line of thinkers who, over the centuries, engaged in creative ignorance. Socrates spoke of creative decisions. St. Augustine first and Nicholas of Cusa then dwelt on the ignorance learned. Johann Gottlieb Fichte at the turn of the eighteenth and nineteenth centuries wrote that not knowing is an infinite journey. The reformer of education in the United States, John Dewey valued genuine ignorance. Hans Magnus Enzensberger, one of the great thinkers of the twentieth century, argues that creative ignorance is due to gestures of rejection. Stuart J. Firestein, the chair of the Department of Biological Sciences at Columbia University, argues that to overcome the limits of the known is neces-sary the ability to remain in the mystery and the unknown, which, to adopt a saying of Confucius, can be compared 'to find a black cat in a dark room, especially if there is no cat'. Hence Firestein's idea of an entire course dedicated to and entitled *Ignorance*, a science course in which a visiting scientist talks for a couple of hours to a group of students about what he doesn't know. Firestein, who has published a book titled *Ignorance: How It Drives Science* (New York, NY: Oxford University Press, 2012), tells his students, 'Have the ability [which he calls negative capability'] to remain in mysteries and unknowns without any irritable reaching or grasping'.

Creative Markets

Creative markets are social communities of collaboration and sharing in various cultural fields, supported by technological platforms.

They involve individuals of the most diverse ages who are passionate about entrepreneurship associated with technology and culture. Wanting to be self-fulfilling by creating new ideas for a better society, they are both producers of ideas worth sharing and cultural consumers.

They are responsible for building digital communities that sell their collaborative creations directly to customers in online marketplaces.

Co-founded in 2012 in San Francisco by Aaron Epstein, *Creative Market* has brought together around 9,000 independent creators.

Creative Thinking

Creative thinking is a skill that, once learned, translates into unconventional and sometimes unique business ideas. To ideators, we owe the launch of original activities that are mutant species of the business community. The set of disciplines that study the functioning of the mind is at the origin of training and research initiatives to be mobilised to give a decisive impulse to innovative processes of entrepreneurial ideation.

Four Stages of Creative Thinking

Preparation – the phase in which the problem is investigated.
Incubation – the phase in which the problem is thought about unconsciously.
Enlightenment – the phase in which ideas converge to form a possible solution.
Verification – the stage where the result is evaluated and deemed acceptable.
Source: Graham Walls, *The Art of Thought*, Tunbridge Wells: Solis Press, 2014; original edition: *The Art of Thought*, London: Jonathan Cape Ltd, 1926.

Creatives

Surrounded by an atmosphere of uncertainty, innovation is knowledge in action learned by practising the game of imagination and possibility. Creatives and the companies they found are giving innovation a boost. Together, they translate talks into action to innovate.

Creatives stimulate heterodox and imaginative thinking that fosters 'creative creation' – a ceaseless exercise in uncertainty, as the poet and Nobel Prize winner for Literature Joseph Brodsky would put it.

A new idea springs up suddenly and with great excitement of mind and spirit. However, you have to keep your mind well trained to come up with original ideas. In the gymnasium of mental gymnastics, following the method of lateral thinking developed by the Maltese physician and psychologist Edward de Bono, you can keep your creativity exercised with mental experiments to look at reality from different angles, from one or more sides rather than from the face.

Creatives are explorers of unknown lands. Their mental maps provide ideas, projects and potential entrepreneurs to the path of innovation that changes the state of the world. New enterprises arise from and among scientists and engineers, academics, researchers and analysts, poets and writers, architects, designers and stylists, artists and actors. They combine the most diverse technologies, such as those that have changed the way we communicate (Apple's iPhone) or play the most varied sports at home with more fabulous fun and less difficulty (Nintendo's Wii software – from the English word 'we').

Crowdfunding and Crowdsourcing

The willingness combined with the ability to do great things individually and in a crowd with others traces and opens up the paths of crowdfunding and crowd-sourcing. The latter represents a crowd of volunteers and passionate people, ready to respond to the need expressed by a company to outsource the design, implementation or development of an idea.

Crowdfunding is the contemporary version of ancient charities like the Irish Loan Fund launched by Jonathan Swift in the eighteenth century, and modern societies such as the Grameen Bank microcredit, arising from a research project conceived in 1976 by its founder, Muhammad Yunus, together with some of his students in Bangladesh.

The 'do-it-with-the-others' rather than the 'do-it-yourself' of the aspiring and the isolated new entrepreneur is one of many social technologies immersed in the Internet world that aggregates and organises crowds of people towards achieving a particular goal. Crowdfunding adopts innovative methods that change the way we allocate capital. Collective financing by a group of individuals pooling their money can support the emergence of entrepreneurial, social and cultural initiatives with many small sums granted by many small investors.

Money is not a fruit hanging from the trees that one can freely gather. However, today it is indeed more manageable for a potential entrepreneur to obtain funding through crowdfunding sites (such as Kickstarter, IndieGoGo, MicroVentures, Profounder and Peerbackers) embracing a broad community of small investors. They are eager to see success in a venture that otherwise might be a potential loser for lack of financial oxygen in the capital market.

The wave of people involved with networking and pooling their money via the Internet to support individual or collective initiatives is an overwhelming force. An assessment made by the World Bank raises the annual world potential of crowdfunding to US$300 billion by 2025, of which $13.8 billion is attributable to Europe and $47.6 billion to China.

Collecting small sums of money from many people – successful entrepreneurs have taken the lead of this movement. The founder of Starbucks, the largest international chain of coffee shops, has pulled millions of Starbuck's customers to accumulate millions of dollars that swell like an avalanche. Starbucks started the snowball effect with five million dollars donated by its Foundation, followed by a mass collection of 50 million resulting in loans to entrepreneurs seven times as much.

With the potential return on investment expected to rise, equity crowdfunding is set to grow. The United Kingdom, Finland, Australia and Italy have opened the way to the legality of equity crowdfunding.

Culture

Voices and words accompanied by symbols and gestures create a culture that enlivens innovation. Culture stimulates innovation processes, particularly in open innovation modality. The perspective of innovation changes according to the cultural system of reference.

Knowledge is one of its components, along with language, beliefs, customs, practices, codes of conduct and institutions. If the cultural norm is unhealthy, knowledge is affected. In turn, a knowledge malaise has negative repercussions on culture. The culture is not, therefore, an ornament – beautiful but useless. On the contrary, it is beautiful and valuable since it presents the human mind predisposed to openness to different minds and, therefore, inclined towards collaboration. It also shows us the virtue of altruism which, by defeating predatory behaviour, benefits all players in the collaborative game. This reminds us of a comment widely attributed to Peter Drucker, the management thinker, who considered himself a historical writer: culture eats strategy for breakfast – and, we might add, structure for lunch. Alternatively, by recalling Greek mythology, we could say that culture allows us to enjoy Athena's favours, the goddess. She, among her many attributes, presides over strategy.

Only subject to cultural conditions will open innovation have the opportunity to speak, in the framework of strategy and structure, the language of technical skills and methods acquired through experience and from books, articles, databases and dossiers. Finally, culture is the key that gives access to open innovation beyond the boundaries of business, making it accessible to society as a whole.

Cultural Consumption

The enthusiastic creation of machines, and an equal fervour for the consumption of new commodities and luxury goods, are the driving forces that, in the society and culture of the Renaissance, spurred the attitude to the new sciences of artificial life. What we now call 'second life', with their strong effect on entrepreneurship.

Cultural consumption encapsulates words inherited from the Renaissance that still permeate our ways of thinking, communicating and interacting in the presence of alternative choices in the production and consumption of goods and services that occur as often as they change rapidly. Today's Renaissance generation consists of millions of individuals of the most diverse ages who share a passion for entrepreneurship combined with technology and culture: an intersection that inspires confidence and encouragement for entrepreneurial intentions. Far from the anxiety and threats that culture was thought to face in the field of entrepreneurship when the age of digital reproduction of cultural content arrived.

From the perspective of consumer goods – from glazed pottery to pictures and furnishings – Isabella d'Este, Marquise of Mantua, a contemporary of Leonardo, is regarded as the 'First Lady of the Renaissance'. It is the patrician Isabella, patron of the arts, the illustrative embodiment of the 'cultural consumer' who attends the marketplaces in person. Here, a new class of direct customers, the patricians, who are no longer or not only represented by their intermediaries, joins the commoners. Isabella d'Este does more, promoting a new shopping channel, one operating by mail, a forerunner perhaps of e-commerce.

Curiosity

Curiosity treads unprecedented paths to invention, innovation and entrepreneurship. The curious person forgets about the patterns and rules generally used to approach problems and leaves more room for unconstrained observation to find innovative solutions.

Curiosity is a source of risk. Originating from the fascination of an experiment conducted on a horse, research into cardiac catheterisation (an invasive test used in cardiology) won Werner Forssmann the Nobel Prize for Medicine. Ulf Larsson (*Cultures of Creativity: The Centennial Exhibition of the Nobel Prize*, Science History Publication, 2002) notes that the medical community ostracised the scientist for the curious way of conducting his experiments. In Berlin, the Charité Hospital, Larsson recalls, fired him, pointing out that he could teach a class in a circus with his little tricks, but never in a respected German university.

Digital Craftsmen

Each of us can take the opportunity to evolve from a passive consumer to the active status of a craftsman producer of things that we know. The enablers are low-cost digital devices such as the Arduino board, an open-source electronics platform based on easy-to-use hardware and software. The platform allows us to make interactive projects and rapid prototyping – and high-tech laboratories equipped with 3D printers, laser cutting machines and other devices. We can thus create things for ourselves and the community faster, at a lower cost and with higher quality than large companies.

In the age of mechanisation, there was a bottleneck between doing and thinking: a mental impairment as defined by Robert Sennett in his essay *The Craftsman* (London: Allen Lane, 2008). The digital revolution exalts the figure of the technological craftsman whose hand-working and thinking head are intimately connected. *Homo Laborans* and *Homo Faber* (see the corresponding entry in Chapter 4) live together in his person. He is the owner of a craft in which the interaction between fingers and mind combines technical education with the liberal arts. The technique used to do things well is material culture capable of creating mental images without the use of the senses, while waiting, according to some visionaries, for better oculometric technologies and the digital evolution of cranial implants that configure a head that replaces the hands.

In the vast field of new technologies, the craftsman is an artist. Going back to the time of Leonardo da Vinci, being a painter and engineer is what distinguishes the craftsman. It is to say that the technology that has its root in the Greek word *tékhne* (i.e., art, craft) is married to the liberal arts. Painting, drawing, graphics, architecture, sculpture and other plastic arts, music, literature, psychology, and history give us an idea of the human nature of technology. These are the sources of design that provide a technological product with a touch of creativity and empathy indispensable for its success. Here echo the words advanced by Steve Jobs as he presented the iPad2 resonate:

> It's in Apple's DNA that technology alone is not enough. It's technology married with liberal arts, married with the humanities, that yields us the result that makes our heart sing, and nowhere is that more true than in these post-PC devices.

In the entrepreneurial neo-renaissance of the twenty-first century, innovative digital artisans create artefacts that are works of art.

Diplodocus

A dinosaur whose intelligence (as measured by its relative brain-to-body weight) was amongst the lowest of the dinosaurs.

Excessive regulation is a creature similar to Diplodocus. The many rules dictated by state bureaucracies swell the body of the 'bureaucratic diplodocus' and shrink its brain as they prevent experiments being conducted to bring about change in the cultural, social and economic climate.

Discontinuity

Discontinuity entails removing established certainties, favouring the Renaissance values of dynamism, diversity and versatility, and cognitive conflict. It is a culture that affects society's whole and whose horizon is much broader than the narrow horizon of the practices mastered by experts pursuing innovation strategies.

The education received and the experiences made convey ideas along the lines of thought traced by that education and those experiences. That leads to the conception of novelties that are a correction of the existing state of affairs, not a radical change. The revolutionary ideas – those beyond the horizon of our age's conceptual background – come to light once embraced uncertainty and doubt.

Discontinuity is such because it rejects indoctrinated thinking and proceeds along a path that takes back to a concept of the ancient Romans embedded in the verb *patere*. *Pateo*: 'I am accessible', 'I am exposed' to imagination, exploration, experimentation and creation. Along this open space path, wayfarers create or search for opportunities and find solutions to complicated or convoluted problems.

For organisations and individuals called upon to expose and express themselves on the scene of open innovation, a journey of exploration begins into the vast field of conditions and habits of mind challenged to confront external reality under conditions of uncertainty that raise serious questions about whether and how to present themselves on that scene.

Discovery and Invention

'Discovery consists of looking at the same thing as everyone else and thinking something different'. According to the Hungarian physiologist and Nobel Prize winner for Medicine Albert Szent-Györgyi, this is the preparatory path to the future. A future that is unfathomable, ambiguous and open to all alternatives.

If today's business is like a well-kept garden, with neat flowerbeds and high walls, this is not enough. Apparently, in stable equilibrium, that garden sees its survival threatened even by a light wind. Instead, a gust is an opportunity for those who are heedless of balance because they are voluntarily exposed to unexpected disturbances rather than constant adaptation.

Discovery (the act of observing or finding something unknown), the invention (the process of creating a new technology), and transformation into entrepreneurial innovation (the process of actually bringing the discovery and invention to market): it is on the fine-tuning of these events that the knowledge value chain depends.

Do a discovery and invention happen precisely at the right time, at the right speed and pace to result in an entrepreneurial event that is also unique, unlike anything else? Are discoveries and inventions immediately visible and usable, or how much time elapses between their emergence and the ability to understand them from a business perspective? At the crossroads of the economy and society, these kinds of events, once they are recognised and translated into innovative entrepreneurship, jeopardise the arrangements of production factors and consequently upset the behaviour of those involved. Accidentality, error, having or lacking imagination, absolute doubt and Socratic doubt are factors that intervene to trace the trajectory and fix the length of the path between the manifestation, perception and entrepreneurial translation of discovery and invention.

Accidents and mistakes create an aura of mystery that leaves the new event nameless. This is what happened in the late nineteenth century to Wilhelm Röntgen, professor of physics in Würzburg, Germany. The rays he discovered remained nameless: 'X' rays. The 'X', however, was not synonymous with doubt so that Röntgen's discovery was in the blink of an eye translated by the doctors of the time into ground-breaking practice: 'perhaps one of the fastest translations of any scientific discovery into practice', commented Robert Friedel ('The Accidental Inventor', *Discover*, 1 October 1996).

Either use the toolbox that goes by the name of 'Possibility' or stick to the rigid rules table that shapes our beliefs: the former speeds up the time of perception; the latter delays it by a long way. The great open-mindedness of Joseph Priestley, credited with the discovery of oxygen, his desire to share ideas and research among friends of science and freedom – the credo of their 'Honest Whigs Club' – was not enough to translate that discovery into innovation and to make it usable. Around 70 years passed between that event in 1772–1774 and, in its wake, the pioneering use of anaesthesia in dental care by the American dentist Horace Wells, who imaginatively triggered a learning process through experimentation.

Disrupter

He is a debunker and visionary who sees the I&R pair (Incrementalism and Return on Investment that measures the gain or loss generated by an investment relative to the amount of money invested) as the worst enemy of innovation. As Andy Grove preached, 'What's my ROI on e-commerce? Are you crazy? This is Columbus in the New World. What was his ROI?' (Anderson, 1997).

The disrupter finds the time to leave the risky paths of forecasting, which he has taken with his mental baggage, and take paths strewn with uncertainty.

A stubborn and unorthodox experimenter in facing the hindrances encountered along the way, the perturber calculates time by measuring the width of the window open on a varied and discontinuous landscape that offers a glimpse of overwhelming opportunities at the edge of a precipice.

It only takes a few disruptors to give a solid impetus to human events so that they can happen suddenly, thus marking the destiny – the inevitable decadence – of the incrementalists.

The forest regenerating itself with small, new trees is the cultural habitat of this disrupter. While, during the 1970s and 1980s, the gaze of the incrementalists was on the already tall and ever more luxuriant trees of the Japanese economic miracle, in their garages the unknown Steve Jobs and Steve Wozniak (Apple), Bill Gates (Microsoft), Michael Dell (Dell Technologies), Larry Ellison (Oracle) and others were gathering the seeds of the new and original plants that the incrementalists would initially denigrate with the nickname 'toys for boys'.

It is not always the case that technology alone feeds and boosts the disrupters of the status quo. Other elements are involved in shaping the killer innovation, either in addition or as an alternative to the technological nutrient. Soft values come into play. For instance, ethics is the nutrient chosen by Lyft to scale, to Uber's detriment, the 2017 ranking of the top 50 disrupters drawn up by CNBC, featuring private companies in a wide range of industries from biotechnology and machine learning to transport and retail (https://www.cnbc.com/2017/05/16/the-2017-cnbc-disruptor-50-list-of-companies.html).

Doubt

The passage that accelerates the encounter between the unique event and its recognisability is obstructed not by Socratic doubt, motivated by the search for truth, but by absolute doubt – the defender of the faith, of the status quo. Through artificial expedients, it constrains the understanding of discovery and the potential impact on the terrain of innovation. It took decades to convince physicians and nurses, confined within the bastion of the miasma theory of disease, of the validity of the theory of infectious germs developed by the French scientist Louis Pasteur.

Broad ambitions allow us to look beyond the horizon of absolute doubt and achieve outstanding results. The brave and visionary experimenter, walking on a tightrope across faith in science, curiosity and creativity, is overwhelmingly ambitious. The invention of the radio was obscured by dense clouds of doubt mixed with controversy and scepticism. There were doubts about the value of the pioneering work on long-distance radio transmission and a radio telegraph system conducted by Guglielmo Marconi. He stood on the shoulders of two giants of physics – James Clerk Maxwell, credited with the modern theory of electromagnetism, and Heinrich Hertz, who discovered and demonstrated the existence of electromagnetic waves. Scientists thought the earth's curvature was an insurmountable obstacle to long-distance communication through wireless telegraphy.

Overcoming or bypassing such high barriers requires unbridled ambition – what Marconi had, quite possibly inherited from his mother, Annie Jameson, of the Irish entrepreneurial family known since 1780 for the celebrated whiskey production. The first experiments by Marconi, on the hills of Bologna between 1894 and 1895, were followed in less than three years by the foundation in 1897 of the Wireless Telegraph and Signal Company (subsequently the Marconi Company).

As a 20-year-old, Marconi attended the University of Bologna, which included him among its illustrious physics personalities, but he did not graduate. It is fitting to reiterate here what we said in the first part (Chapter 2) about his university studies. Marconi recounts that he had never attended Professor Augusto Righi's lessons, a pioneer of electromagnetism. When Marconi told him his idea of wireless telegraphy, Righi replied that it was not feasible. Since then, Marconi never spoke with him about that subject (*Guglielmo Marconi. Memorie 1895–1899*, edited by Gabriele Falciasecca, Bologna: Pendragon, 2020). At the top of their field, renowned and revered, yesterday's pioneers remained in place, losing the mental agility to jump from known space to an unknown one.

Marconi did not fall into the trap of treating his invention as a toy or a game, unlike many scientists and senior corporate executives over time. The then-president of Western Union described Bell's phone as a toy, a word still used in 2007 by BlackBerry to describe Apple's iPhone.

Drone

As promised by Jeff Bezos, the ape's artificial male, the drone, is now in sight, delivering home purchases made in online stores. In the space of a few years, Amazon promises to deliver, on a large scale, with miniaturised helicopter-robots the products we request. If not the sunset, first, of a long sequence of horses – those, for example, of the Pony Express, fast postal service from Missouri to San Francisco – and, then, of trucks in the streets, what is certain is that, with bits moving goods, companies are trying to figure out the best way to integrate e-commerce into their operations. Even those companies already dipping a toe (or an entire leg) into the waters of digital commerce are recognising that a long journey has just begun. Bezos' little drones prove it.

Ecology of Entrepreneurial Species

The shaping of innovative and novel environments depends on the intensity and quality of the relationships between the entrepreneurial populations living in the same habitat.

The 'Commensals' species do not contribute an endowment to the habitat, do not disturb it, and do not interact with other species.

'Predators' hunt other species in the habitat.

'Symbionts' live and grow in close relationship with other species; they seek complementarity in their habitat.

'Parasites' exploit the attractiveness of the habitat in which they locate.

Economy On-Demand

With the advent of digital technologies, the on-demand economy is emerging.

We can affordably avail ourselves of a professor's lectures and a taxi driver's transportation without going through the university and the company of taxi drivers. A book can be purchased directly from its author. The same is true for an exponentially growing number of products and services. Thus, a vast field of opportunities opens up before us for one-to-one interactions between consumer and producer that mutually switch roles.

Ecosystem

We owe to Arthur George Tansley, an English botanist and pioneer of ecology, the term 'ecosystem'. In the ecosystem, organizations and individuals interact with each other and other organisms of the external environment involved in its sphere of influence. The flow of knowledge is the connecting medium. Resources, perspectives, aspirations and commitments are shared in order to pursue a profitable future for all.

Energies

There is today a whole world of novelties sprung from different energy sources.

Intellectual energies move discoveries in the direction of entrepreneurship with high expectations and strong growth potential.

Productive energies exploiting the new generations of robots and 3D printers give back strength to local economies that had lost the old manufacturing industry's whole sectors.

Communicative energies exploit new sensors and new materials to connect people and things.

Social energies set in motion the engines of sharing.

Between events of this magnitude, relationships are anything but linear. The ensuing effects are not proportional to their causes and can even be chaotic.

Entreprenaissance

Jacob Christoph Burckhardt, an influential historian of art and culture, called the Renaissance 'anthropocentric', interpreting the age in terms of individual human values and experiences at the centre of the universe. 'Anthropocene' represents the age in which we live today, an age in which the protagonists are people who, through their activities, have modified the physical, social, cultural and entrepreneurial environments significantly.

By launching projects which combine scientific and humanitarian approaches to creativity, the entrepreneurs of the twenty-first century are bringing into being a new renaissance, described by Creel Price, perhaps one of the most dynamic entrepreneurs in Australia, as the 'Entreprenaissance' – namely, entrepreneurship which marks the reawakening or the rebirth of learning and culture, building a bridge between past and present renaissance men: from Leonardo da Vinci's invention of the flying machine to Elon Musk's advanced rockets and spacecraft.

Such is the underlying scenario that gives us a glimpse of extraordinary results – both substantial in scope and altruistic – that contrast with short-term perspectives, concerns for quarterly results and, in particular, the lower production costs achieved through economies of scale that defined the journey.

Entrepreneurial Education

Business education, brought forward to start in primary schools, stimulates the inventiveness of young people and helps them to gain control of their futures.

To combat the weakening of the entrepreneurial pulse and low growth of the start-ups, the European Union Commission has identified, amongst the priority action to be put in place, investment in business training. It is an investment with high returns. About 15–20% of students who participate in mini-business programmes organised by secondary schools go on to launch a start-up. Moreover, this percentage is between three and five times higher than that of the population as a whole. In Finland, primary education incorporates business classes, and assessment of students appears significantly better at a relatively small overall cost per student. We learn from Harvard University that interest in attending university increases by 32% after taking part in a business course, while the desire to find a job that combines employment with entrepreneurship increases by 44%.

Entrepreneurial Enterprise

In the Renaissance landscape of the twenty-first century, the entrepreneurial enterprise stands out. The protagonists are the young entrepreneurs of today, who can converse in the mathematical, physical and natural sciences and the humanities.

Tradition dictates that massive doses of managerial culture must be injected into the fabric of the company. Entrepreneurs cannot do everything. Managers must support them to entrust the company staff with specific tasks and rigid bonds. In short, the company is born entrepreneurial and grows up managerial. However, it was one of the founding fathers of that culture, Peter Drucker, who regretted 'Much of what we call management consists of making it difficult for people to work' (http://econ.st/1pTnyR1). Nowadays, it is the Drucker Society, an international society that analyses the birth and growth of companies, which puts the human being at the centre of company development, breaking down the barriers which management functions raise between one department and another in the company.

As the protagonist of this new Renaissance scenario, humanism makes entrepreneurial activity flourish again – a living, incandescent matter compared to the cold, soulless practices of the bureaucratic company. What is destined to grow is the enterprise that maintains its entrepreneurial character, born of an entrepreneur.

Rather than passive executors of tasks, the entrepreneurial enterprise relies on co-creators and entrepreneurs. It will nurture the growth of baby companies in the human dimension of entrepreneurial enterprise. The coexistence and clash of different talents make that enterprise a lively place where the confrontation of opinions opens the door to would-be exploited opportunities.

Entrepreneurial Fertilisation

Human and social capital resources produce virtuous links between inventors, academics, researchers, young graduates, and entrepreneurs: all protagonists in the process of entrepreneurial fertilisation in university classrooms and laboratories. A process triggered by radical innovation in academic organisations: something similar to the interposition that occurred in the transition from convent education to medieval universities' birth.

From the tree of research hang the fruits of entrepreneurship. To reap them, the number of entrepreneurs ready to dance with the researchers and talents who accept to run the business risk on the ground of the innovations born from their research must grow: a virtuous dance, also because it could give oxygen to the always ailing budgets of research institutions. Academic innovation is a potentially rich source of entrepreneurial projects that translate into companies with high growth expectations.

Entrepreneurialism

Entrepreneurialism – the mind and creative faculty for entrepreneurial actions, and the underlying Entrepreneurship, the process of designing and starting a business – has the purpose of changing the performance of resources, giving them the ability to create new wealth. Entrepreneurialism is not just about material prosperity. It is a way of perceiving the world that contributes to the broader design of society.

Entrepreneurialism is a human pursuit, a multifaceted cultural movement, a polar star to navigate the sea of new model enterprise creation at the intersection of science and the humanities.

The culture of entrepreneurialism is to take care (from the Latin *colere*, whence culture) of the socioe-conomic environment while respecting the natural environment. It conceives thoughts that lead to blue actions, associated with the colour of sea and sky (viz, the safeguarding of the Planet) and, in the dark blue shade, to the ideas – the ideator's intellectual momentum – that shape those actions.

The culture of entrepreneurialism feeds on the thoughts of polymaths, who aim to keep all knowledge under their domain. The German Jesuit Athanasius Kircher, a scientific star of the Baroque age and a traveller in many worlds of knowledge, guides us towards that culture, preparing us to flutter like a butterfly from one field of knowledge to another. As a precursor to the contemporary world, Kircher moved between the study of volcanoes and fossils, the observation of microbes under the microscope, mechanical inventions such as automata, the magnetic clock and megaphone, Egyptology, music theory and comparative religion.

Entrepreneurialism ushers a new age of education, moving away from the 'front-loaded' educational system. It is a journey heading towards the reimagined school (see the corresponding entry in Chapter 4), a rebirth of Renaissance learning by forging revolutionary paths for human and relational capital that changes the student's mind.

If we were to compare the agents of entrepreneurialism to the artistic avantgarde of the early twentieth century, we would see them as Cubists – those who depicted the subject from a multitude of points of view to frame it in a broader context. Further, we would attribute to them the characteristics of the Dadaists who rejected society's standards of the time, believing that imposed societal norms and established expectations had become outdated. The protagonists' culture of entrepreneurialism gives rise to a constant buzz of creativity that arouses motivations and expectations based on knowledge at the eventide of probability and in the dark night of uncertainty. Furthermore, we would say that those agents constitute a parallel with the cultural movement of the Surrealists to whom we are indebted for representations of illogical scenes, strange creatures, surprising elements and unexpected juxtapositions.

Entrepreneurship

A word that lies at the heart of the commercial exploitation of the colourful results of the big bang caused by the collision of bits, atoms, neurons and genes.

The convergence of chemistry, biology, physics, computer science and robotics opens up dizzying prospects for innovation that explorers and opportunity creators will exploit if they are enabled to do so.

By acquiring the new digital means of production, anyone can rise to the role of an entrepreneur without the need for intermediaries. The process of democratising entrepreneurship is, therefore, on its way.

Emerging entrepreneurship is an integrated system with multiple and overlapping dimensions of entrepreneurship. Different entrepreneurial species converge and associate. There are:

- Business owners and their descendants.
- Capitalists who invest at their own risk in the enterprise.
- Employers who employ human resources.
- CEOs who, with their managers, implement business strategies, and
- Revolutionary entrepreneurs who create entrepreneurial enterprises rather than replicating the modus operandi of managerial enterprises.

Inventions have their outlet in technological entrepreneurship. Social entrepreneurship takes over the no man's land between the economy and society. The international mobility of talent is the source of the geographical entrepreneurship of global start-ups that move products and services to and from various places on earth. Sharing communities are the basis of new enterprises such as social roads. Smart, knowledge-based, digital, wired, ubiquitous city projects and their implementations promote civic entrepreneurship that transforms local government processes and procedures.

Highly educated, borderless entrepreneurship is becoming increasingly crucial in economies open enough to accommodate the waters of a great river fed by numerous tributaries. These are:

- International twinning of successful scientists and entrepreneurs.
- Researchers and students using their global mobility to create unorthodox entrepreneurial alliances with colleagues in other countries.
- Investors providing venture capital to internationally conceived entrepreneurial projects.
- Experimental laboratories for building new enterprises.
- Pioneering technological infrastructures, hosting incubated start-ups. At the meeting point of mobile talent and new international entrepreneurship, research results translate into commercially viable goods and services, yielding significant financial benefits for universities and, most importantly, having a beneficial, entrepreneurial effect on research communities.

Entrepreneurial Reaction

Entrepreneurship is not a simple set of conventions (nomos, as the ancient Greeks used to say). It has a genuine nature (a physis) visible in converting resources from input to output, a process occurring from an 'entrepreneurial reaction'.

The 'entrepreneurial reaction' leads to exploring the emerging science of eco-physics, which employs physics tools to study markets. In particular, the sub-field of interest to 'reaction' features microscopic elements whose configuration resembles atomic structure. Artificial as it may seem, there are analogies between business ideas, the units of entrepreneurship, and atoms, the units of matter. At the centre (the 'core') of a venture creation is a positively charged idea whose instigator must have a vision and give it meaning. Almost all of its 'mass' is made up of highly interactive 'particles' that are not easily distinguishable from each other, such as the motivations and attributes of entrepreneurial behaviour. Orbiting around the 'core' are the experimenters (the entrepreneurial teams with their coaches) responsible for the idea's 'chemical' properties, such as practicality, profitability and sustainability.

The 'particles' of motivations and attributes must be placed in a 'magnetic' entrepreneurial field and possess entrepreneurial energy, the ability to do entrepreneurial work to move from the state of the intention to the state of entrepreneurial action. 'Entrepreneurial energy' (E) and 'Mass' (M) are two sides of the same coin. The cube of creativity (C) in business (creativity in technology x creativity in process x creativity in marketing) is the conversion rate between E and M.

This is the equation of entrepreneurship:

$$E = MC^3$$

An entrepreneurial reaction occurs when the 'core' changes, releasing a significant amount of energy needed to transform ideas into real business projects.

Entrepreneurial University

The entrepreneurial university acts as an open-circuit enterprise of ideas, developing small science and not just big science, i.e. also engaging in transfer sciences (such as engineering) that link basic and applied research. It enters the body of knowledge to extract entrepreneurial DNA from it and manage entrepreneurship and innovation, generating knowledge whose output is companies founded by graduates, researchers and academics. These spin-offs also assist in financing university departments, as Oxsoft, a company created by a professor of cardiovascular physiology at Oxford University. Ultimately, a university aiming at research results turned into attractive goods to which technology marketing strategies are applied, with financial spillovers on its balance sheet and, above all, with innovation spin-offs indispensable for developing the local communities in which it is rooted.

John Seely Brown and Paul Duguid ('Space for the chattering classes', *The Times Higher Education*, supplement, 10 May 1996) have designed the entrepreneurial university as a network of freely associated and complementary bodies. Precisely:

- The Agency sets quality standards, hires teachers and enrols students in numbers compatible with the available resources.
- The Faculties are independent contractors of one or more Agencies.
- The Service Companies manage classrooms, libraries and research laboratories.
- Laboratories test innovative start-ups initiated by professors, researchers, graduates and students in collaboration with industrial partners and international investors. In addition, the laboratories make entrepreneurial use of studies and research carried out at the entrepreneurial university.

In the entrepreneurial university, former students participate in the network activities through 'learning contracts' signed by themselves and their employers.

Experimental and Conceptual Innovators

David Galenson's in-depth studies on artistic creativity led to the expressions 'experimental innovators' and 'conceptual innovators' (*And Now for Something Completely Different: The Versatility of Conceptual Innovators.* NBER Working Paper No. 12034. National Bureau of Economic Research, Cambridge, MA: USA, 2006; *Old Masters and Young Geniuses: The Two Life Cycles of Artistic Creativity*, Princeton, NJ: Princeton University Press, 2007).

Experimental innovators develop innovations slowly. Aiming at a single, uncertain goal, they take a long time to refine their innovations by incessantly reviewing their work by trial and error. According to Galenson, in painting, the typical character, motivated by aesthetic criteria, is Paul Cézanne. In science, Charles Darwin 'spent decades accumulating evidence on evolution and its mechanisms' (Galenson, D. W., and Pope, C. L. 'Experimental and conceptual innovators in the sciences: The cases of Darwin and Einstein'. *Historical Methods: A Journal of Quantitative and Interdisciplinary History, 46*(2), 102–112, 2013). In the film industry, Alfred Hitchcock is a prominent name.

Conceptual innovators bring radical innovation to their field from an early age. They exhibit highly abstract reasoning and are keenly focused on reaching the goal regardless of obstacles and errors they might encounter along their creative path. They are characterised by their versatility, jumping from one subject to another, producing a great variety of innovations. They run counter to existing beliefs and depart from those who cling to outdated ideas and obsolete definitions.

According to Galenson, in visual art, Picasso is the archetype of the conceptual innovator. Painting objects not as he saw them, but as he thought them, with *Les Demoiselles d'Avignon*, he inaugurated the Cubist movement – 'a startling and radical stylistic innovation'. John Cage stands out in the art of music because of 'the diversity of his many innovations' (Galenson, 2006, p. 19). The American composer used to say that he was afraid of old ideas, not new ones. To simplify problems and put forward bold ideas out of the box of consolidated thinking, Albert Einstein is on the podium of conceptual innovators in science, as is Walt Disney in the entertainment industry and theme parks.

Experimental Laboratory

Experimentation promotes value creation through innovation. In the laboratory, relationships between aspiring entrepreneurs with high growth ambitions are the engine of innovation. Experiential knowledge (having experience) and experiential learning (gaining experience through experimentation) interact in the development of a business model.

Every single moment of the experimental process of creativity has to do with a different face of the prism of innovation.

There are various aspects to experimentation:

- Putting together scattered pieces of accumulated knowledge to improve the products and processes in use and the organisation and governance of the system.

- Targeting with new products the lower segments of the market neglected by incumbents.
- Designing content to serve a new medium.
- Combining ideas from different fields to conceive something new, not reflected in acquired knowledge.
- Creative recombination of elements from the past.

The experimentation of innovation among peers gathered in open communities leads to entrepreneurship generating economic value and shared social benefits. The innovation resulting from experimentation is, in fact, a social product, the distribution of which is supervised by the participants so that the resulting wealth is not monopolised by a few holders of economic and extra-economic power in the experimental process. In addition, the experimenters (see the corresponding entry in Chapter 4) have the opportunity to reproduce the creative process with the same or other protagonists, taking their cue from discarded works in the course of the now completed experiment.

Just as the experiments in physics at CERN in Geneva unearth new particles, the experimental laboratories of entrepreneurship with high growth expectations discover the variables of entrepreneurial innovation. In the laboratories, people from the most diverse backgrounds are engaged in experiments to establish companies that exploit the opportunities opened up by the entrepreneurial knowledge society to solve humanity's problems accumulated since the latter part of the last century.

Accelerating the transformation of the present requires experimentation rather than reliance on experience with prediction underneath. Laboratory operations make logical leaps, freely combining and linking the most diverse thoughts and data.

Modes of experimentation to decipher the 'what', the 'why' and the 'how' should replace or, at least, complement modes of prediction. As Richard Davenport-Hines writes (*Universal Man: The Seven Lives of John Maynard Keynes*, William Collins, 2015), Keynes, acclaimed as the founding father of modern macroeconomics, preferred experimentation, tempered by intuition, to experience that runs on roads so travelled that they are no longer capable of arousing emotions.

An experimental lab initiates and facilitates the two main phases of the entrepreneurial process aimed at innovation: i.e., the creation of an idea and the initial testing of possible dissemination paths to determine its potential feasibility and probability of success.

Heterogeneous groups of people with the most varied and complementary skills participate in the laboratory.

In an experimental lab, participants ignore the obstacles that hold back the race in the field of innovation occupied by experts sunk in their wells of knowledge. The scenario revealed by the expert is a guide to innovation that improves on the existing. The experimental scenario is a beacon that sheds light on the unknown of innovation that changes state of the art and achieves the impossible. To those who asked him, what laboratory rules do you want me to follow, Thomas Edison replied that there were no rules, 'We are trying to do something'.

People from different fields and professions observe with curiosity and without prejudice what one of them is doing. Many changes take place through repurposing and adapting the idea of one experimenter to the ideas of others. Thus, by crossing business ideas and building one on the making of another, the laboratory increases the number of ideas that can be successful.

Solid networks of experimenters freely exchanging ideas are made possible by the increased capacity for interaction. A small idea fed into the network can turn into an excellent entrepreneurial result. To benefit from the multiplier effect of sharing – 'I am going to use my idea in my field of use, and you are invited to use it in your field, which is different from mine' – one has to abandon the bad habits of mortifying the ability to interact, thus forcing the entrepreneurial idea to be carried out in an isolated environment. There is no shortage of historical cases to consider to understand how vast the field of use of an idea can be. The idea of steam as an energy source moved, in the course of about a century, from the mine to the blast furnace and then to the steamship and the electric locomotive.

The laboratory is based on the principle that there are no failed experiments, only experiments with unexpected results, as argued by the American inventor Richard Buckminster Fuller. Following in the footsteps of the physicist Richard Feynman, experiments are carried out in the laboratory in search of what invalidates the initial hypotheses, rather than focusing only on the evidence that confirms them.

Experimentation does not leave one in the dark in the tunnel of a prolonged crisis that brings about significant transformations in a depressed economy. Franklin Delano Roosevelt was well aware of this. On 22 May 1932, speaking to students at Oglethorpe University, he said:

The country needs and, unless I mistake its temper, the country demands bold, persistent experimentation. It is common sense to take a method and try it: If it fails, admit it frankly and try another. But above all, try something.

The Framework of an Experimental Laboratory within an Open Innovation Community

- Meetings of minds facilitated by network connectivity and physical contacts are at the heart of experimentation. People from different backgrounds and experiences test business ideas by working together. The choices of one group are connected to those of others ('social influence').
- Network relations are visible to all parties involved and are performance driven. The laboratory 'temperature' is taken by applying mathematical rigour to assess the influence of the laboratory community on personal interactions. The mathematics of networks quantifies the intensity of connections between lab members.
- The evaluation process assigns the degree of compatibility to a given idea concerning its relevance in the network and connection to it.

- The network learns through its exposure to the most varied situations. Signals are transmitted from one business idea to another.
- Models of business ideas are discovered. This makes it possible to move across adjacent market boundaries. Permutations and combinations of ideas are then possible. Witness the case of Johannes Gutenberg, who abandons the best practices of the time and replaces them with the process of pre-adaptation (or ex-adaptation), applying to printing techniques and tools used in other sectors – from the punch in goldsmithing to the winepress.

Experimenter

Whether as an innovator or as an entrepreneur, the experimenter has a hybrid cultural identity. Like Lemuel Gulliver, experimenters embark on extraordinary journeys. By practising the art of play, the exploring experimenters put questions answered with the 'Four Knowns': Knowing How To Do, Think, Imagine and Understand. Thus, experimenters discover new territories where the similarities and differences between individuals overlap and interact.

The experimenter appreciates purposeful and lasting interactions with those from different cultural backgrounds. The more connected and the more intense the dialogue and the questioning of existing propositions and theories, the more experience will be acquired from participation in communities that promote the sharing of experiments.

In an open innovation environment, experimenters focus on exploration. In the open field of exploratory experimentation, they try to chart new paths by relying on their mental power and imaginative observation and sharing and learning from each other. The result is a dynamic and adaptive ecosystem that creates, channels and transforms ideas into practical innovation.

Formulating the idea is the first stage of experimentation. Next, the experimenters put a rudimentary business idea to the test. Finally, the lightning bolt of inspiration has the advantage of creating a link that moves the experiment forward, thanks to the formulation of a strategy and interaction with other teams. At the end of this phase, a prototype will be available.

Reformulation or re-evaluation of the idea is the second stage, thanks to the feedback from a few potential customers.

In the third stage of the experimentation, that of fine-tuning the growth potential of the idea, the experimenters build a bridge between the tiny base of pioneering and enthusiastic customers and the broad platform of pragmatic followers.

Expert

The ascent to Paradise followed by the fall to Hell of the expert champions is well known. Yet, to the present day, the sailing syndrome – a term derived from the perseverance of sailing ship manufacturers in investing in technology that had been long in use, in the conviction that steamships were nothing but an ugly duckling (reference is made here to one of the most renowned economic historians Carlo Maria Cipolla in his essay *Guns, Sails, and Empires: Technological Innovation and the Early Phases of European Expansion, 1400–1700*, London: Collins, 1965) – has affected a large number of experts.

'In the beginner's mind there are many possibilities; in the expert's mind there are few', said Shunryū Suzuki, Sōtō Zen monk and teacher. Albert Einstein believed that the more experienced and famous one becomes, the more stupid one is; 'the intellect gets crippled, but glittering renown is still draped around the calcified shell' – as Walter Isaacson reports in his biography on the illustrious physicist (*Einstein: His Life and Universe*, New York, NY: Simon & Schuster, 2007). That is the consequence of the expert who descends into the deepest darkness of the well of parcelled knowledge. The pit syndrome acts as a barrier to prevent the expert from practising the sport of contact between humanities and sciences. In entrepreneurial universities, professors and students, once out of the well, weave and merge the most disparate knowledge forms. New scientific assets are gained that the same protagonists turn into innovative entrepreneurship.

Explicit and Tacit Knowledge

Pioneering studies (*The Knowledge-Creating Company: How Japanese Companies Create the Dynamics of Innovation*, Oxford: Oxford University Press, 1995) by Ikujiro Nonaka, organisation theorist, and Hirotaka Takeuchi, professor of management, have designed two forms of knowledge: the explicit and the tacit.

Explicit knowledge is formal and systematic, articulated in words and numbers, and available in manuals, books, databases and files.

Tacit knowledge can be acquired orally, by direct experience, trial and error. It is a set of intuitions, sensations, and points of view that come to light through the use of metaphors, images or experiences. It is subjective, not easily perceived and expressed, below the level of awareness, and is therefore difficult to communicate.

'Festina lente'

Making haste slowly: the promptness of action combined with the slowness of careful reflection.

The 'slowness is inseparable from his genius', said Thomas Mann, of Johann Wolfgang von Goethe, whose work on *Wilhelm Meister's Apprenticeship* lasted for more than 16 years and on *Faust* for almost six decades (Thomas Mann, *Goethe impolitico*. Milan, Italy, 2017).

A proponent of an open world, the slowness-espousing Goethe aspired to rapidity when it came to driving forward the progress of what we now call globalisation. Impatiently, he sighed at the thought of having to wait for decades to see the realisation of innovative events on the scale of the Panama and Suez Canals.

Emperor Augustus, who wanted to change the face of Rome for the better, in his official letters, noted Desiderius Erasmus, recommended to his ministers the solicitude of action together with the slowness of reflection. The promptness of the action time with a reflective slowness is the legacy Erasmus attributed to the great leaders. Innovation must run at a speed that enables it to achieve effective results efficiently. We could portray innovation as a dolphin whose way of flying over the water's surface like an arrow and of being stable by entwining around an anchor fuse together.

'Festina lente' is the behaviour that takes over from the production speed of an abundance of mediocre and superfluous goods (how many of them are in our possession but forgotten) and multiple choices urged by a mass of information captivating and debilitating at the same time. Losing the hoarding of goods attraction among the new generations, the values brought by thought activities with a much lighter environmental footprint and a robust local character will be reinvigorating to the cultural tissue worn out by the old economy's functioning.

Fictions: The Coffee Red Thread

Narrative fictions possess an irresistible power to move the landscape of innovation far and wide in time and space. Between the real and the fictional, the history of coffee is a case in point.

The world is an open-air laboratory of experimentation in which those passionate about the art of innovating are involved. It is a long red thread that unravels the skein of events that, through stories handed down, historical events, readings and intentional or accidental occasions, have united the many characters on stage in the theatre of innovation recounted here: coffee. Our present theatrical tale, performed in the theatre of innovation, concerns a universal commodity: coffee.

Our red thread has at one end a Yemenite shepherd of ancient times and, at the other, a latter-day entrepreneur of the digital era who has given a unique and memorable taste to the two aspects of coffee: the place and the drink. In order of appearance, the characters of this story are:

Kaldi: a young shepherd of Ethiopian origin.

Avicenna: an Arab doctor of high repute.

Prospero Alpino: a botanic doctor.

Leonhard Rauwolf: a doctor of Augsburg.

Francesco Procopio Cutò (dei Coltelli): an Italian chef from Sicily.

English and French cultural representatives and businessmen, workers and technicians of the Bologna engineering industry.

Starbuck: First Officer of the 'Pequod', the whaling ship hunting Moby Dick.

A trio: Jerry Baldwin, Professor of English; Zev Siegl, Professor of History; and Gordon Bowker, writer.

Mr Howard Schultz: a manager and entrepreneur.

What is unique about our characters? What do they have in common? Each is a rare member of its species, living in our story in a period of time different from their usual environment. History – the steamroller of time – has forced together, in our virtual world, natives and non-natives alike, innovatively combining their characteristics so as to create a vision that is always greater than the sum of its parts. Coffee is the name of the whole: its parts are coffee as a drink and coffee as a place of entertainment.

The next 'big idea' might arise in any part of the world, from any individual – even one unaware that their idea has started an irreversible process of change. Do not seek places and individuals having a monopoly on ideas: you will not find them.

Our story starts with an inexperienced drover who, without realizing it, releases the innovative potential contained in some seeds.

Once upon a time, a young Yemenite shepherd named Kaldi fed his flock with coffee berries. 'Those fruit must be the work of the Devil', he pondered, noticing how the animals became agitated after eating them; and it was known that monks at the nearby Cheodet monastery regarded the berries as devilish and put them on their fires.

Great ideas travel on the wagon of chance. Seated on the wagon, supported by the wheels of casual occurrence and unpredictability, the idea of coffee began its journey through time and space. The roasting process of the Cheodet monks caused the aroma of coffee to fill the air. Time passed, places changed, and others were discovered, but, from that moment, the coffee cup entered society, marking time in the mornings and then encouraging socialisation – with people enjoying it whilst engaged in idle chatter or playing cards – wherever coffee was made.

The first to benefit from this natural harvest were the monks. Scientists then arrived and started to reveal the book of nature and understand its secrets. Reading that book, Avicenna, a Persian scientist and doctor of the eleventh century, promoted the therapeutic qualities of coffee, including it as a remedy in his *The Canon of Medicine*. Many other doctors were to follow his example and prescribe coffee as a medicine.

Ideas and things run with the mind and legs of human beings. From Islam to Catholicism, from the Arab peninsula and the Eastern world to Italy, coffee continued its journey through different, changing places and times. Towards the end of the sixteenth century, men (and it was men) from the Middle East would be the first to start conversations and read from books about coffee. The Venetian botanical doctor, Prospero Alpino, taught his fellow Venetians about coffee as a medicinal plant after having been to Cairo. Leonhard Rauwolf, an Augsburg doctor, published one of the first books about coffee after visiting the East between 1573 and 1578.

In places of conviviality, ideas come together spontaneously, discoveries are made, and entrepreneurship germinates: this is the 'coffee-machine effect', particularly prevalent it seems amongst students and academics in universities and colleges in the UK and the US. However, the effect is older than Anglo-Saxon places of learning.

'Arabian wine' or 'wine of Islam', names of the coffee beverage, arrived in Europe on the echo of the first Ottoman cafeterias, which served coffee instead of wine, forbidden to Muslims. Between 1683 and 1686, a period of war and peace between the West and the East, 'Viennese coffee' was first served (in 1683, the year the Turks were defeated); the first coffee shop opened in Venice (also in 1683); and, in 1686, the first literary café in Paris – Le Procope – was opened by a Sicilian chef, Procopio dei Coltelli. With customers such as Voltaire, Diderot and Fontenelle, Le Procope became the cradle of literary, philosophical, scientific, political and artistic events. Since that time, coffee has become a seemingly indispensable accompaniment to intellectual discourse and debate, to the extent that Pellegrino Artusi, the Italian master chef of his time, was moved to observe that

> ...this precious drink spreading a joyful excitement throughout the body was called the intellectuals' drink, the friend of academics, scientists and poets because by shaking nerves, it clears ideas and makes imagination more lively and thought quicker.

In the eighteenth century in England, the new coffee houses would play their part in the industrial revolution, underpinning advances in science and engineering with the liberal revolution taking place in general society. In the period of Enlightenment and Rationality, the so-called Age of Reason, people like Joseph Priestley, who discovered oxygen, James Watt, the Scottish engineer who refined the steam engine, and Josiah Wedgwood, an entrepreneur who developed ceramic tableware and decorative items, would meet in the English coffee houses to drink coffee and smoke tobacco ('drink the smoke' or 'chi yan' as tobacco smokers called the practice in China in the seventeenth century).

Thus, in Europe, in the eighteenth century, immersed as the continent was in Newtonian physics' scientific method, the introduction of coffee, to be sipped together, was volcanic in effect. Inventions and discoveries seemed to spread like molten lava, arising from conversations between intellectuals stimulated by caffeine to such an extent that the author Tom Standage has described the coffee houses as the *Internet of the Age of Reason*. Here was the starting point of the phenomenon that was to become known as the cross-fertilization of scientific, industrial and financial ideas.

The Age of Enlightenment and the first industrial revolution had come and gone before Italy became involved with modern industrial development. In the 1920s, coffee, tobacco and card games would be the three critical ingredients of socialisation between ordinary working people, whatever their employment. More so than with current academic and professional conferences. Their rituals of exchanging business cards and drinking coffee while playing cards in city bars gave rise to informal relationships among different people, often getting unexpected results. For example, in just such bars in Bologna, employees with generalist and specialist career paths first developed and then launched packaging machines that would eventually reach global markets.

In Italy, Naples and Palermo are reputed to have the best coffee-houses globally: naturally, their native clientele, as frequent visitors, know this. Everyone has their preferred coffee-house, usually run as a small, self-contained business. There are numerous coffee bars in these cities, with many local clients, in contrast to the few foreign tourists and business people who visit such establishments generally on their way to elsewhere.

These tiny, artisan coffee houses in the historic neighbourhoods of Naples and Palermo provide companionship for the regular customers and genuine concern for the welfare of their less-fortunate neighbours. Naples has become famous for its 'suspended' (that is, 'to be drunk' – see the corresponding entry in Chapter 4) coffee.

Geographical distances are also cultural distances. In Naples and Palermo, drinking coffee is a pleasure, a symbol of an oral tradition's spontaneity that encompasses casual conversation at the bar and social solidarity. The artisans are like a brotherhood, protecting traditions in order to pass them on to their successors. Their world is ancient: their cities have high walls to defend the status of their craft.

If Italian artisans keep alight the flame of tradition, intellectuals in the US can be considered as having started a latter-day fire of innovation. In 1971, in Seattle, thousands of kilometres from Naples and Palermo, Jerry Baldwin (a professor of English), Zev Siegel (a historian) and Gordon Bowker (a writer) opened their 'Starbucks Coffee, Tea and Spice' stall in the city's main market square. Initially, they sold only the raw materials – coffee beans, leaf tea and spices – and did not offer brewed drinks or food. Unlike the neighbourhood-based artisan coffee houses in Naples and Palermo, which thrive on close relationships, with nicknames or family names often being used as the name of the shop, the three founders of Starbucks chose to create a corporate logo with no reference to themselves at all.

Legend has it that Starbucks derives from Starbuck, the First Officer under Captain Ahab of the whaling ship *Pequod*, in Herman Melville's novel *Moby Dick*. The prudent Starbuck, a Quaker, stands in stark contrast to the demented character that is Ahab. So, Starbucks is a coffee house where imagination rides on romanticism waves, roams and hunts in deep waters on the routes of the pioneers of the coffee trade between East and West. It is an enterprise arising from driving and deep ambition and similar to Captain Ahab's quest, but always with the controlling influence of a First Officer such as the fictional Starbuck. Starbucks' true story is as epic as Melville's novel, a story which, from its beginnings in 1971, contributed to innovation and change in coffee houses worldwide, resulting in the now instantly recognisable, international brand and logo that are Starbucks.

The chain reaction which led to Starbucks becoming a global brand started when the creativity of Baldwin, Siegel and Bowker came into contact with the commercial acumen of Howard Schultz. Schulz contributed business efficiency, complementing the intellectual skills of the three founders. He visited Milan in 1983 and was struck by the fact that coffee houses were rooted in their local communities, as in Palermo and Naples. They commanded their customers' loyalty, with solid relationships being formed between these customers and the owners and staff of the coffee shops. Schultz had a vision that Starbucks could emulate this globally, irrespective of locality or political, religious or cultural influences. The common factor would be the Starbucks brand and what it represented.

The thread linking Kaldi, the Arab shepherd, and Schultz, the American entrepreneur, is long. It represents the distance between 'suspended' coffee and global coffee. All characters along this thread have been participants in a tale of innovation that has influenced many generations' lifestyles.

Flexibility

Flexibility assumes constantly changing forms. Sometimes it appears as the personage of Ability to adjust, with Lean, production volumes. On other occasions, it impersonates Speedy, changing the product mix of the range of products and models. First, taking on the role of Kinesis, it moves production from one site to another. Then, assuming the role of Kronos, it reconfigures production timing.

Flexibility and Lean scan the horizon of change. New algorithms of the age of knowledge force many science provinces to converge to form NIBC – Nanotechnologies, Information and communication technologies, Biology and Cognitive sciences.

Raw materials now consist of the ideas generated and flowing in research laboratories, art and design workshops, and networks woven by young talented individuals inhabiting the digital world. Therefore, there is the need to provide innovative education, instigate and instil in young people the desire for creativity, provide resources to discover talent, and set up a 'find the talent in you' programme.

Fragilista

Word invented by Nassim Taleb, a Lebanese-American essayist and mathematician, as opposed to 'antifragilista' (*Antifragile: Things That Gain from Disorder*, New York, NY: Random House, 2012) to describe a person who loves 'order and predictability', and who suffers as a result of 'random events, unpredictable shocks, stressors, and volatility'. Since any change seems awful at first glance, one chooses to be wrong with infinite precision rather than being on the side of reason, albeit in a rough manner. Whereas the antifragilista do things without understanding them or with an incomplete understanding – and do them well.

According to Taleb, with its sense of security, the fragilista make us engage 'in policies and actions, all artificial, in which the benefits are small and visible, and the side effects potentially severe and invisible'.

Future Universities

Schools in churches sowed the seeds of Medieval University. Centuries later, the Prussian linguist and philosopher Wilhelm von Humboldt created the modern university, where the new physical and natural sciences were mastered alongside classical culture. Finally, with the books of management science opened by Peter Drucker, the 1950s gave us business schools.

In the distant 1910s, Giovanni Papini (*Chiudiamo le scuole*, Vallecchi: Florence, 1919) anticipated the prototype of the university of the twenty-first century as follows:

> Here, then, is how I imagine the future university founded on perfect freedom. First of all, the young person who enters it will not be obliged to enrol from the first year onwards in a given number of fixed and established subjects. It will be possible, for example, to enrol in only one course if one wishes to devote all one's time to the one subject of interest. The system I propose overturns current habits. The university should not be, as it is today, a state-run factory of candidates for stupidity or employment. Universities should become less and less academies and more and more collections of special seminars with special libraries and special laboratories as classrooms where students should present the results of their inquiries to their fellow students and teachers.

At the dawn of the twenty-first century, the outlines of a new academic setup began to emerge, in which scientific discoveries and their transformation into high-growth enterprises live in symbiosis.

New conduits of knowledge, along which pearls of knowledge flow to the markets, are the hallmark of the future university: a foundation with a scientific and entrepreneurial mission, agile, flexible and not subject to the pressures of bureaucracy and corporate interests; a foundation promoted and financed by entrepreneurs who want to renew their companies and invest in the entrepreneurial renaissance. They contribute to the training of young people to enter the most promising markets opened up by the knowledge economy with the mindset of the Nobel Prize winner for Physics and Chemistry, Marie Curie, a scientist with a marked propensity for entrepreneurship.

These are its distinguishing features:

- Learning. Learning processes attuned to the acquaintance with people and social strategies, not only centred on taking up technicalities.
- The project. Cultivating specific projects in learning is carried out with a few lectures, many seminars, workshops and in-company activities.
- Recruitment. Select not only people but also ideas and projects, which are practical experimentation funds comparable to cash funds.

- The contract. Offer 'learning contracts' to participants. These are contracts to develop a continuity of relationships between participants and the local community (not only academic) in several ways, formal and informal.
- The outcome. The result of the training course is (1) an entrepreneurial project that is complementary to the conventional qualification (certificate, diploma or degree) and (2) in new innovative enterprises, which, in turn, lead to a continuous improvement of collaborative behaviours, and thus to a higher performance of the local innovation system.

fu xing

The Chinese renaissance smouldered under the surface up to the early twenty-first century. Now, like a frog leaps from the depths of a well into the open air, the word 'renaissance' – *fu xing* in Mandarin Chinese – has emerged and has been wholly accommodated in the vocabulary of Xi Jinping, Secretary-General of the Communist Party of China since November 2012. He used the word three times in his first press conference.

The entrepreneurial renaissance in China seeks to redraw the geopolitical map of the distribution of power. If Chinese philosophers inspired the old and cultured Europe of the Enlightenment, entrepreneurial spirits were released by the metaphorical statement by Den Xiaoping (architect of Chinese economic reform between 1978 and 1992): 'It doesn't matter whether the cat is black or white, as long as it catches mice'. These spirits are observed with curiosity and desire to emulate them by both the old and the new generations of the advanced Western world.

Great Government versus Big Government

Innovation requires a high calibre of a public environment, such as to encourage the free flow of ideas and their entrepreneurial translation. In short, it is a government that is great, of high quality, rather than big and intrusive.

2021: in developed economies, fiscal and monetary stimulus averages 40% of GDP. Is it the return of the government to the throne of the economy, with the court of politicians infiltrating the fabric of society? The question has only a conjectural answer. In the Financial Times on 26 April, Ruchir Sharma, head of the Emerging Markets Equity team at Morgan Stanley Investment Management, argued: 'The idea the state has been shrinking for 40 years is a myth. The 'neoliberal' era that began with Ronald Reagan and Margaret Thatcher has instead presided over ever-bigger government'. If there is one idealised fact with a pervasive participation charge that has polarised the aspirations of an era, it is GDP. When we call for a post-pandemic economic revolution, we need to go beyond GDP by adopting new economic thinking that gives voice to nature by extolling the value of natural capital, the totality of our planet's natural resources. What matters is to rely not on a big government but on a great government that is such by taking care of the natural capital resources that provide ecosystem services.

Since nature has no national borders, public interventions should not be designed using the yardstick of national self-sufficiency. It is the old ideas that are frightening. In the name of economic retreat, it would be self-defeating to return to the past with industrial policies designed to support particular sectors and regions of a country. 'Self-sufficiency was what Nehru and Indira Gandhi tried in the 1960s and 1970s. It was a horrible, terrible flop', said Adam Posen, president of the Peterson Institute for International Economics in Washington. Rather than a retreat from the market economy, it would be good to work towards demobilising business practices that run counter to nature's voice. Resilience, the quick return to the initial state of a supposed golden age of more and better jobs and a more productive economy, should be viewed with deep scepticism. A great state cultivates the art and practice of experimenting with actions that can move the economy to another, fundamentally better stance than it is today. The big government has produced a feudal society that has locked workers into particular roles, preventing them from adapting to changing circumstances following new ideas. It would be detrimental to relax monetary and fiscal policies to serve the representation of interests organised in non-competitive, hierarchically ordered categories, created, recognised or authorised by public authorities. Worse still if those categories enjoy monopolistic privileges in return for compliance with certain controls on their selection of leaders.

When launching and implementing expansionary policies, the public authorities must ask themselves what value should be attained. This is where Adam Smith comes to the aid of policymakers. The Scottish economist, a profound and subtle moral philosopher, understood that not only was greed an evil but that empathy and behaviour that takes account of others are the essential glue that holds society together. Smith extolled 'the ingenuity of the makers of the machines who managed to anticipate the advancements of science' and was concerned about 'The man whose whole life is spent in performing a few simple operations, of which the effects too are, perhaps, always the same, or very nearly the same, has no occasion to exert his understanding, or to exercise his invention in finding out expedients for removing difficulties which never occur. He naturally loses; therefore, the habit of such exertion, and generally becomes as stupid and ignorant as it is possible for a human creature to become. His dexterity at his own particular trade seems, in this manner, to be acquired at the expense of his intellectual, social and martial virtues'.

If he then addressed himself not to the benevolence of the butcher, the brewer, or the baker in providing us with dinner, but to their interest, he did not fail to point out that 'People of the same trade seldom meet together, even for merriment and diversion, but the conversation ends in a conspiracy against the public, or in some contrivance to raise prices'.

One discovers the New World by borrowing the thoughts of classical economists and paying attention to the research of the Institute for New Economic Thinking. That research brings economics closer to physics, biology and computer science to model economic life in much more realistic ways, not forgetting that this approach has much to do with *Homo oeconomicus* (see the corresponding entry, Chapter 4) in his relations with nature.

Gulliver's Watch

Innovation rejects the status quo, proposing as it does new ideas that question established and accepted custom and practice. Custom and practice prevented the Lilliputians from understanding the innovation represented by Lemuel Gulliver's watch, the fictional protagonist and narrator of *Gulliver's Travels*, a novel written by Jonathan Swift, first published in 1726. It takes Lynceus' long sight to see beyond tradition, enabling innovative entrepreneurs to reduce the gap between research and its applications, between the worlds of academia and business. The familiar path is likely to be a cul-de-sac: the rate of progress is now determined by business people equipped with high levels of technical and scientific competence, whose enterprises have high expectations of growth.

These pioneers of innovative entrepreneurship meet at the frontiers of innovation. They are explorers who build bridges between the old entrepreneurial generation – the creators of, for instance, the German *Wirtschaftswunder*, the Italian *miracolo economico*, and other similar economic and social successes in Europe after World War II – and the age of knowledge with its rich assortment of artificial intelligence, microtechnologies, robotics, new raw materials, nano and biotechnologies, post-computer devices, telecommunications, etc...

Happiness

People who conceive of cities enriching the future with creative products – those that absorb innovative cultural influences and provide new stimuli, thus making life delightful – privilege the complex structure of happiness indicators over the simplifications of aggregates such as GDP.

Since Bhutan's kingdom first came to measure its well-being in 2004 with an index that, borrowing from GDP, it called Gross Internal Happiness, there has been a proliferation of statistics on peoples' happiness.

The Global Happiness Council, an international group of independent experts, annually publishes the Global Happiness Policy Report. While the GDP thermometer moves in tune with the intensity and direction of the flow of goods and services, the happiness index rises and falls with the importance of relationships, kindness towards others and mutual help. Devoted only to themselves, not seeking friendship but only profit, the bar of happiness turns downwards.

To happiness, positive education contributes significantly. It is a range of educational programs that train elementary school children and secondary students to engage in various activities. Interventions include:

- Remembering what went well today.
- Writing letters of gratitude.
- Learning how to respond constructively.
- Identifying and developing character strengths.

These activities are part of training in meditation, mindfulness, empathy, coping with emotions, decision-making, problem-solving, and critical thinking.

By investing today in positive schools and teachers, tomorrow we will rely on citizens committed to developing family relationships and proximity networks (thus enriching the dowry of social stress inherited from past generations – see the corresponding entry in Chapter 4). Following Seneca's thought, happiness should not be confounded with the means to achieve it. Economic growth is only a tool whose good use depends on social innovation, whose name is 'positive schooling', which transmits optimism, confidence and hope for the future.

For the English philosopher John McTaggart, 'With a proper cake the more you eat the bigger it gets'. The ideal to be cultivated is the abundance in an economy of happiness instead of scarcity in an economy of sadness, to leave behind the 'dismal science', as the Scottish philosopher Thomas Carlyle had succinctly christened the economy. The communities that will know how to navigate the ocean of Happy Abundance will unveil a new age of Enlightenment, bringing to the surface the thought of Italian and French philosophers and economists of the eighteenth century who attributed great value to public happiness. The French economist Anne-Robert-Jacques Turgot had defined political economy as the 'science of public happiness'.

Homo Faber, Homo Laborans

The *Homo Faber* asks questions about why things happen; the *Homo Laborans* about how they happen. For the latter, 'making things' is an end in itself and is dictated by the needs imposed by technology. Subjugated to technology or pleasantly attracted by it, they are a slave of the tasks by which the will of technology absorbs them (*Animal Laborans* is the definition given by Hannah Arendt in her essay *The Human Condition*, Chicago, IL: University of Chicago Press, 1958). Their work is comparable to the manual labour of past industrial revolutions. Just consider, for example, intelligent machines that alert their operators when they need maintenance and the cyborg, a person equipped with prostheses – bionics and computer prostheses, which give the human body the machine's characteristics.

Homo Ludens

Business creation is art. Art is a ludic game. The creator of enterprise is *Homo Ludens*, figured by the cultural historian Johan Huizinga.

The game will improve affective, educational and working life. The new generations will be thus entitled to aspire to a job that is all the more enriching for its playful quality. Like the hunter-gatherers of the Paleolithic era, today's students should be trained to become hunters of ideas, having to exercise, tomorrow, a multifaceted profession. At that time, hunting and gathering were not regarded as work; they were done with enthusiasm, not grudgingly. Nowadays, the new work path is a combinatorial game between the composition of the most varied stories, artistic creations and the construction of things. Along with that path, one can glimpse a horizon different from the occupations that physically and mentally exhaust people.

Homo Innovatus

He or she is the bearer of the open innovation culture. The mental space they inhabit is not that of a specialist plunged into the well of knowledge. As they descend into the well, the specialists take possession of smaller and smaller pieces of their cognitive field and protect them from the gaze of others. The protection is a high wall, raised with the bricks of accumulated experience. *Homo Innovatus* escapes from the experiential space and occupies the experimental space as extensive as the imagination that circumscribes it. As an experimenter, Homo Innovatus is well aware that facts and ideas cultivated reflect the past. On the other hand, dreams and speculations about the future are fantasies that confront reality.

Homo Innovatus transcends dogmatic reason and conventional wisdom to challenge the existing state of affairs, experimenting the entire journey from fantasy to realization.

Social adaptability and the willingness to plant cooperative roots make the language of innovation evolve. Among its words, fluctuation, perturbation and imbalance stand out. These words belong to the cultural baggage of *Homo Innovatus* along the path that, starting from the organisation closed in its bubble, leads to innovation that, by opening up to dialogue, designs a possible future. With the evolution of language, the argument supporting evolutionary perturbations of economic relations takes strength in place of the economic calm ensured by rational preferences, profit maximisation, and the full availability of relevant information: three climatic conditions that should keep storms away.

Homo innovatus learns to shoot the arrows of doubt, thinking, action, and construction being immersed in intellectual innovation's cognitive field. The opening up and expansion of the innovative field depend on the direction and the speed of the four arrows. There is not a linear time sequence that, starting from doubt, leads to achievement. The uncertainty of judgement (doubt), the weight (*pensum*, from the verb *pendere*, meaning 'to weigh' – used by the Romans about 'thinking') of the subject to be treated, the will to change (action), and its concretisation intersect and become integrated along a circular path.

To their better fusion, *Homo Innovatus* contributes with the courage to diverge from peers, being aware of the value attributed to personal diversity and the distinctive feature of his or her culture to achieve more creative, more sustainable and more equitable performance. In this way, *Homo Innovatus* shapes the environment of open innovation that, in turn, shapes his or her personality.

Homo Innovatus confronts and influences a variety of subjects and, in turn, are inspired by them. Nesta, which describes itself as 'an innovation foundation' (https://www.nesta.org.uk/about-us/) has identified five innovators in the UK, each with its particular attitude towards innovation (*Innovation Population. The UK'S Views on Innovation*, 1 April 2014).

Futurists are committed to the debate on innovation and can see the benefits of change in all aspects of life.

Creatives, who are younger than average, display high personal creativity levels and propose new ways of solving practical problems. They cultivate solid social interests.

Romantics are stimulated by innovation, 'but are not long-term planners and tend not to be concerned about the future, and they are the least likely to have participated in innovative activities'.

Realists, the largest group, appreciate innovation but are not enthusiastic about it per se, 'believing that ethics and rights are more important than innovation and progress'. They recognize that it is necessary to keep pace with change and balance innovation's shortcomings with the benefits.

Sceptics are ' particularly concerned about the pace of change in society. Cautious and practical, they attribute relatively little value to innovations until they are confident of real-world benefits'. They consider new ideas less critical than problem-solving by making the best use of existing ideas and technologies. Sceptics, therefore, tend to adopt new products and technologies belatedly.

Homo Oeconomicus, Homo Socialis

Homo Oeconomicus is a selfish individualist who tends to maximise his or her utility. In the traditional theatre of the entrepreneurial economy, Homo Oeconomicus is the incremental innovator. This meticulous calculator pursues ever-higher pecuniary rewards, in addition to social prestige, by strengthening the competitive position over time through improvements and upgrades of the activity pursued.

Narrow self-interest cannot fully explain human behaviour. In the new theatre of the economy of respect, *Homo Socialis* bursts onto the scene, whose propensity for altruism and spontaneous socialisation is a decisive added value for the common good of society. *Homo Socialis* ushers in the age of a renewed civilisation of cooperation.

Ideation

Meeting people from diverse backgrounds, engaging in new and more effective dialogues, and also clashing — the intersection of artistic, scientific, business and policy ideas is the outcome of the creative process dubbed 'ideation'. This process was triggered by the social phenomenon that Frans Johansson called the 'Medici effect' (*The Medici Effect: What You Can Learn from Elephants and Epidem*ics, Brighton, MA: Harvard Business Review Press, 2004), revisiting the driving force of across-the-board innovation attributed to the Medici. In fact, in the Florence of the Medici ideation performs the whole cycle: from the generation of the idea to its realisation which, as Romer would say, comes in the guise of a recipe better than those hitherto produced.

Ideas awaken the world; they do it as if being reborn. They are, in short, 'renaissance' ideas. 'No matter what anybody tells you, words and ideas can change the world'—so said the late Robin Williams, the great actor, in the movie

Dead Poets' Society. Further to his seminal work of 1986, three years before that movie was released, the economist Paul Romer explained that due to the non-rivalry of ideas – the fact, that is, that one person's use of an idea does not prevent others from making another use of it – innovations that arise from them enable the economy to be freed from the chains of the law of diminishing returns (doubling the input, the change in output is less than proportional). By exploiting ideas, increasing returns (additional production inputs yield more than proportionate returns) change the economic world for the better because they raise material living standards.

Hence, ideas, not objects, make the world move. The world is no longer caught between scarcity of resources and limits to growth. On the contrary, it is a playground for almost unlimited opportunities, where new ideas create new products, new markets and new possibilities for generating wealth. Free spaces for fruitful collaborations have brought and continue to bring surprising results. Think of ecosystems such as IdeaSpace (https://www.ideaspace.cam.ac.uk) in Cambridge, UK, and Vivid Ideas (https://www.vividsydney.com/ideasguide) in Sydney, Australia.

Ideation will gain more space in the enterprise as management does not aim, following a shock, to return to the previous equilibrium, preferring to go through moments of imbalance by walking the path of ideation conducive to entrepreneurial outreach.

Imagination

We live in the Knowledge Age, which pushes us into the Age of Imagination that violates established thoughts and standardised procedures, thus generating new ideas that override those established by tradition.

Imagination enables the mind to create mental images as symbols, metaphors and concepts that enrich tacit knowledge assets. Our imagination pushes us beyond the visible horizon, and it does so by seeking interactions with others, the bearers of different cultures. In this melting pot of diversity, new knowledge is modelled through careful handling of the fertility of imagination, the critical spirit and the consequent cognitive conflicts among the participants in the open innovation process.

The technological wave is rising, and with it, the wave of change affecting both the economy and society. When the two waves will reach the shore where knowledge meets ignorance and how to ride them are questions that require us to imagine the future. Therefore, we must board the vehicle of imagination, abandoning the cargo that contains what we know and understand. Those who give less weight to knowledge than to imagination feel intolerant of the traditional education that suffocates them with its teaching kit, exams and specialisations.

Innovation with imagination eradicates a disease deeply rooted in the social body. Symptomatic of the disease is the notion that 'something is happening to us'. The future is conceived as a succession of events that swoop down on us. From a diametrically opposite perspective – that we can construct our own tomorrow – open innovation looks towards the future, drawing fresh ideas from the resources of the imagination.

Conventional thinking addicted to customary rules prevents apprehension through imagination. That is why, in the course of history, an avalanche of nonsense has smothered the new thought that overturns existing knowledge and methods. As Armen Petrosyan (Within a Nutshell (The Mental Roots of Human Insusceptibility to New Ideas), *Journal of the Knowledge Economy, 6*(1), 2015) documented, the adoption of the Gregorian calendar sparked protest, with opponents arguing that, as a result of the changes of date, migratory birds would no longer know when it would be time to return. The medical faculty of Bavaria feared that the rapid speed of the train would damage the health of travellers. The invention of the gas lamp was rejected because it did not accord with existing scientific knowledge: how could a lamp burn without a wick? Radioactive β decay, discovered by the physicist Enrico Fermi, was thought by many scientists to be far from reality. In times closer to us, consolidated knowledge has conflicted with discovering microorganisms in the stomach by Marshall and Warren, the Australian university scientists and recipients of the Nobel Prize in Medicine in 2005.

Imagination is a source of ideas and a way of combining them, some of which flourish in the field of a renewed entrepreneurial renaissance. The actors are those who, being crazy enough to think they can change the world, actually change it (sic, Steve Jobs). The prominent protagonist is the imaginative entrepreneur.

Building bridges between those who have imaginative power and those who translate the imagined into reality is a distinctive trait of open innovation. Science fiction writers have contributed much to this work of intellectual engineering, fulfilling the requirements of innovation. From the future of flight envisioned by Jules Verne, Igor Sikorski created the helicopter. Inspired by *Star Trek*, in the early 1970s, Martin Cooper, Director of Research at Motorola, designed the first mobile phone. *Snow Crash*, a novel by Neal Stephenson, provided the cue for the conception of virtual reality.

The unusual combination of unconventional writers and scientific experts is an endless source of inspiration, bringing imagination onto the stage of reality. From the heights of their experience, experts standing alone lose sight of the entrepreneurial opportunities ignited by a bottom-up imagination that produces what may sound like a puerile idea. It is not the result of judgement based on experience. The unknown finds the expert extraneous, unprepared and therefore distressed.

The literary imagination shatters the certainties of business, which has shut itself away, using well-defined maps with well-defined routes that delimit its territory in order to institutionalise the production of economic knowledge. Maps and routes result from an abstract, logical way of thinking imbued with mathematical symbolism. Having raised high barriers along the perimeter of its disciplinary enclosure is a painful countdown for business to encounter the imagination. Literate business people, through fictions and storytelling, bring people closer to business and elicit those insights that change the traditional way of doing business.

Imaginative Entrepreneur

The currents of beauty and knowledge meet and mingle. In order to nurture both, it is not enough to ask oneself what one sees, the 'why' of something, but also what one imagines and wants to achieve, and therefore the 'why not'. This is what the imaginative entrepreneur does.

The manager adopts a logical approach that moves the company from A to B. The entrepreneur's imagination seeks to take the company everywhere. The action of the former is as circumscribed as knowledge is. In the words of Albert Einstein,

Imagination is more important than knowledge. For knowledge is limited to all we now know and understand, while imagination embraces the entire world, and all there ever will be to know and understand.

Knowledge is even more important in the uncertain time between the emergence of an innovative idea and its entrepreneurial application, when the evaluation of the idea is, therefore, shrouded in mystery. That is rough terrain for the manager's logical-rational thinking in search of certainty, the antechamber to fanaticism according to the French philosopher Ernest Renan. At the same time, it is the window of doubt that overlooks uncertainty that guides the entrepreneur's action towards a correct assessment of the facts. In this regard, the words of the Italian poet Giacomo Leopardi in his *Zibaldone* appear far-sighted:

> ...our reason can absolutely not find the truth save by doubting,
> that it distances itself from truth whenever it judges with certainty,
> and that not only does doubt serve to uncover the truth, but that
> truth essentially consists in doubt, and whoever doubts knows, and
> knows as much as one can know.
>
> (1821/2013, p. 760)

The one who enters the infinite field of ideas and takes one or more of them – this is the entrepreneur endowed with imagination and fantasy – is bound to clash with the one who has to keep the house in order – the manager within the fence of acquired knowledge. Entrepreneurial imagination is the way out of old ideas. This action is fraught with obstacles because, as John Maynard Keynes (Preface, *The General Theory of Employment, Interest and Money*, London: Palgrave Macmillan, 1936) argued,

> The difficulty lies, not in the new ideas, but in escaping from the
> old ones, which ramify, for those brought up as most of us have
> been, into every corner of our minds.

Incrementalist

The incrementalist is rich in money but lacking in time. Like the Germans of whom Publius Cornelius Tacitus wrote in his ethnographic work *De origine et situ Germanorum* (*On the Origin and Situation of the Germanic Peoples*), the incrementalists are a community uncontaminated by intermarriages with other communities, but remains 'a people pure, and independent, and resembling none but themselves'.

Doubt and uncertainty are covered by the veil of knowledge accumulated over time. Doing what is necessary to safeguard the continuity of the original vocations, the incrementalist is adept at warping assonances, practising the art of forecasting. This technique is all the more arduous the further the time horizon. Forecasting based on 'tendentialism' (a trend that is not likely to continue) is a light that, while corroborating one's point of view, can be deceptive, leading one to look where it quickly spreads but where the world-changing innovation is not to be found. By wearing such a cultural garb, the priests of incrementalism calculate time according to financial considerations that reflect the expected return on investment. Their calculations reflect the prejudice that losses hurt more than gains of the same magnitude bring benefits. Not to mention that, as the investment innovator John Maynard Keynes warned, 'wordly wisdom teaches that it is better for reputation to fail conventionally than to succeed unconventionally' (*The General Theory of Employment, Interest, and Money*, Chapter 12, 'The State of Long-Term Expectation'. London: Palgrave Macmillan, 1936).

According to an article in *The New York Times* of 22 June 1902,

> Five or six years ago [...] there were fewer than fifty motor vehicles of various patterns (types, models) in the whole of what is now the Greater New York. It seemed that it would not be easy to persuade people accustomed to travelling by horse and carriage to change to the car. A mere two decades later, however, cars had spread beyond the most optimistic expectations. The New York Times reported on 6 June 1924 that the US$23 million of capital invested 20 years earlier in the automotive industry was worth almost US$2 billion in 1919, and that the number of workers in the industry had increased from 13,000 to 161,000.

In Silicon Valley, incrementalists are called 'farm workers', meaning those who work day to day picking the low-hanging fruit, i.e., Wall Street operators focused on the quarterly results produced by companies.

Incubator

A public, private or mixed organisation that systematically supports the creation of new enterprises by providing them with a range of integrated support services, physical (spaces, equipped laboratories) and intangible (services for the development of the business idea).

University-based incubators nurture a new entrepreneurial generation of scientists who plan to turn their discoveries into businesses and others who want to tap into the source of scientific developments for business opportunities. They complement each other, each perceiving the strength of the others as an opportunity and, therefore, showing interest in each other's successes.

Entrepreneurship and scientific research are not in conflict. The fact that academic entrepreneurs publish more and of higher quality is not a negligible result of the marriage of science and entrepreneurship, as shown by scholars from the Universities of Rome Tor Vergata and Naples Parthenope (Giovanni Abramo et al., *An Individual-Level Assessment of the Relationship between Spin-Off Activities and Research Performance in Universities*, R&D Management, 42, 3, Blackwell Publishing, 2012).

Industry 4.0

It is the future of networked factories with connected robots deployed in fully automated production lines. In the digital ecosystem thus created, the extension of the Internet to the world of concrete objects and places (what has come to be known as the Internet of Things) makes it possible to connect the physical environment of the factory with virtual reality.

The digitised factory bridges the gap between doing and thinking in the age of mechanisation sprung from the first industrial revolution. It is necessary to row with imagination and dexterity in the sea of work. In the waters of innovation, not the individual but the whole crew separates the winner from the loser. It is the critical change facing the workforce that calls for teamwork. The team must row strong and in tune as the factory job faces the transition from 'full subtraction' (removing parts of material by turning and milling) to 'vacuum filling' (additive manufacturing), which involves adding layer upon layer of material to achieve the desired product.

Work is no longer broken down into small tasks requiring increasing levels of control. Much of the work is executed through horizontal processes that cross different business functions and specialities. Therefore, success no longer depends on the control of each worker. What makes the difference is the ability to align all actors in and out of the company. For the new manufacture, the eight rowing crew, the boat with a helmsman (the entrepreneur) whose rowers are the manager, the technologist, the engineer, the technician, the craftsman, the scientist, the educator and the student, will be decisive.

The paradigm shift brought about by a range of digital technologies has far-reaching educational implications, including 3D printing, which allows three-dimensional objects to be produced using additive manufacturing, starting from a digital model. With three-dimensional printers at ever-lower costs, promising business prospects are opening up. Artisans, workers and technicians can now design and produce customised objects on demand. Widespread manufacturing in homes, which also become tailor-made factories for the prosumer (the consumer who is also an actor in the production process), is one of the hallmarks of the new entrepreneurial renaissance.

Info-Enterprise

The transition from the 'machine tool' to the 'information machine' leads to the info-enterprise. Here, processes are not set in motion by physical facts; they are activated and revolve around information, which governs the transformation of matter and energy from one form to another.

In the info-enterprise, future exploration does not occur along the path of questioning the extent of deviations from past data. To what extent will next year be different from today is not the question to ask. The info-enterprise asks itself what innovative actions to take – what needs to be done differently next year to get closer to the target. Instead of predicting the future, it wants to master it.

Intellectual Entrepreneurs

They are the talents who migrate from university lecture halls and laboratories towards entrepreneurship.

Highly educated entrepreneurship without frontiers is becoming increasingly crucial in economies that are sufficiently open to accommodate the waters of a large river fed by numerous tributaries. These are: international twinning of scientists and successful entrepreneurs; researchers and students exploiting their global mobility to create unorthodox entrepreneurial alliances with colleagues from other countries; investors who provide risk capital to internationally conceived entrepreneurial projects; experimental laboratories for new venture creation; pioneering technological infrastructures that host newly launched enterprises in incubation; and other tributaries.

It is at the meeting point of this mobile talent and the new international entrepreneurship that the results of research translate into commercially viable goods and services, offering significant financial rewards for universities and, above all, with a beneficial, entrepreneurial effect on the research communities.

Intellectual Salons, the 'Mind Salons'

Ambitions for economic growth and social progress are nurtured in informal places where debates between conflicting viewpoints become so heated that they result in unusual connections of ideas that will later give rise to innovative enterprises. It is there that creativity manifests itself, setting the productivity bandwagon in motion. In this respect, there is much to be learned from the salons of many madames. They were the driving force behind the conversations that accelerated scientific progress and brought about the Age of Enlightenment.

The civilisation of conversation had its golden age in the seventeenth and eighteenth centuries. As the literary critic and writer Benedetta Craveri wrote in her essay *La civiltà della conversazione* (Milano: Adelphi, 2001), the elective place of conversation was, first, the 'Chambre Bleue' of the Hotel de Rambouillet and its hostess, Madame de Rambouillet. In the following century, the intellectual salons of Madame de Tencin and Madame Geoffrin were the places designed to conversation fruition where the primacy of the intellect eradicated social differences. Conversations were competitive pastimes that acted as a powerful stimulant for thinking, listening and speaking. People also listened with their eyes to see new uses for past ideas and discoveries. Women showed remarkable capacity for empathic listening, thus managing to develop personalised ways of thinking and doing.

The French economist and encyclopaedist, Abbot André Morellet, recalls Craveri, saw in the art of conversation practised in these salons an ideal investment that enriched all the people involved in lively conversations. In the salons, wrote Morellet ('D'un Essai sur la Conversation', In *Éloges de Madame, H. Nicolle, Librairie Stéphane. Nicolle*, Paris: Librairie Stéréotype, 1777), the attention of the participants in the conversation was alive. The 'salonnières' entertained each other, instructed each other and compared their ideas with those of the other creators. They grasped connections between different ideas that together developed more than each creator initially thought of his or her idea; the intellectual exchanges broadened and deepened the field of knowledge; what turned out to be a unique and original way of building mutually beneficial long-term relationships, highlighting the personalities involved.

In Italy, the eighteenth-century intellectual salons that hosted scientists were meeting places for discussions, debates, exchanges of ideas and projects at the basis of advances in science and engineering. In their Venetian palaces, Caterina Dolfin Tron, Giustina Renier Michiel, niece of the penultimate doge of Venice Paolo Renier, Marina Querini Benzon, and Isabella Teotochi Albrizzi gathered a cosmopolitan and polyglot community that developed the art of conversation as a social good.

Intelligence

Carlo Cattaneo, patriot, political thinker, economic theorist and brilliant practical economist, called for concern with the psychology of wealth, not just its physicality symbolically represented by the labours of the body and the sweat of the brow. His remains are an appeal to consider the intelligence that manifests itself in the formation of ideas. Cattaneo wrote: 'There is no work, there is no capital, that does not begin with an act of intelligence'. It depends on intelligence, whose effectiveness is directly productive, whether wealth grows or declines. If both the thought that gives rise to intuition and the human faculty of learning decline, the dulling of the intellect closes a virtuous circle of ideas, no matter how great it may have been. And once it is extinguished, the process of wealth comes to a standstill.

We come from years in which we have overworked our left brain to binge on the news produced and offered by the digital information age. It is time to activate the right brain, whose qualities of invention and empathy with cultures other than our own are indispensable. They are needed since the language of innovation rewards the critical faculties of young people so as not to make them impervious to ideas and thoughts deemed dangerous by the defenders of the status quo. This is how eccentricity wins out over standardisation, which leads to immobility.

Of the ideas that change the language, it is often impossible to identify the inventor's name. David Krakauer, President of the Santa Fe Institute, states,

Consider the following conundrum: the more important an invention, the more anonymous are the inventors. We cannot name the inventor of language, numbers, classical architecture, logic, Chess, Go, the clock, or the wheel. One possibility is that useful objects outlive biographical influence. And it is to be expected that provenance is lost. Another more likely possibility is that most truly great ideas are collective and accretive, and the reason we cannot name an inventor is because we should be naming an invention's history.

Those ideas are born and grow in communities that go back in time and meet Carlo Cattaneo at the intersection of physicality and the psychology of wealth.

International Entrepreneurship

It is the discovery and exploitation of business opportunities across national borders. It adds a new dimension to the entrepreneurial economy, with parts of the business activity set in foreign locations.

An entrepreneurial behaviour oriented towards internationalisation requires knowledge management so refined as to grasp cultural, linguistic, corporate governance systems, public policy frames, and other differences.

New companies engaged in internationalisation since the beginning of their activity are called international start-ups or global start-ups. An innovative form emerges from the networks of would-be founders of multiple nationalities. For instance, groups of students enrolled in entrepreneurship training programmes organised by universities and business schools in different countries.

Internauts of Social Networks

The language of the Internet originated with the British computer scientist Tim Berners-Lee at CERN (the European Organisation for Nuclear Research) in Geneva in 1989, and its evolution into Web 2.0, a term coined in 1999 by Darcy DiNucci in his article *The Fragmented Future* (http://darcyd.com/fragmented_future.pdf), have led to the blossoming of new forms of community: the social networks, set in motion by the Internauts of cyberspace. Today, the community that frequents the Internet square is shaken by attacks on people. The Internauts who navigate in the sea of social networks are threatened by predatory attacks that must be fought with antibodies (including ethical codes) that raise barriers against the spread of social epidemics whose viruses are cultivated in the laboratories of the new information and communication technologies.

The physical and virtual spaces designed by the Internauts of the digital age are amplifiers of change. Trust is the signal that runs through the amplifier: trust in the social contract that binds the community members and trust in the future.

Internet of Things

A combination of physical and virtual reality, the Internet of Things (IoT) is now the Internet of Everything. IoT connects people, processes, data and things. On average, there are about 200 things per capita in the world. Sixty-four per cent of these things are in developed economies, even though these countries together account for only 14% of the world's population. Around halfway through the last decade, Cisco Consulting Services estimated that IoT was putting up $14.4 trillion, of which $9.5 (66%) was generated by individual industries and $4.9 (34%) by cross-industry interactions. In addition, asset utilisation was estimated to improve by 2.5 trillion and labour productivity by the same order of magnitude; supply chain logistics by 2.7 and consumer satisfaction by 3.7.

Things are increasingly becoming objects of thought, knowledge and communication. Low-cost sensors, more innovative software and increasingly powerful networking are opening the door to energy savings, fast and safe transport, home healthcare and many other innovations.

Things that are familiar to consumers – such as electrodes, the clothes we wear, cars and many others – and manufacturers will communicate with each other. To mention one of the most publicised cases today, think of the fridge that sends a message to the smartwatch to remind us to buy milk.

Things are presented as physical devices and objects connected to the Internet and each other, thus enabling intelligent decision-making. The IoT teaches the customer how to create more value and, as a result, gives the company the information tools to produce what the customer wants. The more complex the product, the more opportunities the company has to learn what makes the difference. As the customer becomes a prosumer (co-producer and consumer), the approach to sales and marketing changes radically.

The Internet of Things generates new jobs: systems developers, transport network engineers, medical device consultants, data analysts, electrical engineers for smart grids, and many others.

The IoT will produce value if and to what extent it makes everyday life easier, more convenient and therefore healthier, whether in the workplace, at home to perform household chores or during leisure time. Not things but human beings should be at the centre of the digital ecosystem teeming with IoT devices. If we are to be indeed at the centre, data privacy is the main problem to solve. With so many devices talking to each other, transmitting a massive amount of information, much of it sensitive (think of the fallout from the disclosure of our health status), the lack of security would sting us causing pain.

The IoT involves many multilateral and transdisciplinary collaborations, including scientists, computer scientists, sociologists, economists from academia and industry, and entrepreneurs. They are all jointly engaged in broadening and deepening the connections between the physical world and virtual reality.

Intrapreneur

The knowledge professional, responsible for entrepreneurial work.

Intrapreneurship transforms the profile of the employee, who takes on the proactive role of inventing the entrepreneurial mission to be carried out within the company that employs him or her.

The intrapreneur triggers cognitive conflicts that contribute primarily to breaking entrenched rules. Abandoning opportunities that conform to prevailing habits and navigating in the sea of uncertainty, intrapreneurs strive to achieve something that does not yet exist.

Inventive Entrepreneurs and Incremental Innovators

The American economist William Baumol draws a dividing line between founders of business firms who are 'inventive entrepreneurs' responsible for novel innovations (breakthroughs) and those who are 'incremental innovators' engaged in cumulative incremental improvements ('Education for Innovation: Entrepreneurial Breakthroughs vs. Corporate Incremental Improvements', NBER Working Paper, June 2004).

The educational preparation of the incremental innovator leads to mastery of the already available paths of scientific knowledge and methods. The inventive entrepreneur needs an unorthodox approach to education that favours the free-wheeling exercise of the imagination. In Baumol's words,

> We know little about training for the critical task of breakthrough innovation.

In Silicon Valley, the visionary has the temperament of the farmer whose projection of the future is long-term. He tills the soil, cuts the weeds, plants trees, carries the water and nurtures the crops, often ridiculed for years by the incrementalist before benefiting from his creative work. Nevertheless, as Steve Jobs once said, the visionaries end up changing the world and taking over the fields.

For disruptive visionaries, the admonition of Andrew Grove, co-founder of Intel, applies. He wondered what happens when the pace of change is so rapid that, before one technological innovation unfolds, another spreads out and creates destructive interference with the first. Falling on top of each other, the two create a traffic jam where users, suppliers and investors all end up trapped.

Let us observe two images of innovators through the prism of culture that reflects the paradox of Achilles and the Tortoise attributed to Zeno of Elea. T, which stands for Tortoise, is the cluster of incremental innovators who are conservative reformers. T has a long manufacturing tradition in the transport industry. The continuous improvements made to their horse-drawn carriages give hope that they can one day reach the speed of 100 km/h. Likewise, by continuing to invest along the known technological trajectory, incremental innovators aim to increase the cruising speed of their sailing vessels.

A, which stands for fleet-footed Achilles, is the community of visionaries. Unlike T, A has no extensive and deep industrial roots. Its innovators are free to move around. Their mental models depict transport driven by internal combustion engines rather than the muscular energy of horses and wind energy. Will

A's cars and steamships overcome the challenge with coaches and sailing ships of T? Post mortem, the answer is obvious. It is not ex-ante when the contenders are not yet in the race but just on the starting line. Even during the competition, the answer is not unambiguous. What is really at stake is the culture of the two communities.

The realist Tortoise does not care if his race is slower than the faster visionary Achilles. As recounted by Aristotle, Tortoise believes in Zeno's paradox: 'In a race, the quickest runner can never overtake the slowest, since the pursuer must first reach the point whence the pursued started, so that the slower must always hold a lead' (*Physics* VI: 9, 239b15). He is though the visionary fleet-footed Achilles who has the best on the practical Tortoise. The fallacy of the argument will only emerge once the race is over – when it is clear that pursuer A has achieved his or her goal because, in practice, it was a race composed of finite parts. The winner is the visionary innovator, an eternal child who does not cling to the accumulated experience – as the Spanish philosopher George Santayana might have said.

The English-style Romantic gardens, so-called because of their free and irregular forms, as well as the visionary paintings of Romantic artists Caspar David Friedrich and William Turner are associated with visionary innovators. Such innovators, contemptuous of accepted realities, create commercial paths in territories unknown to the rulers of the current business regime.

Invisible Horizons

Distant, unseen horizons are the destination of explorers who are so naive that they throw away the rules dictated by experience.

When Pope Julius II, born Giuliano della Rovere, offered him the task of frescoing the Sistine Chapel ceiling, Michelangelo Buonarroti first replied that, since he was a sculptor and not a painter, he lacked the experience to engage at fresco painting. If there is something profound and significant that then pushed Buonarroti to accept the task, well, this something can be found in the folds of inexperience. It is 'not knowing' that leads the rebels to commit themselves in any case. Furthermore, the undertaking requires seeking solutions outside the box to break with the dominant tradition.

Journey

Journeys are powered by the winds of curiosity and creativity. Curiosity leads to visiting different countries; creativity leads to moving towards new places to observe the most varied scientific panoramas. Ulf Larsson (see the entry 'Curiosity') mentions travel as a source of inspiration in his quotation of George de Hevesy, Nobel Prize winner for Chemistry.

The exchange and intertwining of reflective knowledge and exploratory freedom are on display in the theatre of innovation. We cast an eye over the play starring the couple Karl and Bertha Benz. The engineer and engine designer Karl Friedrich Benz is regarded as the inventor of the passenger car. In the first public test run, the car crashed into a wall. This was enough to convince the people of

Mannheim that Benz's was the work of the devil. As Benz descended further and further into the well of knowledge, subsequent tests yielded better results. However, to turn the prototypes into a marketable product was his wife Bertha's freedom from what is already known. Her entrepreneurial mind inspired her to take a trip with her two young sons in the car designed by her husband, driving over 100 km from her home to her mother's house.

The freedom Bertha felt was the source of vicissitudes that stretched the journey into the night, as well as inventive insights that improved the car's performance. The publicity relaunch of the event marked the beginning of a success story that Mercedes-Benz still enjoys today.

Knowledge in Action

The new age of knowledge carries a vital meaning: the value derived from innovation, which is the process by which knowledge moves to action. Shared knowledge and collective intelligence have substituted the three traditional columns for the creation of value: land, work, and capital. These three scarce resources were the guiding factors of progress in the industrial economy, with knowledge incorporated fundamentally in the machines and the other physical or tangible activities. In the age of knowledge, the primary source of the creating of value resides in the hyper-mobility of knowledge, which controls access to opportunities and progress. While the industrial culture focuses above all on the production of things, of static objects, knowledge, on the other hand, continually flows, like an electric current, restoring and redefining markets.

Driven by chaos and adopting new patterns drawn from the imagination, knowledge breaks out of the prison of reason associated with the habit of thinking, researching and doing as we have always done.

According to the Austrian philosopher and sociologist Paul Feyerabend (*Against Method: Outline of an Anarchist Theory of Knowledge*, London: NLB, 1975; *Der Wissenschaftstheoritische Realismus un die Autorität der Wissenschaften*, Braunschweig: Vieweg & Sohn, 1978), there is no knowledge without chaos and no progress without a frequent rejection of reason. The reason has to be defeated in favour of other instances. No rule remains valid in all circumstances.

> Given any rule, however fundamental or necessary for science, – states Feyerabend – there are always circumstances when it is advisable not only to ignore the rule, but to adopt its opposite. Experience counts to a certain extent. It is what we perceive in normal circumstances in a normal environment and which we describe with words of everyday use. Extreme events drive the human being out of normality.

Shared knowledge and collective intelligence have replaced the three traditional value creation pillars: land, labour, capital. These three scarce resources were the drivers of progress in the industrial economy, with knowledge embedded in machines and other physical or tangible assets. In the knowledge age, the primary source of value creation lies in the hyper-mobility of knowledge, which controls access to opportunities and progress.

Knowledge Commercialisation

The talent in mastering knowledge enables us to attribute meaning to data, to offer innovative solutions to problems in both current markets (observation activities) and prospective markets (creating visions of the future in the medium and long term).

As we will see in Knowledge and Information, knowledge is not traded as a material product. What reaches markets is knowledge in a myriad of forms, illustrated under 'Knowledge and Information'.

Knowledge Entrepreneurs

They epitomise the aristocracy of intellectual work that enriches new technologies with content. Knowledge entrepreneurs create value in the unlimited markets of knowledge, striving for social and economic growth and improving the environment. The transversal strategy pursued by knowledge entrepreneurs makes them agents of cultural integration. One of the scarcest resources in a knowledge-based economy is an organisation's ability to create new knowledge. Thus, knowledge entrepreneurs tap into the talent of the creative class on a global scale.

Confidence-builders, creativity and innovation capacity of their human capital are primary drivers of productivity. They rarely act alone. Entrepreneurs are traditionally regarded as individualists; on the contrary, knowledge entrepreneurs usually participate in networks of ideas and people who complement them. They build and manage transversal relationships in which there is no authority or order. By breaking down cultural, institutional and geographical barriers to knowledge sharing, they build bridges between different communities and countries.

Knowledge Growth

The germination of knowledge is a process of expansion and deepening in space-time (see the corresponding entry in Chapter 4) with remarkable epidemiological aspects.

Let us look at three notable protagonists of revolutionary changes: Harrison in Yorkshire, Arkwright between Derbyshire, Lancashire and Nottinghamshire, and Watt in central and eastern Scotland.

John Harrison was a carpenter passionate about the mechanics of clocks he worked on in his spare time.

Richard Arkwright began working as a barber and wig manufacturer but showed great interest in spinning and carding machinery that turned raw cotton into thread.

James Watt, an instrument maker at the University of Glasgow, was interested in steam engines' technology.

Three personalities with a strong practical sense and united by a passion for discovering new paths to tread. Their actions mapped out a shortcut that allowed innovation to travel faster from one point to another. In the 14 years between 1761 and 1775, Harrison's marine chronometer (it was successfully tested in 1761), the patent of Arkwright's first automatic spinning machine (1769) and the development of Watt's steam engine (1763–1775) contributed to changing the configurations and performance of the leading industries of the time. Those outcomes unlocked the doors to that phenomenon which the French economist Adolphe Blanqui, followed by the British historian and economist Arnold Toynbee, dubbed 'Industrial Revolution'.

The space-time of three protagonists of revolutionary changes, 1761-1775

D: Derbyshire; L: Lancashire; N: Nottinghamshire; Y: Yorkshire; S: East-Central Scotland

Know How to Do

This is the mantra of companies that strive for continuous improvement and whose foundation is the ethic of stability.

Know How To Do (KHTD) is learned by running in the 'STEM' field, i.e. by training in the intellectual gyms of Science, Technology, Engineering and Mathematics. However, the 'STEM' option alone can no longer sustain human labour eroded by artificial intelligence, which has penetrated deeply into various fields – from drug discovery and medical analysis to civil engineering. This motion will accelerate in the years to come.

KHTD rests on two pillars. One is the column of the enterprise founded by workers and technicians, the representative class of that knowledge. The other is the vocational and technical schools pillar, the cradle of education of those founders.

The interaction between companies and schools, both centred on technical culture, has produced a set of tacit and implicit knowledge in which anecdotes, stories, suggestions, intuitions, feelings and individual points of view mixed with manual skills and a willingness 'to grease their elbows with machine oil'. This is how, in Bologna, a centre of manufacturing excellence in Italy, the inventor Bruto Carpigiani, learning through direct experience, trial and error, ushered in the prosperous Bolognese age of packaging by building the first machine for dosing and packaging *Idrolitina* powders to obtain effervescent drinking water.

Knowledge and Information

Information is a static resource or a static activity of reading, duplicating and broadcasting news. Knowledge is a human process concerned with mental objects; a process that requires awareness and intuition. Knowledge is a purposeful and dynamic process of selection and interpretation of information, and of face-to-face interactions through which knowledge is continuously recreated, and meanings assigned to facts that otherwise would remain unintelligible. There is no information without rendering it explicit. Conversely, there is knowledge, although not explicit.

Distinctive Attributes of Knowledge and Information

Knowledge	Information
Mental tools that make sense of things	A message that reduces uncertainty
An evolving set of beliefs about the world	
Knowledge is a crucial production factor that changes old habits into new ones	
Knowledge makes mere information valuable	
Dynamic	Static
Dependent on individual	Independent of individual
Tacit	Explicit
Analogue	Digital
Must be recreated	Easy to duplicate
Face-to-face communication	Easy to broadcast

Source: Leonard, D. (1998). 'Mining knowledge assets for innovation', *Knowledge Management, 1*(1), August–September. Sveiby, K. E. (1997). 'Knowledge management and EU. Challenging the perspective', In *Seminar on knowledge management and the European Union–results of the workshops*, Utrecht, 12–14 May.

Industrial culture has mainly focused on the production of things, of static objects. Knowledge, on the other hand, is in constant motion; it is a flowing river that reforms and redefines institutions and markets. Reformed markets are the result of the reformulation of existing ideas. Enterprises that arise from new ideas reshape the markets.

The producer of knowledge, unlike the manufacturer of a physical product, still keeps it, once knowledge has been surrendered in exchange for money. This raises two points.

From one point of view, knowledge goods are, in economic parlance, non-rival (that is, they can be used by their vendors and buyers simultaneously). 'Knowledge – as knowledge experts say – is not given up in exchange for money in the same way as a cream cake. You can't eat your cake and have it, but you can sell your knowledge and keep it' (Hampdem-Turner and Trompenaars, *Mastering the Infinite Game. How East Asian Values Are Transforming Business Practices*, Oxford: Capstone, 1997). In fact, the more you give, the more you have. Conversely, material products are rival in that two or more persons cannot use them at once.

From another point of view, knowledge is not a market like agriculture, mining and bulk goods, whose limited resources constrain trade. Knowledge markets are not affected by a short supply of ideas: the potential for finding new ideas is infinite.

There are different types of knowns listed below by Rob van der Spek and André Spijkervet (*Knowledge Management. Dealing Intelligently with knowledge*, Utrecht: Kenniscentrum CIBIT, 1997):

- Know-how: skills in managing practical processes, which means selling the knowledge of how information must be processed.
- Know-what: knowledge about facts – that is, what sort of information is needed.
- Know-why: explanatory science – that is, why a given type of information is needed.
- Know-where: where information can be founded to achieve a specific result.
- Know-when: by what time information is needed.
- Know-who: knowledge about socially related understandings.

Knowledge Map

As conceived by the American researcher Xenia Stanford ('The Knowledge Management Strategy Vee: A Framework for Creating a New Strategic Direction'. In Debra Amidon, Piero Formica, and Eunika Mercier-Laurent, *Knowledge Economics: Emerging Principles, Practices and Policies*, Vol. 2, Tartu: Tartu University Press, 2005), a knowledge map differs from a graphical representation of information or data in its function and purpose. Generally, the purpose of an information map is to show what we have available and where to find it. A knowledge map helps us learn, construct, infer, share, create and store knowledge.

The map, comprising text linked to symbols, directions, and routes, shows the relationships between concepts, and its value is commensurate with what it allows us to know about:

- What you own of what you need so that you can exploit it.
- What you have that you do not need, so that you can eliminate the excess and concentrate on the most critical elements.
- What you do not have that you need so that you can get it.

Knowledge Markets

Knowledge is transmitted to markets through a variety of ideas expressed in conversations and in recipes, formulas and techniques whose common denominator is the ability to reorder physical objects in low- to high-value configurations. One thinks of silicon, first used mainly to produce glass and then become a decisive element in producing microchips and optical fibres.

As a driving force for economic development, knowledge markets, as were product markets throughout the industrial era, represent the conceptual space in which bits are exchanged across continents in a wide range of contents. The Internet, undersea fibre optic cabling and satellite communications are the infrastructures that make access to knowledge markets possible. A wide variety of offerings and expanding connectivity give participants an unlimited capacity to weave relationships and profit from their development.

Heterogeneity is a distinctive feature of knowledge markets. End-users can profit from the availability of more choices and a wider diversity of outlets that allow them to spend their money somewhere else and from price reductions that sellers can sustain as a result of accelerating growth in those markets.

Knowledge and Technology Transfer

Knowledge transfer (KT) is the process of putting knowledge into action, designing a virtuous circuit between productivity, economic growth and entrepreneurial activity. Knowledge in action that ensures the availability of relevant experience at the point of action, and just in time, has the power to produce innovations from the imaginative exploitation of discoveries.

The KT key is used for the purpose of effectiveness so that the enterprise is enabled to conceive things that others cannot. Instead of information, knowledge is transferred through a close dialogue between the provider and the user. Therefore, the key must be in the hands of knowledge brokers with excellent interpersonal skills, business awareness and contractual experience. Mutual trust is a fundamental part of success, as the field of knowing 'how', 'what', 'when' and 'to whom' to transfer is elusive.

Technology transfer (TT) emphasises information and efficiency rather than knowledge and effectiveness. The TT key uses technical concepts to transfer information, either unbundled or embedded in technologies, and data extracted from scientific research results. When implemented efficiently and quickly, the information and data-oriented approach help to develop applications that solve practical problems in the industry. The goal is to increase efficiency while reducing costs by doing better what one already knows how to do.

Knowledge Workers

An expression coined by Peter Drucker around the 1960s to denote those who possess the knowledge and can also allocate it to productive uses.

Knowledge workers operate on knowledge applied to itself – not just to tools, processes and products, identifying what new knowledge is needed and how to make it effective. Tasks and commitments characterised by originality, variety, chance contingencies and exceptions, rather than routine, regimented causality and predictability, characterise knowledge workers. Their work requires cooperation, understood as an exchange in which the participants benefit from the interaction.

Knowledge workers prefer the bumpy terrain of meritocracy to the flat plain of bureaucratic equality.

Due to their transversal competencies, they are well connected to the high added value content industries (interactive multimedia, infotainment, virtual reality) and the borderless networks that innervate the fabrics of the knowledge economy.

Latin

As Steve Jobs hoped, Latin and other so-called dead languages are starting a learning process to combine technology with the liberal arts, technologists with humanists. *Alienus Non Diutius*, alone no more, is the Latin motto of Pixar University, which has made Jobs' wish its own. On the same wavelength, in Tampere, Finland, from the Latin word trivium, the meeting point of three roads, the University's Trivium Centre was founded, inaugurated in January 2015, with the mission of encouraging transdisciplinary dialogue and promoting medieval and Renaissance culture.

Here are just some of the facts which highlight the resurrection of the Latin language:

- Turning back to the Classical Lyceum of Tampere, founded in 1901, whose tradition continues with the Classical School where the study of the Latin civilization and language is still one of its hallmarks, Finnish YLE Radio 1 has, since 1 September 1989, broadcast a programme in classical Latin called *Nuntii Latini*, with listeners in over 80 countries.
- Similarly, Radio Bremen in Germany has broadcast a programme called *Nuntii Latini Septimanales* since 2001.
- Google Translate provides a service in Latin which attracts a more significant number of users than Esperanto.
- In 2004, a Polish journalist started *Ephemeris*, an online journal in Latin, with contributors in Germany, Colombia, Chile and the United States.
- *Schola* is a social network in Latin, operational since 2008. Launched by Benedict XVI on Twitter in January 2013, the account Pontifex Latin records hundreds of thousands of followers.
- According to David Butterfield, a Latin scholar at the University of Cambridge, Latin is ideal for those who want to post 140 characters on Twitter; as Butterfield says, 'Five Latin words can often say more than ten English ones'.

Laws of Knowledge Dynamics

Knowledge is abundant, provided it operates as a multiplier – i.e., the more it is shared, the more it grows and the more it can be used innovatively. Otherwise, human knowledge also remains a scarce and expensive commodity.

Three laws of knowledge dynamics have been formulated (see Debra Amidon, Piero Formica, and Eunika Mercier-Laurent, *Knowledge Economics: Emerging Principles, Practices and Policies*, Tartu: Tartu University Press, 2005).

The First Law of Knowledge Dynamics states that knowledge multiplies when shared. The resulting knowledge energy, which triggers organic growth, is manifested through a broad range of mechanisms. These include Innovation Management, Leadership for Value Creation, Knowledge Pattern Recognition, Knowledge Mapping, Knowledge Networks, Social Cybernetics, Mental Models, Situation-Handling, and Capital Systems. Since knowledge is inherently a human process, we must optimise its creation and flow to minimise the loss in the transmission process.

The Second Law of Knowledge Dynamics states that value is created when knowledge moves from its point of origin to the point of need or opportunity. The real benefit of knowledge lies in action, and innovation is the process whereby knowledge is put into motion or used. This process of innovating knowledge requires high-powered knowledge energy flows (see First Law) supported by comprehensive bandwidth connectivity and rich interrelated actions. The Second Law emphasises effectiveness whereby actions aiming to do the right thing (effectiveness) prevail over those addressed at doing things correctly (efficiency).

The Third Law of Knowledge Dynamics states that mutual leverage provides the optimal utilisation of resources, both tangible and intangible. It asserts that collaboration and the value of leveraging the knowledge of one another create greater wealth and sustainability for us all. Unlike vested interests playing against the competition, collaborative efforts made by those agents who put knowledge into action are incentives not to collude but to combine cooperation and competition to enhance precompetitive forces working for the general interest of the knowledge society. There are multiplier implications that operate within and across network boundaries. Synergy and symbiosis are natural outcomes of human interaction in ways that provide profound network effects.

Leadership

The leadership is dead, long alive the leadership. A new leadership whose life blossoms in the age of innocence at the time of the knowledge economy. As Narcissus turns to Goldmund, the new leadership says to the old:

We are sun and moon, dear friend; we are sea and land. It is not our purpose to become each other; it is to recognize each other, learn to see the other and to honour him for what he is: each the other's opposite and complement.
(Hermann Hesse, *Narcissus and Goldmund*, first published in 1930)

The new leadership comes to light when the debate between two corporate social responsibility visions is still hot. The followers of Milton Friedman, who received the 1976 Nobel Memorial Prize in Economic Sciences, identify it with profit enhancement. The opponents of Friedman's doctrine aspire to leadership that serves society's broader needs. Mistrustful of each other, the two sides are obsessed with differences. The new leadership breaks down the barriers erected by the two camps and thus grasps the echo of what is or could happen. From the heights of renewed knowledge, one senses a change in the air, with the economy nearing its Copernican moment.

Not everything can yet revolve around the corporate mission of making profits and the consumer goal of satisfying all their selfish material desires. At the same time, labour fails to provide stable and adequate incomes for a growing number of people, as evidenced by stagnant wages, irregular incomes, non-existent financial reserves for emergencies, low job security and even harsh working conditions. From the peaks of a reinvented knowledge, we will learn that our material needs' desirability is worth less than our social needs, such as the need to care and be cared for, belong to a community, and shape one's destiny joint efforts. The Copernican shift shakes the foundations of business schools.

Learning

How can I rethink the way I see the problem? How many different ways can I solve it? These are questions that are answered not having to comply with the authority of the canons defined in the teaching manuals. Learning prepares the mind to formulate questions rather than to give answers, starting with those that do not admit to being questioned; to cultivate abstruse questions that reveal unusual paths to explore.

Learning provides the mind with an understanding of ignorance as something normal rather than something that departs from the norm. Learners exploring ignorance 'agnotology', from the Greek ἀγνῶσις (agnōsis), is the term coined by science historian Robert Proctor – take pleasure in not finding what they are looking for, and they are not afraid to confront the uncertainty that comes from the 'unknown unknowns'. In this way facts classified as immutable, fixed once and for all, are challenged and may be proven wrong.

In the learning process, the leading actor is the experimenter who enters the ballroom with light baggage, not burdened with accumulated knowledge, where the questions that are not known dance the can-can, as Mark Forsyth writes in his *The unknown unknown: Bookshops and the delight of not getting what you wanted*, London: Icon Books, 2014.

In the early twentieth century, the Italian writer Giovanni Papini spoke against the school that 'does not invent knowledge but prides itself on transmitting it'. Papini shifted the emphasis from teaching that takes students from giving the right answer to learning in experimental laboratories which provide a basis for raising, by both students and teachers, unspoken and unprecedented questions, and determining from errors.

Lunar Society

In the Age of Reason, under the spotlights of Enlightenment and Rationality, a club was founded in Birmingham, an informal learning society so-called because the meetings, held regularly between 1765 and 1813, took place at every full moon, at dinner time. The Lunar Society was a diverse body of visionaries. It included scientists, inventors, entrepreneurs, artisans, artists, and politicians who shared ideas in an entirely free mode because they were unfettered by interference or influence arising from monetary incentives. Among the Lunaticks, there were personalities the likes of the chemist Joseph Priestley, the inventor James Watt, the entrepreneur Josiah Wedgwood, the manufacturer and Watt's business partner Matthew Boulton, and the physician, naturalist and poet Erasmus Darwin. By making science, art and commerce interact, those brilliant minds intertwined the new technologies of the industrial revolution with the commerce of the liberal revolution. Their achievements extended to fossil classification, telescope manufacture, and experimentation with electricity.

Managerial Enterprise

The words that hallmark management are accuracy, diligence, scruple, zeal, efficiency. The managerial enterprise responds to the wishes of the customer. To this end, the knowledge map is used by managers to improve the performance of products and services and to win new customers. By mastering the market, knowledge accelerates incremental innovation – what makes products more attractive to offer to customers who want upgraded versions of them.

Informed entrepreneurs are subject to the rational ignorance that arises when the cost of leaving their market-oriented knowledge maps and entering the field of creative ignorance is deemed too high. Once the path ahead is mapped out, getting to the finish line in time determines the success of incremental innovation, which runs the risk of turning into decline when its culture survives on tradition, imitation and pride.

Manufacture

With the start of the industrial revolution, manufacturing had its symbolic place in the factory populated by a mass of workers and machines. Above it, the sky appeared starry, each star alluding to a new job, a new machine in operation; in short, more jobs and more investment. But not only that. In the Smithian vision illustrated in Book Three of *The Wealth of Nations*, manufacturing is the bearer of good governance, order, security and freedom from which the lower classes benefit. Thus, economic development has been able to proceed at a faster pace than in the past.

Manufacturing is still a front player in the future of growth and innovation. Increased demand for manufactured goods stimulates technical progress, boosts productivity and investment. This relationship was highlighted in the early 1960s by Cambridge economist Nicholas Kaldor. Moreover, it is the booming manufacturing sector that allows exports to expand.

By accumulating experience, the cost-effectiveness of the production process has significantly increased (in the order of 20–30%). As learning widens and deepens, productivity rises. Falling costs and soaring productivity increasingly depend on operators' ability to use digital simulators and test innovative ways to improve performance. Well-combined mind and matter improve the cost and productivity performance of the production plant.

Mass production and markets are shifting towards customised production and sales activities, consisting of small batches, carried out close to customers and in flexible ways, leveraging 3D printing technologies.

In the incoming age of interaction between the economy's health and the preservation of nature, biotechnology companies, medical and environmental devices, precision instruments and communication equipment acquire a strategic value above that of the market.

Method of Freedom

Luigi Einaudi described as decadent societies those which had adopted the model of the state-monopoly university. His preference was for the Anglo-Saxon world, which had opted for the 'method of freedom' by creating universities as private foundations. A sign of freedom was the demolition of the myth of the legal value of a degree. So wrote Einaudi, economist and practical preacher:

> It is enough to appeal to the truth, which says that the source of scientific, technical, theoretical or practical, humanistic, professional suitability is not the sovereign or the people or the rector or the dean or any public authority; it is not the official parchment declaring the possession of the degree. The judge of the truth of the declaration is he who intends to avail himself of the services of another man; whether or not he has more or less authoritative declarations of academic habilitation. Was there a need for a state stamp to accredit young people who came out of Giotto's or Michelangelo's workshop?
>
> (*Prediche inutili*, Torino: Einaudi, 1959)

Millennials

The Wonder Generation or Generation Y, born between the early 1980s and the early years of the current century. Three different generations preceded the

Millennials. First, the Silent Generation of workers and technicians born between 1925 and 1945 who, in the absence of media noise, rolled up their shirt sleeves and contributed to post-war reconstruction, especially in Western Europe. Then came the baby boomers, children of the so-called 'economic miracle', born between 1945 and 1964: they were, first and foremost, a generation of managers. The third generation, Generation X, roughly those born between 1960 and 1980, produced the first wave of entrepreneurs in the new economy. They are educated people, highly motivated to exploit the knowledge acquired at university, willing to change jobs frequently to enrich their portfolio of skills and experience.

Millennials have discovered the seeds of entrepreneurship in the fissures between digital tales, teenage novels and naïve stories of love. As children, they played and taught themselves on computers, game consoles and mobile phones. We could call them the 'digerati' of the Worldwide Web: the new creative technology elite, future serial entrepreneurs and knowledge nomads. If Generation X has been prolific in initiating entrepreneurial projects – four out of five new business founders in the US come from this generation – Generation Y seems to have entered the arena of business creators at an earlier age.

The attitudes of the Millennials contradict the pessimism of conservatives, for whom the balance between economic and social life makes it too precarious to undertake revolutionary experiments.

Mozart Effect

Studies carried out by the Norwegian Institute for International Research in Stavanger and the London School of Economics and Political Science have found that key factors in innovation are outward communication channels and open-mindedness to new ideas and changes by those different from us. Interacting only with people of the same social status and age only enlarges the number of Indian reservations. Communities of citizens harnessed in this way suffocate in selfishness and marginalisation. The creation of value is the result of the meticulous sowing of intelligence. Among these, the motivations, attitudes and skills of the discriminated against should certainly not be overlooked. Music contributes to opening up communication channels.

An innovation community is all the more open, the more it pursues the art of music. Like other art forms, music brings together different feelings and helps find common denominators for exchanging insights, images, and ideas that weaken resistance to change.

It has been called the 'Mozart Effect' (Don Campbell, *The Mozart Effect: Tapping the Power of Music to Heal the Body, Strengthen the Mind, and Unlock the Creative Spirit*, New York, NY: Harper Collins, 1997) the broader and better understanding of the orientation and distance of relationships that one gets from listening to the music of that great composer. Exposure to musical art would thus be an invaluable opportunity to build bridges between communities seemingly distant from each other.

Multilingualists

The model of technology transfer from university research to the commercial world developed by Oxford University University – the University of Oxford's technology transfer company has paved the way in bridging the gap between two cultures as different as research and business by deploying the 'multilingualists', intermediaries capable of understanding and practising the two cultures. 'Multilingualists' pursue entrepreneurial goals. Their entrepreneurship is a contribution to the economic impact of academic research.

Multiversity

It was the first chancellor of the University of California, Clark Kerr, who coined the term 'multiversity' to describe the multiple and parallel missions that universities have to fulfil. These missions range from education to moving the frontiers of knowledge forward.

In the meantime, the mission of extracting entrepreneurial values from the raw material of progress in the different branches of knowledge has taken hold. 'Multiversity' is an innovative learning network that benefits all participants.

Nature

Nature's voice reaches us through bees and other pollinators. From them, we learn how to listen to and understand it. Yesterday's thinkers display the stage space by raising the curtain on tomorrow. Only the evolutionary surge in culture can enable humankind to surmount the constraints of economic and lifestyle models that have led to our failed relationship with nature.

Between 1961 and the present time, from the midst of post–World War II economic expansion to the globalisation of the 2000s, the human load on nature increased 2.5 times in terms of population and seven times when measured with GDP at constant prices. To the demographic and economic weight must be added the ponderousness of technology combined with hyper-specialisation. The race for quantity at the expense of quality extends to the limit of the biosphere, which under a heavy burden would no longer sustain us. It is imperative to balance economic values with environmental concerns to assess the compliance of human initiatives with the conservation of nature. It is equally vital to promote a generation of multifaceted thinkers and creators, polymaths familiar with different fields of study who have open minds to resolve complex problems creatively.

From the thinkers of the past, we hear voices that deserve to listen, for they make us reflect on how to innovate together with, not against, the nature that appears endowed with its subjectivity and intelligence, as the poet Titus Lucretius Caro maintained. If tomorrow must be designed with nature as a partner, not as an object, then in the discourse of design, the imagination of artists and the intellect of scientists must converse.

In *The Love Poems* (Book III, a translation into English by A. S. Kline. PiT (*Poetry in Translation* – www.poetryintranslation.com, 2001), Ovid puts it this way:

> Human nature, you've been skilful, against yourself, and ingenious, in excess, to your own harm. What use to you are towns encircled with turreted walls? What use to you to add the discord of arms, at hand? When was the sea yours – land should have contented you! Why not seek out a third region then in the sky? Though you honour the sky too, Romulus, Bacchus, Hercules, Caesar now have temples. We dig the earth for solid gold not food.

Following Goethe's thought,

> Nature is living, [it is not] pure quantity…game to be captured…a tool to be forged according to the usefulness of man.
> (*Teoria della natura*, Milano: SE, 2020)

In his essay *On Liberty*, John Stuart Mill holds that human nature

> …is not a machine to be built after a model, and set to do exactly the work prescribed for it, but a tree, which requires to grow and develop itself on all sides, according to the tendency of the inward forces which make it a living thing.

Human beings have fought to hoard natural resources by neglecting conversation with nature to focus on whatever can bring personal gain. Lack of collaboration toward a shared vision of resource allocation and environmental sustainability has narrowed the range of opportunities that nature offers humanity.

Networks

We owe Ray Miles and Charles Snow ('Causes of Failure in Network Organisations', *California Management Review*, Summer 1992) the design of three types of network.

Internal network: dedicated to partners interacting with each other. The network administrator plays a central role due to her experience, strategic ability and strong personality.

Stable network: formed by independent and specialised partners linked to a central unit through long-term relationships and contractual solutions. Each partner maintains and develops its distinctive competencies, also in the service of other actors outside the network. The central unit has the same characteristics as the administrator of an internal network.

Dynamic network: arises from short-term or one-off relationships. The partners are contractually bound for a particular project, each operating in a specific value chain segment. There are no unique or privileged relationships. The central coordinating unit plays a mainly administrative role.

The networks' code of conduct requires:

Voluntarism: Partners are free to withdraw from relationships they consider unfair.
Openness: Relationships are external and therefore highly visible to all parties.
Explicitness: Relationships, external and visible, tend to be explicit.
Simplicity: 'The less you sign, the more you get'.
Performance: Performance rather than procedures drive relationships.
Accessibility: Information systems ensure that all decisions are made objectively and fairly.
Self-renewal: Work units reorganise quickly to solve new problems.

New Cultural Movement

Under the Song Dynasty (960–1279), Hangzhou was the Chinese version of Renaissance Florence. Many centuries were to pass before the re-emergence of the Chinese Renaissance, seemingly from oblivion, in 1917. Influenced by India and variously known as the New Cultural Movement, New Thought, and New Tide, its identity was linked to a group close to the leadership of the Chinese philosopher Hu Shih. The movement was strongly characterised by its efforts to promote a culture of reason, freedom and human values in contrast to the existing traditionalism, authoritarianism and suppression, through a monthly magazine Renaissance, founded in 1918 by a group of government students at Beijing University.

Its spirit had smouldered under the ashes until the present day when the word fu xing appeared on the horizon.

Nibelungs

A metaphor from Germanic mythology, we give the name Nibelungs to managers who hold the rich treasure trove of customers and consumers. Siegfried, the visionary innovator, will take possession of their wealth.

Nibelung managers are the experts on the hard things of today. Speculating on the coming tomorrow, they stop innovation at the border of incrementalism, doing what is necessary to safeguard the continuity of the original vocations. Their attitude is a light which, while confirming their point of view, can be deceptive, leading them to look where it is quickly spreading, without there being anything more than the improvement of what is already skilfully practised.

Olivetti Lettera 22

Between art and business, innovation experiences moments that are sometimes virtuous and some others vicious. If, as in the Middle Ages, the deity governs art according to objective criteria and the corporations determine the production process with fixed rules, then neither artists nor artisans have freedom of action. Innovation is curbed to the point of being prevented.

When, in the Modern Age, artists and craftsmen free themselves from super-human chains and corporate constraints, respectively, innovation is exalted.

From then on, the two freedoms, the artistic and the entrepreneurial, conquered new spaces and interacted to such an extent that, as the art critic Gillo Dorfles said in the 1950s, the meaning of art can even be identified with the industrial product. To confirm this assertion, in 1959, the Olivetti Lettera, 22, a portable mechanical typewriter designed by Marcello Nizzoli, was awarded by the Illinois Institute of Technology as the best design product of the last 100 years. From another viewpoint, several entrepreneurs and business executives have said that business is their art.

Online Markets

Several species of Internet-based companies populate online markets. The most popular are those that sell a product or service to a retail customer (Business-to-Consumer or B2C) and those supplying a product or service to another company (Business-to-Business or B2B). Two other market segments are Consumer-to-Business (C2B) and Consumer to Consumer (C2C).

Some companies offer solutions to end-users, while others provide Internet infrastructures and infrastructures for online vendors to navigate in cyberspace. There are online enterprises that rely on advertising (e.g., a portal). Others are only successful to the extent that visitors make purchases.

Online marketplaces can also be organised around independent purchases or exchanges. The former are one-way networks in which large buyers hold market power. The latter tend to be two-way networks that occupy a central position between buyers and sellers, mediating between the two parties.

Online markets built around independent transactions show fragmentation on both sides of supply and demand. They have been labelled as butterfly-shaped neutral marketplaces, focused on specific industries (called purely vertical portals) or on specific business functions and processes in different sectors (purely func-tional portals). Online intermediaries create these kinds of portals within less established industries, where no one or few prominent players have a significant market share. With the balance of power divided between several competing buyers and sellers, all participants share the benefits of independent and neutral e-commerce.

In online markets, information is a vehicle for buying and selling physical products. Physical items trading puts online businesses under the umbrella of the 'brick-and-mortar culture'. They personify the hybrid solutions of the Web.

Pure online marketplaces arise from people's ability to buy and sell informa-tion. The expression People-to-People (P2P) has been coined for these markets. Information transactions between people that directly generate revenue can be designed for serious matters such as treating a disease or for trivial ones such as gossip from the star system.

Open Innovation

Borrowing from Einstein's playful comment during banter with other physicists after a famous dinner with the King and Queen of Belgium, as Gabriella Greison reports (*L'incredibile cena dei fisici quantistici*, Milano: Salani Editore, 2016), we could depict classical innovation as apricot jam and open innovation as the grapes that make up a bunch. His joke referred to the concept of discontinuity (quantum physics), which stands in contrast to that of continuity (classical physics).

Open innovation with its cultural attributes is the spirit of the times we live in, characterised by an emphasis on the broadest possible access to new knowledge and resources and their entrepreneurial translation. What emerges is a hybrid culture enriched by options reflecting different aspects of innovation. Among these, altruism deserves to be taken into account, and with it an openness to experimentation with irritating and non-prescriptive solutions.

Popularised in the early 2000s, open innovation is a systematic process through which ideas penetrate from one organisation to another and travel on different vectors of opportunity for value creation. The network is at the heart of open innovation: a socio-economic process in which people interact and share information to recognise, create and act on business opportunities.

Open innovation is congenial to a community in which cognitive conflict arises from the unfettered debate raised by the authority of the canons. The bearers of antagonistic ideas compete to assert personal prestige and help to enhance cooperation so that antagonism does not lead to stagnation. The egoism of competition coexists with the altruism of cooperation. In doing so, the proponents of open innovation are motivated by the knowledge that their ideas may be buried if they decide to act in isolation. Defection from cooperation would, in fact, restrict their margins of manoeuvre.

The mental space of open innovation, therefore, requires the breaking down of offences. 'Walls are in mind' – this is one of the suggestions deployed along the 'Path of Meditation' on the Island of San Giulio in Lake Orta, northern Italy. Playing the game of open innovation, we change our minds. As Virgil says in The Aeneid III, line 72, 'terraeque urbesque recedunt' ('leave the cities and the shores behind').

How does the innovator move in the psychological space of open innovation? A solution lies in the game of chess. The innovator's move resembles the characteristic movement of the knight as it jumps over squares and other pieces. The innovator has endless possibilities to exploit and the feasible reactions of the other players are unlimited. In the radical uncertainty surrounding them, each relies on simple rules of thumb.

One can move around in the spaces adjacent to one's domain. In such a way, Nicholas Callan invented the induction coil in 1836 – a result obtained by combining two adjacent ideas: the discovery in 1831 of electromagnetic induction by the physicist and chemist Michael Faraday and the electromagnet invented in 1825 by the physicist William Sturgeon.

Adjacent mental spaces may give rise to physical spaces that are sources of unlikely combinations. As Christina van Houten recounts (*Adjacent Innovation-Unlikely Connections That Move Our World*, Diginomica, 5 October 2016), the concentration of Venetian glass artisans on the island of Murano turned out to be an 'accidental creation of a colony of highly skilled glassmakers'.

Socialising in the neighbourhood cultural space could lead to a 'sole mode of thought' syndrome of loyalty to the scientific community or industrial district to which one belongs. Those who espouse anti-discipline move into wide and 'white' (uncontaminated) spaces.

Seven Currents of Thought That Flow through Open Innovation

Various currents of thought make up the threads that weave the culture of open innovation. Here we have chosen seven.

LAO TZU (sixth–fifth century BCE)

The supreme good is like water

Like water, open innovation benefits everyone. It adapts to the ground and irrigates it with altruism. We descend into the well of non-knowledge and come back into the sunlight bringing new knowledge.

DUNS SCOTUS (1266–1308)

Knowledge born out of actions

Open innovation multiplies actions.

FRANCIS BACON (1561–1626)

Inductive hypotheses

Open innovation makes inductive hypotheses rise to the surface from sources of imagination and creativity.

JOHN LOCKE (1632–1704)

The mind at birth is like a blank slate

The minds of participants in open innovation communities are a blank slate on which they write as they experiment with new ways of communication and conceiving new lines of thought.

DAVID HUME (1711–1776)

Relations amongst ideas are at the basis of human knowledge

Open innovation is a relational field.

PAUL FEYERABEND (1924–1994)

Multiple alternative hypotheses compete with one another

There are circumstances in which it is best to adopt an idea that is opposite to the usual practice. Open innovation is a field where competition and cooperation reinforce each other. Open innovation changes the rules of the game.

'BA' THEORETICIANS (Kitarō Nashida, Hiroshi Shimizu, Ikujiro Nonaka and Noboru Konno).

Living organisms live in the 'ba' space (whether physical, virtual, mental or any combination of these) of non-separation of the self and the 'other'.

Carried along by the current of open innovation, open innovators attract each other, adapting to the conditions of mutual cooperation. In the field ('ba') of open innovation, unpredictable and impromptu creations may emerge from the entrainment process.

Open Innovation 2.0

The European Union's Open Innovation Strategy and Policy Group (OISPG) unites industrial groups, academia, governments and private individuals to support policies for open innovation. Its philosophy embraces the Open Innovation 2.0 paradigm: creating open innovation ecosystems where the serendipity process is fully fledged.

The OISPG defines Open Innovation 2.0 as a new paradigm based on principles of integrated collaboration, co-created shared value, cultivated innovation ecosystems, unleashed exponential technologies and extraordinarily rapid adoption. Innovation can be a discipline practised by many rather than an art mastered by a few.

As the result of advances in digital technologies and developments in cognitive science, this type of innovation marks the transition from marginal and incremental gains to radical change – long shots that make a big step forward in economic and social development possible. There are many cases of collaboration whose outcomes produce a sum of the parts that is less than the sum of each of the individual components. In open innovation 2.0, two or more entities interact to produce a combined effect that is greater than the sum of their parts.

It aims to produce benefits for society, not just the economy, by identifying and implementing innovations that collectively move us towards the trajectory of an intelligent and, therefore, sustainable way of life. In doing so, it makes clear how new services and markets can be co-created in open ecosystems where win-win outcomes ('I win, you win') outweigh situations that separate winners from losers ('I win, you lose').

Organisational Knowledge

Through dialogue and discussion, cognitive conflicts and disagreement raise, which questioned the existing premises. It is what makes possible the transformation of personal into organisational knowledge. The long-standing, healthy rivalry has been at the origin of healthy collaboration – that is, collaboration to share complex information on an ongoing basis for a common goal.

The key players in organisational knowledge are 'strong heart' individualists endowed with a hedgehog-minded personality and focused on their projects, but also ready to collaborate to bring about change beyond the conventional wisdom horizon.

Throughout the 1920s, Enzo Ferrari spent much time judiciously creating his commercial and engineering connections. He also began surrounding himself with a group of close collaborators. Among them was former Fiat technician Luigi Bazzi, a man who would survive into the 1960s as possibly Enzo's longest-standing lieutenant, having joined him in 1923. Bazzi had joined Alfa Romeo as long ago as 1922 after a spell in Fiat's experimental department, and would later become tagged as the man who conceived the fearsome twin-engined Alfa Romeo Bimotore in the 1930s. Not only was Bazzi an invaluable technical guide, but also his long collaboration with Ferrari helps smooth out differences of opinion and respective temperamental problems, which made working with his boss an increasingly unpredictable, sometimes stormy, challenge in the following years.

Otto von Guericke, the Vacuum Experiment

Otto von Guericke, mayor of Magdeburg and scientist, conducted a scientific experiment in public which helped to demolish the *horror vacui* theory according to which nature abhors a vacuum.

At the 1654 fair, Otto amazed the spectators. In the middle of a large square, he placed a sphere made up of two brass hemispheres adhered to each other. If not held together, the two hemispheres would have fallen to the ground. Using the air pump he invented, Otto removed the air from inside the sphere. Each hemisphere had an inner ring to which a string was attached. The other ends of the ropes were attached to the harnesses of two teams of horses. The horses, no matter how hard they pulled, pressed and snorted, to everyone's surprise, could not separate the two hemispheres (www.thermospokenhere.com - B654). Even with all the force exerted by willing citizens pulling in opposite directions, the two hemispheres would not have detached.

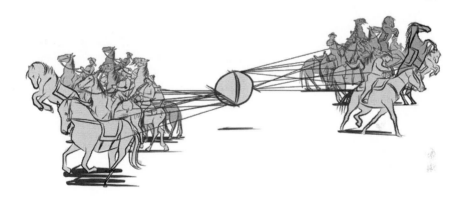

Referring back to that experiment, let us assume that one hemisphere contains passions for innovation; the other, innovative projects. Once the air of bureaucratic regulation is removed, no force in the world can detach the two hemispheres. By creating a vacuum, we give breath to innovation by jamming passions and projects together.

Passion for Innovating

Passion combined with determination can produce exceptional results. Referring back to one of Stefan Zweig's five 'historical miniatures' ('The First Word to

Cross the Ocean', In *Genius and Discovery: Five Historical Miniatures*, London: Pushkin Press, 2016), by harnessing the power of electricity, it was passion combined with the will to succeed that enabled Cyrus West Field to finally and successfully lay submarine cables in the Atlantic Ocean for the transmission of electricity between Europe and America. Between 1858 and 1866, it took eight years and several unsuccessful attempts to achieve the desired result. Field accomplished a remarkable feat in raising as much money as such an ambitious project required. If other doors of innovation had been opened alongside the financial ones, the time might have been shortened. What is now known as 'Open Innovation 2.0' should help speed up the journey from conception to realisation.

Patents

Patents are centuries-old windows open to innovation. Their words evoke the perennial making of the world's reality. They encourage inventors to reveal their innovative ideas in exchange for a monopoly on their use for a given time from the moment the invention is revealed. Researchers can observe and analyse patents, unlike trade secrets which are challenging to study because they are a secret.

The Santa Fe Institute (SFI) – an independent, non-profit, research institution based in Santa Fe (New Mexico, USA), dedicated to the multidisciplinary study of the fundamental principles of complex adaptive systems, including physical, computational, biological and social systems – defines patents as 'one of the best sources of data on technology development — an open-ended, historical and adaptive system that shows us how and why inventions have come to be' (https://santafe.edu/news-center/news/opening-centuries-old-window-innovation).

According to the SFI, Artificial Intelligence (AI) is already being used to support patent examiners, enabling them to respond more quickly to clients' needs.

Path Creators

'Every act of creation is, first of all, an act of destruction', said Pablo Picasso. Path creators do not merely accept received knowledge as truth. Adept at using a transdisciplinary approach to venturing, they rely on a series of iterative experiments to observe the world beyond the visible horizon. Discontinuity (see the corresponding entry in Chapter 4), randomness, breakthrough and disruption are familiar words to them.

Disobedient innovators, route makers feel like René Magritte's *The Ignorant Fairy*: the portrait of a person who represents the promise of new knowledge and perceives in herself a creator intentionally pursuing alternatives to paths already trodden. While immersed in calculations for plotting courses on the navigation charts, the geographer painted by Johannes Vermeer suddenly decides, by intuition, to take the broad line. He turns his gaze elsewhere, to the window that opens onto an unknown landscape, playing the part of the visionary and not only that of the meticulous specialist. Perhaps, just outside the window, an idea is in flight that would like to enter the room, to be grasped by the geographer. That is how a thrill-seeking journey begins, a unique journey to a world that the knowledge maps ignore. Vermeer himself was a path creator. He used a camera obscura, an optical device that helped present reality objectively and impartially.

The freedom of action distracts path creators from the laws and rules of knowledge. 'There is no map, and charting a path ahead will not be easy', so Amazon founder Jeff Bezos said after buying *The Washington Post*. The lenses path creators wear are not intended for predicting a future that is a projection of the past: their lenses, once worn, enhance the imagination. The future is no longer a particular place identified by exercises in logic and anchored to the past. The future is everywhere with imagination, revealing uncertainties not quantifiable in manageable risks based on the knowledge maps mastered.

Path Dependency

Success is addictive. It arises from positive feedback confirming the soundness of established practices of thinking and doing things. 'You can't change a winning team' is the leitmotif attributed to the Serbian footballer and coach Vujadin Boškov. That is how the achievements of the past turn into losses of assets. Know-how and skills, experienced workers, specialised infrastructure, inter-company links, all the institutional, social, cultural, economic and technological factors that once ensured success now cause path dependency. One finds oneself 'lock-in', confined in a room with no light and therefore no vision.

What more can you expect once you reached the top? Whether one has reached the heights is a matter of fact. However, once one tenaciously trusts the facts, resistance to change takes over: the more robust the latter, the more reliable the pedestal of beliefs on which the former rests. Attention is paid to the facts, which after all represent what has been, while the rapid changes underway take on the task of making them less and less usable. There is a need to give voice to creativity, to new entrepreneurial vocations that break with the past to project themselves into the future. On the contrary, the community remains stuck on the line of the crude rationality of facts to push the past into the future. The sense of profound insecurity and bewilderment that discourages action exerts a subtle fascination on society's various protagonists.

Several authors have recognised this syndrome. For example, according to Ron Martin and Peter Sunley ('Deconstructing Clusters: Chaotic Concept or Policy Panacea?' In *High Technology Small Firms One-Day Clusters Conference*, Manchester Business School, 18 April 2002; *Journal of Economic Geography, 3*(1), January 2003, 5–35),

The competitive strategies of firms in clusters, which are initially highly innovative compared to firms outside clusters, tend to converge (for example, through mimetic and normative isomorphism) and to be less innovative over time because cluster firms define their field of competition as the cluster to which they belong, rather than as the wider external industry. This restricted collective perspective gives rise to competitive 'blind spots' which limit cluster firms' innovative potential, strategic positioning, and ability to anticipate and react to industry-wide shocks.

Bologna is the capital of a community in the top group of regions in the European Union. Its packaging machines are on display in the best factories of multinational pharmaceuticals, tea, tobacco, confectionery, et cetera. Dating back to the industrial revolution, the city was at the peak of its success in developing the silk processing for which it was known throughout Europe. The precepts and forms of the new scientific and technological domain and working practices introduced by the industrial revolution caused a deep and prolonged crisis in the local economy. Immersed in the culture that Richard Feynman called 'Cargo Cult Science' (see the corresponding entry in Chapter 4), the Bolognese community struggled in assimilating the principles of the scientific and industrial age that was advancing at a fast pace. The transition from artisan manufacturing to the industrial age enterprise left many dead and wounded on the ground.

Polychromatic Culture

It is marked by transdisciplinary and international distinguishing features. Thus, it can break down the high and often insurmountable barriers that separate disciplines, languages, countries and ethnicities. To be truly effective, such a culture must go hand in hand with sympathy – in other words, with an inclination and instinctive attraction towards people, things and ideas – to counterbalance those human attitudes that relate more to personal interest than to the common good. As Bernard Lewis (*The Middle East: A Brief History of the Last 2,000 Years*, New York, NY: Scribner, 1995) writes, the Islamic world of the High Middle Ages, despite being a polychromatic culture, showed more of a closed attitude than openness to the (re)-invention of printing with moveable type during the fifteenth century in the context of the monochromatic culture of Christian Europe. That closed attitude prevailed in order to protect the interests of the scribes and calligraphers who were powerful members of society. From one round to the next of human history, this is a phenomenon that we see repeated in many different places, often in the far corners of the world.

Today, selfish interests that are in opposition to emerging lifestyles, entrepreneurial models and technologies continue to hinder open innovations for altruistic purposes. Those innovations jeopardise privileged positions, whose holders claim acquired rights once and for all. At stake are positional goods and services (Fred Hirsch, *Social Limits to Growth*, Cambridge, MA: Harvard University

Press, 1976), those which (since not everyone can access them) confer social status and higher incomes on those who possess or have access to them. The scribes and calligraphers of the Medieval Islamic world have their epigones in the many positional professions fighting against technologies and organisational designs that give access to innovators.

Possibilist

Unlike the realist, emphasis on the freedom of human action in the use of time and creative disposition, together with a sense of possibility, prompt the possibilist to wonder how things might turn out differently than they did in the past.

The realist is a probabilist who moves on the relatively solid ground of numbers. The probabilist is a fanatic who, at the twilight of probability and the approach of the gloomy night of uncertainty, dives into a foggy sea and starts to swim against the tide. He or she accepts hypotheses that contradict well-established theories and accurate results that confirm them.

The realist is *Homo sapiens* who lives in the present well perceiving what today is. The possibilist is also *Homo Sentiens*, given his emotional predisposition to appreciate subjective experiences that project him into an unpredictable future but one that can be constructed with the resolution of acting extraordinarily. After all, he is an adept of Aristotle. By interpreting the Greek philosopher's treatise Poetics, written in the fourth century B.C., with creative freedom, the possibilist concludes that a plausible impossibility is preferable to an unconvincing possibility. In his famous unfinished novel *Man Without Qualities* ((*Der Mann ohne Eigenschaften* (*The Man Without Qualities*), Rowohlt Verlag – Germany; Picador – UK), 1930–1943), the Austrian writer and playwright Robert Musil compares 'the man with a common sense of reality [to] a fish that takes the bait and does not see the line, while the man with a sense of possibility trawls a line through the water and has no idea whether there is any bait on it. His extraordinary indifference to the life snapping at the bait is matched by the risk he runs of doing utterly eccentric things'.

Is the possibilist a bizarre person, lacking in qualities? Possibilists such as Maxwell Alan Lerner, the celebrated American journalist and educator, hold that 'the key qualities of the possibilist are the ability to generate an idea, the courage to initiate it and the tenacity to sustain and develop it. The possibilist perceives the seed of that idea emerging through the dirty surface of impossibility. Then the time comes when the idea must be watered and fertilised until the day finally comes to harvest its fruit' (https://www.motivationalmemo.com/the-li-fe-of-the-possibilist/).

Project: A 'Promising Monster'

If there is a word with a dubious reputation, it is the word 'project'. In the range of possible meanings derived from the Latin roots of the word – which include 'reproach' (proiectare), 'expose' and 'throw forward' (proicere) – a project is frequently perceived as a displaced fantasy, a means of escaping from the suffocating grip of routine.

Written by an anonymous author, in the *Giornale dell'assedio di Montalcino* (*Journal of the Siege of Montalcino*) made by the Spanish from 27 March to 15 June 1553, on the subject of projects, we read this definition: 'Idea, proposal which may be vague, bizarre or difficult to realise'. Sceptics often refer to the question posed by Giovanni Papini, an Italian journalist and essayist, in *ll Tragico quotidiano* (*The Tragic Everyday Life*, Firenze: Lumachi, 1906): 'Is a project not the tea, the coffee, the opium, the hashish of life? Is it not the substitute, the surrogate, the down-payment of reality?'

In *The Sciences of the Artificial* (Cambridge, MA: MIT Press, 1969) by economics Nobel Prize winner Herbert Simon, the project comes into sight as an artefact, involving phenomena regarded as conditional, subject to change according to their environment. We learn that these artificial phenomena, concerned with the possible (how things could be), are contrary to the natural phenomena that address the need (how things are) and give an impression of necessity in complying with the laws of nature.

Therefore, the project is an artefact for achieving specific objectives, material or even immaterial creation that is not provided by nature. On the contrary, it is intended to make up for its deficiencies. Simon argues that all those who devise actions to transform an existing state of affairs into the desired ones do project. The project goes beyond what seems to be its natural territory of adoption, engineering and architecture, and extends to economics, medicine, law, et cetera.

Some projects move along familiar paths, and others cause discontinuity. In a journey back to the age of the transition from sailing to steamships, we would notice, marked by continuity, the projects for new sailing ships with higher performance than the old ones. In contrast, they resemble 'promising monsters' and 'vital mutants', as Erwin László would say, the projects for the construction of steamships that leveraged emerging technology to replace sailing, achieving their industry accelerating growth rates.

Prosumer

The consumers change nature: they are both producer and consumer of what they produce and exchange with others. What the union representation divides – the person as producer and the same as a consumer, the sharing economy unites in the figure of the prosumer. Furthermore, what technology divides – each one of us that technology rewards by increasing our purchasing power through cheaper goods and services and punishes by cutting jobs and wages with the scissors of artificial intelligence – the sharing economy reunites in the person of the prosumer.

Ptolemaic Knowledgists

They know through the lens that makes them see the received knowledge as an immutable reference system. Everything revolves around it.

Ptolemaic knowledgists search for paths within the boundaries of their maps, triggering processes of discovery or gathering facts through study and experience.

As experts aiming at perfection, they are accustomed to draw extremely detailed knowledge maps, comparable to the cartographic maps described by Jorge Luis Borges in his one-paragraph short story *On Exactitude in Science* (In A. Hurley, Ed. & Trans., Collected Fictions, p. 325. New York, NY: Viking Penguin. Original work published 1946).

In that Empire, the Art of Cartography attained such Perfection that the map of a single Province occupied the entirety of a City, and the map of the Empire, the entirety of a Province. In time, those Unconscionable Maps no longer satisfied, and the Cartographers Guilds struck a Map of the Empire whose size was that of the Empire, and which coincided point for point with it.

Pure and Applied Research

Einstein said that the mind is like a parachute; it only works if it opens. However, if there are walls in our mind, the parachutist lands on a closed space. Researchers willing to cross over into fundamental research after having fought on the other side and vice versa broke down those walls.

As the historian and sociologist Steven Shapin put it in an interview following his book *The Scientific Life. A Moral History of a Late Modern Vocation* (Chicago, IL: The University of Chicago Press, 2008),

> If we look at the pure research done in industry and that done in academia, many of the most popular contrasts describe the situation rather poorly. If autonomy is the issue, many industrial scientists from early in the twentieth century enjoyed as much of that as their academic colleagues. And the same applies to notions of secrecy and openness. A clear contrast of quality between the university and industrial science similarly seems not to hold, while a presumption that applied research and development requires less brain-power than pure research is just dogmatic.

In innovation, what counts is the researchers' reflexivity and speed once they move from pure to applied research, from publication in the most authoritative international journals to the entrepreneurial translation of the scientific discovery by its author.

Quality

Quality is much more than intervening in defects. It is not achieved by inspection but by prevention since control is too late: good or bad quality is already in the product. As the Japanese like to say, 'if water flows pure from the spring and is clear upstream, there is no need to purify it downstream'. In short, quality must be anticipated. It, like health, must be maintained and improved. Nothing helps to improve company performance more than preventive action. Moreover, interventions must be carried out continuously because quality is dynamic, changing the perception that both companies and consumers have of it.

Quality is a long, all-around adventure. Here we present its most illustrious explorers.

The early 1950s: American pioneers.

William Edwards Deming (1900–1993)

- Statistical methods.
- Systematic approach to problem-solving.
- Planning, doing, controlling, acting.

Joseph M. Juran (1904–2008)

- Quality does not happen by chance; it has to be planned.
- Trilogy of quality: planning, control, improvement.

Armand V. Feigenbaum (1920–2014)

- Total quality control as a business method rather than a technical method.

The late 1950s: the Japanese response.

Kaoru Ishikawa (1915–1989)

- Quality circle: a voluntary group of about 5–10 workers from the same team whose activity contributes to the improvement and development of the enterprise.
- The quality circle respects human relations, creates a positive atmosphere and gives satisfaction in the workplace.

Genichi Taguchi (1924–2012)

- Instead of emphasising quality through inspection, it should become routine to optimise the product and process even before production.

Shineo Shingō (1909–1990)

- Interrupt the process whenever a defect occurs; identify the causes and prevent the same error from recurring.
- Identify errors before they become defects.
- Defects should be identified and corrected at the source, upstream, rather than downstream.

The new Western wave.

Philip B. Crosby (1926–2001)

- Quality is not beauty or elegance but conformity to product requirements.
- Doing it right the first time.
- Quality is achieved through prevention, not evaluation.
- The standard performance must be 'zero defects'.
- Quality is not measured by indices but by the price of non-conformity.

Tom Peters

- Leadership is the critical factor in the quality improvement process.
- Quality improvement is the primary source of cost reduction.
- Quality improvement is a never-ending process.
- Organise unlearning.
- Encourage mistakes, focusing on the three f's of Silicon Valley business logic: fail, move forward, be fast.

Claus Møller

- Underlying all kinds of quality is the personal quality.
- There are two standards of personal quality:
- The current level of performance, influenced by the individual's system of self.
- The ideal level of performance, which is influenced by the experiences made during the formative years.

Recombination

It is a process by which new combinations come to light from existing methodologies and technologies. Recombination has innovative solid power.

Take the case of the Venetian gondola as sketched by Joseph Dambrosio (Comment on 'Why innovators should study the rise and fall of the Venetian Empire' by Piero Formica. *Harvard Business Review*, 17 January. Retrieved from https://hbr.org/2017/01/why-innovators-should-study-the-rise-and-fall-of-the-venetian-empire, 2017):

> The gondola was first mentioned in a Venetian letter in 1094. And whereas we don't typically see gondolas sauntering through our waterways, elements of the design were taken from shipbuilders before then, and elements of the design have become foundational to the building of ships, cars, planes, furniture, packaging, jewelry, and even clothing today! It is a great example of one of the three fundamental truths about innovation, that all innovations are a 'creative recombination' of elements from the past.

This is a great example of one of the three fundamental truths about innovation: that all innovations are a 'creative recombination' of elements from the past.

On the same wavelength as Dambrosio, Jason Owen-Smith of the University of Michigan argued that many of today's most exciting innovations are the result of existing knowledge and technologies that have probably not been matched before (*Research Universities and the Public Good: Discovery for an Uncertain Future*, Stanford, CA: Stanford University Press, 2018, cited by Adi Gaskell, *How Universities Support Recombinative Innovation, Innovation Excellency*, 18 November 2018). In Owen-Smith's view, the accessibility of the research work conducted in the university and the expertise of the people involved in those investigations develop an essential set of building blocks. Extensive networks across many disciplinary fields, together with knowledge storage and sharing, ensure that few of those 'bricks' are inaccessible when it comes time to use them.

Reform of the Heart

The heart must be reformed to steer the protagonists of the economy onto the path of innovation in the name of altruism. In the seventeenth century, which cultivated the ideal of sociability, Madame de La Fayette counteracts 'the terribly corrupt mind and heart'. At that time, in the intellectual salons (see the corresponding entry in Chapter 4), there were intimate corners reserved for the heart.

A theme we find again in the America of the Roaring 1920s. As Azar Nafisi reminds us in her essay, *The Republic of Imagination* (London: William Heinemann, 2014), referring to George F. Babbitt, the famous protagonist of Sinclair Lewis's homonymous novel, published in 1922:

> ...Why, despite his success, his loyal family, his status among his community, his prosperity and the promises of the future, does he feel so dissatisfied?... This is where the heart comes in, – argues the author, English literature professor at the Johns Hopkins University in Washington, D.C. – to help Babbitt find an answer..., to warn him that he does have a choice – there are alternatives to his way of life.

Precisely, alternatives to the race for success 'à bout de souffle' in which the Great Predators of value identified with profit excel.

So many business failures arise from the idea that the ultimate goal of business is profit. This, however, is a means of developing entrepreneurial activity. Conceiving, designing, producing, delivering products, providing services, disseminating knowledge and information: this is the business value chain.

Regard Multiplier

In *The Theory of Moral Sentiments*, first published in 1759, Adam Smith asserts that the purpose of economic activity is regard for oneself and others. This means more than giving exclusively for reasons of charity and solidarity. As Smith wrote,

> How selfish soever man may be supposed, there are evidently some principles in his nature, which interest him in the fortune of others, and render their happiness necessary to him, though he derives nothing from it except the pleasure of seeing it.
>
> (Adam Smith, *The Theory of Moral Sentiments*, 2nd ed., London: A. Millar, 1761, p. 1)

The higher the propensity for altruism and reciprocity (reciprocated altruism), the more the regard multiplies the opportunities for discoveries, inventions and innovations that will generate transformative entrepreneurship.

David Bodanis, in his book on Einstein's famous equation ($E = mc^2$: *A Biography of the World's Most Famous Equation*, New York, NY: Berkley Books, 2000), provides us with illuminating examples of the motivations and emotions underlying such propensity. As a result of an unexpected gift received from an unknown bookbinder apprentice, motivated by the excitement of homage and taken by surprise, the English chemist and inventor Humphry Davy opened the doors of science to this apprentice – a gesture that helped to shape Michael Faraday into one of the greatest scientists of his time. Faraday's discoveries in electromagnetism and electrochemistry had major impacts on entrepreneurship. Nevertheless, motivations and emotions show volatility stemming from, respectively, a discretionary nature and transience. So, Bodanis reminds us, years later, after the qualities that would lead to Faraday's success had become evident, the same Davy withdrew his support, accusing Faraday of plagiarism.

Thanks to a friendly and affirmative attitude towards others, and a sympathetic understanding, a teacher recommended that Albert Einstein should attend an unconventional school. That behaviour was a slight but essential nudge that helped the German physicist forward along the path to his revolutionary theory of relativity. By contrast, not motivated by the need to accomplish something that would take him into a frightening unknown, the great French mathematician Jules Henri Poincaré behaved unsympathetically towards Einstein.

Reimagined and Ludic Schools

Such is the institution that educates students to be self-reliant and independent, capable of generating original intuitions and, therefore, not to be uncritically adherent to the lessons of the past masters.

Education develops creative thinking on a third terrain, compared to family and school: the one that allows us to be fully human because we play – said the poet Friedrich Schiller (*Letters on the Aesthetical Education of Man*, 1793). Keywords of the game are sagacity, serendipity and mobility. The first requires training to be ready in intuition. The second asks the heart to beat fast. The third one wants us to get going. Sitting down, we will never stumble on something new.

The reimagined and ludic school is a playground that requires students to think creatively rather than memorise. They should prioritise a proper understanding of the phenomena, not obtain higher scores, and devise models integrating the chosen discipline with all other fields of study. Play is at the centre of the creative effort. Without fear of judgement, a child's creativity knows no limits. Children combine different ideas to the point of exploring what may be a different view of society.

Reimagined education enhances the mission to cultivate what appears to be useless knowledge (see the corresponding entry in Chapter 4).

Students leave the shore of teaching, with its boundaries restricted by knowledge accrued over time, to reach the far shores of experiential and experimental learning, where passions supported by strong motivation can produce outstanding results. Its characteristics date back to the Renaissance, which ushered in a new narrative that altered the state of the world, preparing for the age of experimentation in the footsteps of Francis Bacon.

Bertrand Russell, in his essay *In Praise of Idleness* (London: George Allen & Unwin Ltd, 1935), argued that education is usually in the hands of the state, and the state tends to defend the status quo. To this end, it tries to blunt the critical faculties of young people as much as possible to make them impervious to dangerous thoughts.

Training the mind to think, inciting and instilling in young people the desire for creativity, challenging the authority of the expert, providing resources for the discovery of talents, launching a 'find your own talent' programme: this scenario that demands new models to be displayed in the theatre of education.

According to Einstein, a societal competitive advantage will come not from how well its schools teach the multiplication and periodic tables but also how well they stimulate imagination and creativity.

For the philosopher of science Paul Feyerabend, clinging to facts that neglect the vicissitudes of history and curbing intuitions that could lead to the blurring of the boundaries between one sector and another, the school restrains the imagination of students whose language ceases to be personal.

Cornell University psychologists argue that children's non-conformist predispositions, their inclinations to creative exploration, are annihilated by mechanical learning (memorising). Teachers show a clear preference for less creative students.

Einstein's words echo in a report from Tokyo, on February 1990, by the Italian journalist Tiziano Terzani, who so wrote about Japanese education, *At school, the child is not used to think for himself but trained to say the right thing at the right time. For each question, there is an answer, and that must be learned by heart. 'What happens when the snow melts?' – Asks the teacher – and the entire class, in chorus, has to answer, 'It becomes water'. If one says, 'Spring is coming!', one is reproached* (*La scuola: Piccole foche ammaestrate, In Asia.* Milano: Longanesi, 1998).

Still, in the mature years of industrialisation, the syndrome of 'trained small seals' (so dubbed by Terzani of the students of that type of school) was widespread beyond the 'Land of the Rising Sun'.

Today, in Japan, extracting students from committing facts to memory is pursued by a new primary school, the New International School of Japan (NISJ) in Tokyo. As Shotaro Tani reported in the *Financial Times* ('Japan's New International School gives children a global upbringing'. *Financial Times*, 13 December 2017), the NISJ encourages multi-linguistics: more than one language is used at the same time, an essential factor for seeing things from multiple points of view, improving expression and social skills, and preparing young people for careers in which they may have to take on different roles at different times. Multi-age learning environments are then designed where the older learners help the younger ones.

The reimagined and ludic school is an unmissable opportunity that society and business are called upon to use to develop natural inclinations towards exploration and playfulness fully. These attitudes are repressed by teaching to obey authority, give answers without asking questions, and perform tedious tasks promptly, raising walls in the students' minds. The game that enriches the imagination takes them down. The student who enters this new territory of education invents a path, appreciating the trans-disciplinarity and beauty of imperfection.

The new generations demand the 'salad days' – what in the Shakespearean atmosphere is the youthful 'time of innocence and enthusiasm' associated with the beginning of a new human adventure.

The learning revolution is pervasive hope. The multifaceted entrepreneur Elon Musk has translated it into reality by founding a brand-new elementary school in its contents. Musk named the school 'Ad Astra', 'To the stars', perhaps to remind us of the Latin saying 'Per aspera ad astra sic itur'! 'Through hardships to the stars'! – This leads us to reflect on the hardships faced by those who aim at reaching the stars, that is, the highest level. The vision of 'Ad Astra' is a primary school without grade levels where open-ended questions are at the core of learning. The mission is 'making all the children go through the same grade at the same time, like an assembly line' – a school which, besides, addresses the aptitudes and abilities of learners. 'Some people love English or languages. Some people love mathematics. Some people love music. Different abilities, different times', he argued in an interview with Kossoff, M. (2015). Interview with Elon Musk. *Business Insider Indonesia*. Retrieved from http://www.businessinsider.co.id/.

The wind of the school revolution blows from the East (India, China, Japan) and the West (United States). Of its strength, the Drucker Institute (www.druckerinstitute.com) offers a four-sided image that we have readapted and commented on as follows:

- Physics should be taught to girls and boys of 4–5 years, thus laying the foundations to build their skills to become tech entrepreneurs when they grow up.
- High school girls and boys should be offered self-learning tools to realise their individual and collective dreams. Yes, also collective, for in the richness of diversity and the intensity of interactions within school communities, creative ideas are developed into professional opportunities. Schools, then, should be equipped with permanent experimentation workshops where students can stage original thoughts and motivate their passions to translate creativity into innovative entrepreneurship. Thus, new personalities and styles of entrepreneurs in tune with the twenty-first-century economy can flourish in the entrepreneurial garden.

- Integrative thinking should be promoted among pupils and students to reflect the convergence of various scientific and humanistic branches of knowledge. So much so that the most advanced educational models have broken down traditional notional barriers by building transdisciplinary bridges. Students should, then, get the opportunity to design their custom-made study clothes, merging scientific subjects with the humanities. Thus, themes about the humanities and social sciences (law, sociology, philosophy, psychology, economics, politics, and the like) will climb out of their deep super-specialised knowledge wells. The same applies to the natural sciences. The imagination promotes STEAM (Science, Technology, Engineering, Arts and Mathematics) over STEM (Science, Technology, Engineering and Mathematics) by embracing all subject spaces.
- Patrons, education entrepreneurs ('edupreneurs') and the world's most advanced companies found schools that leverage these principles. At the forefront, India (see the online network of scientific education spread across the globe by the Khan Academy) and China.

In the United States, along with Musk's school, new institutions of higher learning are arising from advances in the scientific and humanities disciplines, intending to combine learning with innovation.

Following the terminology invented by Ben Nelson, a San Francisco technology entrepreneur, which goes by the name of 'reimagined university', we come to the Minerva Schools at the Unreasonable Institute and Singularity University.

The Minerva Schools draw on the spirit of the Roman divinity who also presided over intellectual activities. Those schools take us back to the medieval time of the *clerici vagantes* (see the corresponding entry in Chapter 4) and project us into a future in which innovative technologies enabling video chat lessons – ubiquitous, real-time and interactive – are combined with a learning system made up of critical thinking, creative thinking, experimentation and interaction. Internationally recruited students shape a borderless community, culturally immersed in the cosmopolitan cities (including Barcelona, Berlin, Buenos Aires, Cape Town, Hong Kong, London, Mumbai, New York, San Francisco, Sydney), where they will, at intervals, live. In addition to the curriculum, the Minerva model is also innovative in terms of cost, being very competitive with the US Ivy League giants, with tuition fees in the ratio of 1 (Minerva) to over 5 (Harvard). Minerva took the lead: from 2,500 applications submitted in the 2014–2015 academic year, this rose to around 11,000 in the following year. The selection was also strong, with an acceptance rate of around 2%.

In Boulder, Colorado, the Unreasonable Institute also offers an alternative route to the universities of the second millennium. Here, students learn by participating in an international talent circuit that moves personally cultivated ideas and other learning ideas in the direction of entrepreneurship. The ship *Unreasonable at Sea* transports nascent entrepreneurs from one port to another among the most entrepreneurial cities on the planet. While sailing, programme participants metaphorically sail together with academics, entrepreneurs and innovators, crossing the strait between the seas of knowledge and creative ignorance.

By harnessing the power of exponentially growing technology, California's Singularity University reaches out to young minds from different countries and cultures who show brilliance at the crossroads of science and entrepreneurship. The methods of each culture should blend in a melting pot of ideas and projects between students, academics, scientists, humanists and business leaders.

Renaissance Coworking Space

The place where talents are cultivated; new technologies deployed; new artistic forms are born; competing artists are also ready to co-create, all together.

As in the convergence of art and science expressed in Leonardo's *Vitruvian Man*, the most attractive business opportunities come from encounters between cultural progress and aesthetic beauty. The Renaissance workshop was a transdisciplinary place. It is, in fact, the combination of people's creativity with their diverse skills that plays an essential role in innovation.

Here the experiments conducted to do material things provided information processed by the mind to be translated into innovation.

Andrea del Verrocchio was a sculptor, painter and goldsmith. In his workshop, young artists might pursue engineering, architecture, or various business or scientific ventures. Verrocchio's workshop gave free rein to a new generation of entrepreneurial artists – eclectic characters such as Leonardo da Vinci, Sandro Botticelli, Pietro Perugino e Domenico Ghirlandaio.

The entrepreneurial spirit combined revolutionary ways of designing and producing products and services, as well as seeing the world.

Renaissance Start-Ups

Renaissance start-ups are born from the marriage of technology and culture, drawing entrepreneurial sap from the immense reservoir of cultural resources accumulated during the Renaissance. They enhance the hidden assets that characterise the unique goods brought to light by artistic creativity. The hybridisation of digital technologies and culture engages the interest of visitors who are captivated by the cultural component that characterises the paths of exploration, narration, play and interactive participation traced by Renaissance start-ups.

In the words of Keynes in his speech in Madrid in 1930 on "Economic Possibilities for our Grandchildren" (*The Nation and Athenaeum*, *48*(2), 11 and 18 October 1930: pp. 36–37, later reprinted in *Essays in Persuasion*, London: Macmillan, 1933), start-ups nurtured by cultural heritage give free rein to how to occupy the leisure that 'science and compound interest will have won'.

With the tools made available by digital technologies, these start-ups bring history and renaissance histories to new fruition. In addition to Google's geographical maps, they are placing Renaissance knowledge maps side by side. The creative possibilities are endless. One only has to look at the video games of the entrepreneurs of Tale of Tales (www.taleoftales.com) to realise how protagonists of Renaissance art can be given a new lease of life, outside of time and the museums where they are often kept and even confined. Unfortunately, in Italy, the cradle of the Renaissance, start-ups that draw on the abundant source of Renaissance culture are still very few.

Scale-Up

A baby business that develops quickly. It pursues a non-linear, iterative, intuitive value creation process: in short, a process of discovery, the leaven of its accelerated growth.

According to Andy Grove ('How America Can Create Jobs', *Bloomberg Businessweek*, 1 July 2010),

> Start-ups are a wonderful thing, but they cannot by themselves increase tech employment. Equally important is what comes after that mythical moment of creation in the garage, as technology goes from prototype to mass production. This is the phase where companies scale up. They work out design details, figure out how to make things affordably, build factories, and hire people by the thousands. Scaling is hard work but necessary to make innovation matter.

Science and Art

Creativity unites the scientific process and the artistic method. Artists and scientists share a curiosity for the unknown, appreciate the beauty of both worlds and have a keen interest in creating something new. An increasingly intense dialogue between humanism and science sheds light on their compatibility and virtuous interactions, pulling the fruits of innovation together from the branches of the trees of science and art. Their intersection characterised the free-thinking of Renaissance Man, personified in the *Vitruvian Man*, the famous drawing by Leonardo da Vinci that combines art and science to represent the human body. We like to think of the entrepreneurial Renaissance as an art form in which the spirit of adventure, imagination and freedom makes the entrepreneurial path accessible to artists and scientists together. Today, digitisation is the technological medium that facilitates and expands mutual learning towards experiments that result in business opportunities. Thus, we are witnessing the rebirth of the art of entrepreneurship with the artist and scientist entrepreneurs making a cultural difference and the new technologies assisting them in creative production. Science and the various forms of art have in common their ability to amaze people, to arouse their imagination and passion. In science, as in art, imaginative minds create models that will need to take on a 'second nature' to have a practical impact. The 'second nature' is the aptitude for entrepreneurship.

Even at the dawn of the Renaissance, artists and scientists began the work of dismantling everything taken for granted for centuries. In 1482 and for the next 15 years, Milan could stand on the shoulders of a giant in the service of Ludovico il

Moro. Giorgio Vasari portrays Leonardo da Vinci – this is the name of the giant, a universal genius – as

> ...an admirable painter, sculptor, art theoretician, musician, writer, mechanical engineer, architect, stage designer, master smelter, artillery expert, inventor and scientist.

Leonardo gave Milan and its surrounding area an artistic imprint and helped to mark the transition from feudal to capitalist modes of production.

As writes Vasari in *The Lives of the Artists* (Oxford: Oxford University Press, 1998), engaged intellectually in the birth of the modern age of machines, Leonardo

> ...made designs for mills, fulling machines and engines that could be driven by water-power ... In addition he used to make models and plans showing how to excavate and tunnel through mountains without difficulty, so as to pass from one level to another; and he demonstrated how to lift and draw great weights by means of levers, hoists and winches, and ways of cleansing harbours and using pumps to suck up water from great depths.

This is how the figure of the manufacturing entrepreneur began to emerge in the Milan area.

In the eighteenth century, as Jenny Uglow brilliantly recounts (*The Lunar Men: Five Friends Whose Curiosity Changed the World*, London: Faber and Faber, 2002).

> In the time of the Lunar Men, science and art were not separated: one could be an inventor and designer, an experimenter and a poet, a dreamer and an entrepreneur all at once without anyone raising an eyebrow...when people spoke of the 'arts', they did not mean only the fine arts but also the 'mechanic arts', the skills and techniques in agriculture, say, or printing.

In India, Bengal was the stand-in for Medicean Florence at the turn of the eighteenth and nineteenth centuries. Over about a century and a half, the Bengal Renaissance is an innovative context of religious and social reformers, literary giants and scientists. Characters like the multi-lingual Sir Jagadish Chandra Bose – physicist, biologist, botanist, archaeologist and science fiction writer – and physicist Satyendranath Bose, with their pioneering research ranging from quantitative mechanics (Nath Bose) to radio and experimental science (Chandra Bose), sowed the seeds for the Indian start-ups that enrich the landscape of the digital economy today.

As Guillet de Monthoux reminds us (*Aesthetic Management and Metaphysical Marketing*, Redwood City: Stanford Business Books, 2004), avant-garde painters such as Fernand Léger, Marcel Duchamp, Juan Gris, Pablo Picasso and Georges Braque conducted experiments in the field of non-Euclidean geometry.

Science and Entrepreneurship

Forging links between Science and Entrepreneurship (S&E) is an investment in connecting academic knowledge with the world of entrepreneurship, which is often peripheral or even unknown to it.

S&E is the result of a collective effort that, as discoveries and technologies emerge, constantly traces and changes the paths of scientific entrepreneurship.

S&E reverses know-how into 'knowing why' and 'knowing what to do about' the entrepreneurial exploitation of knowledge.

Entrepreneurial scientists help turn the most complex problems in the research world into businesses. In order to increase the number of scientists setting up companies and find equal interest in research work and its entrepreneurial translation, a country needs laboratories where scientists can combine thought with action.

With the mindset of the nascent entrepreneur, the most educated and ambitious generation is discarding the idea of the workplace and putting on a suit made of entrepreneurial materials and designed with recourse to experience gained in university or industrial research laboratories.

The latent entrepreneurial potential turns into knowledge-driven start-ups by investing in university incubators.

Science and Technology

Who leads whom to innovation? During the Renaissance, science and technology advanced mutually. Then, between the fifteenth and seventeenth centuries, maritime ventures to discover new lands led to major advances in the scientific fields of astronomy and cartography. In that age of discovery, as the time of the great geographical explorations was christened, developments in navigation technologies and techniques through trial and error by seamen triggered the speculative process of scientists.

The formidable naval power of Venice, the innovative urban plan of the city of Ferrara, the inventive genius of Leonardo in Milan, and the city of Urbino expert in military art: four examples of Renaissance cities where science and technology intersected.

Until now, the question of the 'primum mobile' ('first mover') remains open. Is science the locomotive of economic and social progress, or is it technology that drives science? What if science and technology co-evolve and self-organise so that the relationships between the two players allow for a shared life?

Some see science as a queen and technology as a handmaiden. Science explains and predicts natural, social and economic phenomena. At the same time, technology is the practical application of science and uses techniques, tools and machines to solve the problems that science has illustrated and predicted. Science cannot but come before technology since understanding scientific principles is the basis for their practical application. Cases in which technology leads to scientific discoveries would be accidental.

Voices that trace deep scientific insights back to the fruit falling from the tree of technological change are less heard. Yet, technology broadens the field of exploration by science and does so by creating tangible and intangible artefacts that extend our biological and mental capabilities.

Barely audible are the voices that see science and technology as a couple dancing in unison. Cyclically, sometimes science leads the dance; sometimes, the reverse is true.

Economists and scientists themselves have come to believe that technology can organise itself, creating an environment for science to explore. As an autonomous organism – dubbed technium by the maverick science writer Kevin Kelly (*What Technology Wants*, New York, NY: Viking Penguin, 2010) – technology would be the one to raise the waves of innovation that would then be ridden by the inventors and entrepreneurs it found. In this respect, the role of technology as an accelerator of scientific developments and as a link between science, innovation and new entrepreneurship should not be overlooked.

In an article in *The Wall Street Journal*, Matt Ridley ('The Myth of Basic Science', 23 October 2015) writes:

> When you examine the history of innovation, you find, again and again, that scientific breakthroughs are the effect, not the cause, of technological change. It is no accident that astronomy blossomed in the wake of the age of exploration. The steam engine owed almost nothing to the science of thermodynamics, but the science of thermodynamics owed almost everything to the steam engine. The discovery of the structure of DNA depended heavily on X-ray crystallography of biological molecules, a technique developed in the wool industry to try to improve textiles.

Computer technology opened the door to computer science, which in English goes by the very name of the computer: computer science. The technology that led to the construction of the particle accelerator – the 'Large Hadron Collider' – at CERN in Geneva enabled physics to make great strides forward, making it possible between 2011 and 2013 to discover the particle imagined by Nobel Prize winner Peter Higgs (the so-called 'Higgs boson'). On the other hand, the same technology that paved the way for scientific discovery has its roots in earlier developments in physical science. Various technologies have descended from defence-related science – the most reported case being the Internet.

In the light of the above examples, the linear path from science to technology is not as evident as is commonly thought.

Science and Technology Parks

Science and technology parks are places of intellectual production characterised by research and development, training, technology transfer, design and prototyping, and cooperation between companies, universities and public and private research centres.

In 1951, Stanford Science Park, the first science park, was founded on the initiative of Stanford University and the City of Palo Alto. In Europe, the article 'Le Quartier Latin des Champs' by Pierre Lafitte, a French scientist and politician, issued in the French newspaper *Le Monde* on 2 August 1960, envisioned the creation in 1970 of Sophia Antipolis on the Côte d'Azur, the forerunner of European parks and a precursor to the technopolitan city of the twenty-first century, the cradle of a second Renaissance.

Attraction, retention and generation are the three main strategies pursued by the parks.

Attraction aims at establishing higher education and research institutions, multinationals, and other companies operating in the park's nerve centres of international trade networks.

Retention aims at developing local potential by regenerating existing enterprises that otherwise would be attracted to more developed areas or condemned to decline in the absence of renewal of the productive fabric.

Generation aims at creating innovative enterprises, for example, by promoting new businesses from those already existing in the park territory.

The first-generation park is a bridge thrown along the fault line between the end of the path of mature technologies and the beginning of another route. First-generation parks are home to educational and research organisations ('institutional phase'), industrial groups attracted by the research potential and quality of human capital ('first entrepreneurial phase'), and new companies generated by the ideas and projects of the large companies present in the park ('second entrepreneurial phase').

Second-generation parks came into being in the second half of the 1970s when the emphasis shifts from scientific research (development of knowledge) to technological research (development of applications). In order to systematically promote innovative entrepreneurship, the park comprises an incubator. The aim is to reward entrepreneurship and encourage the creation of innovative companies.

Scientific Clairvoyance, Practical Wisdom and Entrepreneurial Creativity

Clairvoyance exudes the perfume of science, but not only this. The economist Carlo Cattaneo wrote that to very shrewd minds we owe inventions that have not sprung up from scientific deductions, including the compass born within the confines of a mere practical sagacity – the result of a fortuitous, disconnected, solitary observation that did not make up the body of science (*Intelligence as a Principle of Public Economy*, Plymouth: Lexington Books, 2003, Dual Language Edition).

Pure scientists and researchers yearn to cross the Pillars of Hercules into the unknown ocean of not knowing. Their long-term commitment is to search for answers to scientific problems that seem insoluble.

Creativity in business is sparked by entrepreneurial ingenuity. In a lecture (the first United Kingdom Innovation Lecture) given at the Royal Society in London on 6 February 1992, entitled *'S' does not equal 'T' and 'T' does not equal 'I'*, Akio Morita asked,

> What difference does it make how fantastic and innovative your new technology is if you do not have the ability to design a useful, attractive, 'user-friendly' product?

In his view, progress in our business knowledge is no less relevant than advances in scientific and technological fields. Creativity in business, triggered by entrepreneurial ingenuity, involves generating new ideas converted into entrepreneurial activities. In business, Morita states, creativity is also concerned with technology, product planning and marketing. These three types of creativity need to be supported by an established and secure entrepreneurial culture. Once developed, a new idea has to be proven commercially. At this point, the following factors come into play: the creation of a prototype, the evaluation of the competitive environment, information gathered from potential customers, fine-tuning of the concept and the search for industrial partners and financial investors.

Seigniories of the Twenty-First Century

With the House of Medici reading 'We are on the side of the people', Medicean Florence reminds us of the Age of Seignories. These powerful magnets attracted artists, entrepreneurs and traders. Having faded with the rise of modern states, the Seignories are reappearing on the horizon of the globalised economy.

The Seignories of today are the city-states of Singapore and Dubai, with the dynasties of Lee Kuan Yew and the Maktoum's, respectively. But that is not all. In San Francisco, as in the other territorial communities where what the British weekly *The Economist* has called the 'Cambrian explosion of digital-age start-ups' has manifested itself most forcefully, the new entrepreneurs who have amassed large fortunes stand in the same way as the Renaissance lords.

The lords of the twenty-first century have as their absolute protagonists the vanguards of economic and social transformation. From photography (Instagram) to music (Apple, Spotify); from books (Amazon) to the exchange of information (Facebook, Twitter, YouTube), and the mapping of human resources (LinkedIn); from accommodation (Airbnb) to local transport (Uber, Lyft); from cars (Google, Tesla) and commerce (Alibaba, Amazon): the entrepreneurs replacing their industrial age predecessors have given a distinctive imprint to their territorial communities, visible in the intertwining of talent attraction and international investment from the rest of the world.

Sensitive Data

Such data are those that reveal private information, like, for example, our choices and preferences. Those who command it wield extreme power. Highly regulated industries such as healthcare, telecommunications and banking handle the most sensitive data. Others, no less sensitive, are at the disposal of Internet titans, from Google to Facebook, acting in unregulated environments. This ownership prompted the MIT Media Lab to campaign for a New Deal in Internet public policy to grant sensitive data the status of a fundamental human right. The individual must be placed at the centre of the data society to avoid the pitfalls (global warming, epidemics, pollution, fraud, corruption, et cetera) by crossing the straits of opportunity (innovative companies, new markets, products and services).

Real-time flows of vast amounts of data tracing unprecedented macro and microeconomic scenarios will enable more people to exercise their economic freedoms and suggest, in a climate of less uncertainty, new things to do other than customary practices. Were it not the case, a Big Data society would develop resembling a Diplodocus (see the corresponding entry in Chapter 4).

Serendipity

A neologism coined by the historian, man of letters and politician Horace Walpole and expanded by Robert K. Merton and Elinor G. Barber (*The Travels and Adventures of Serendipity*, Princeton, NJ: Princeton University Press, 2006). Serendipity means discovering exciting things while looking for something completely different and reaping unexpected benefits. Serendipity is an intangible resource that gives agility and lightness to the accelerated pace of innovation.

Sharing

The sharing of goods and services weaves new social bonds. The use of digital technologies makes collaboration more convenient.

The great web of the global Internet with its exponentially growing technologies – the web is doubling its speed at every stride (2, 4, 8) rather than going one step at a time (1, 2, 3) – has broken down geographical boundaries and educational barriers. The ubiquity of connectivity is revolutionising channels for participation in exchanges. Each of us can connect with everyone and everyone with all things. This is how the economy of sharing is born.

Goods considered indispensable for previous generations are no longer so essential for young people, who show a marked propensity to rely on services that give access to products without having to own them. This orientation is already visible in the case of car ownership. According to a study by Goldman Sachs (http://www.businessinsider.com/goldman-sachs-survey-on-interns-habits-2013-9? IR=T), car sharing appears to be an unstoppable trend, while car ownership would be an outlier. More generally, a large shadow of anomaly is weighing on the economy of ownership, while the economy of sharing is gaining ground quickly.

Sharing communities are a promising platform for launching collaborative businesses with entirely new brands, such as the social streets.

Silk Roads

In 1877, the German geographer and traveller Ferdinand von Richthofen invented the expression 'Silk Roads'. Around that time, the *North-China Herald* published 'Notes on the Silk Trade in Shanghai'.

With the plot hatched by Genghis Khan, many tribes united under the banner of the great Mongol Empire. The unification was the beginning of a dialogue between East and West that stretched along the 'Silk Roads' – a network of trade routes linking Asia, the Middle East, Africa and Europe. Before that time, tribal lords, if they did not kill outsiders attempting to travel these routes, forced them to pay exorbitant transit fees. The Empire launched a foreign and tariff policy that allowed the merchants of the European revival to resume their journeys to Asia in the West, following in the footsteps of Marco Polo. The Venetian merchant and explorer who arrived in the Mongol Kublai Khan China, the fabulous Cathay, synonymous with wealth and power, brought to the West such a revolutionary vision of the world that his contemporaries called him an impostor. Not only merchants but also soldiers, religious philosophers, diplomats and others travelled along these 'Silk Roads'. A dialogue of ideas developed alongside commercial conversations for exchanging silks, gems, minerals, spices, and numerous other products. Material wealth and immaterial wealth made the middle and intellectual classes of Renaissance society flourish.

For some time now, a controversial Eurasian dialogue has been renewed in waves via the Silk Road Economic Belt and the Maritime Silk Road – the two infrastructures resulting from the new Chinese strategic thinking known as 'One Belt, One Road'. Along these routes, we meet the Eurasian cities: those that cross the exchange of goods and services between East and West and that are at the crossroads of sizeable human flows.

The forms that competition and cooperation between the 'Two Silk Roads' cities will take will have a certain weight in determining whether the state powers or the Eurasian cities along those two routes will dictate the Eurasian rules dialogue. What is at stake is noticeable in the entrepreneurship founded on sustainable development. It trespasses national borders to seize, with the formation of global, borderless start-ups, the opportunities offered by the '5 R's' (Recycling, Reusing, Reducing, Restoring and Rethinking natural resources).

Smart City

As the human species evolve, so do cities. Today, the most evolved is the smart city – the knowledge city that, like humans, has cognitive strategies to trigger the process of acquiring knowledge and understanding phenomena through thought, senses and experience. Intelligence, creativity, knowledge, learning and being digital, ubiquitous, hybrid: these are the connotations attributed to it.

With the help of technologies, the smart city turns the wheel of applications of its strategies in a broad field that includes urban mobility, eco-environment, education, health. In particular, leveraging the amount of data growing at an accelerated rate, the smart city design alternative scenarios for its evolution analyse each one's impact and seek consensus among a wide variety of stake-holders: neighbourhood groups, workers' unions, trade associations, real estate developers and environmentalists, to name a few. The favoured scenario reveals potential benefits for the whole urban community by combining traditionally fragmented, dispersed and isolated interests.

Social Streets

Innovation has carved a path out of nothing: new social ties that intertwine by replacing ownership with the sharing of goods and services among the street inhabitants. This proves that innovation, including social innovation, is a contact sport whose approval quickly spreads from all components of the social body.

In the historical centre of Bologna, in Via Fondazza, conceived by Federico Bastiani, the Social Street movement has arisen. The use of digital technologies – in 2013, Bastiani created a Facebook page called 'Residents of Via Fondazza, Bologna' – makes collaboration more convenient. Quickly, people began to connect with it, and soon the page became a place for neighbours to get to know one another and arrange to help each other in various ways. As one article reports, people were soon 'giving free piano lessons, lending washing machines, providing tips to newcomers about services in the city, giving away leftover food when going on holiday, holding street birthday parties', and more.

The imagination of many converges towards doing things together, better than what could be achieved alone.

Social streets provide immediate, proximity-based answers to the well-being of citizens. Their inhabitants benefit from the opportunity to draw on otherwise unused capacities and idle resources. The triple helix of neighbourhood collaboration, the digital revolution and social networks ignites the engine of collective consumption, helping at least partially to offset the decline in individual consumption.

Bastiani and the others he had engaged in this project did not stop at the end of their own street. They publicised the model's success and created a website to guide others who wanted to do the same. As of January 2015, at least 330 other social streets were established in Italy and more than 360 in other parts of the world.

Space-Time of Innovation

Guided by the mind, we pick by hands mental constructs stratified by past innovations and with our legs, we run to discover new things – the building blocks of new constructs. The hands move in the social space in which we live; the time taken by our running depends on the legs.

Space and time can change; as if to say that there is neither absolute space nor absolute time. On a human scale, innovation is not Newtonian but Einsteinian. There is no way to treat space and time of innovation separately; they are interdependent. In short, they are the 'space-time' of innovation.

A seemingly tiny event that allows us to rise a little above the ground is a factor in speeding up a voyage of discovery. That event is the effect of cumulative growth of knowledge occurring in space-time.

Speed

When you think to have arrived at something, you realise that you have arrived at nothing. However, you have to go ahead towards a dream so far away that your path no longer has a beginning or an end. With these words, Indira Gandhi stressed how to reach goals in an interview with the Italian journalist Oriana Fallaci (*Interview with History*, New York, NY: Liveright Publishing Corporation, 1976). The rush to innovate can lead to acting more quickly than necessary, to the detriment of the appropriateness of action. Running a race whose goal is innovation means moving as quickly as possible without sacrificing quality, safety or anything else. The innovator must consider the speed of action – the time needed to complete the journey – and the direction of the movement. If the innovator has taken the wrong path, moving quickly only counts if the danger inherent in the chosen path is grasped in good time. In this case, speed turns into appropriate directional velocity.

In his *Six Memos for the Next Millennium* (Cambridge, MA: Harvard University Press, 1985), Italo Calvino contrasts two Galilean characters. Sagredo is rich in creative imagination and lets his mind roam free, hypothesising on such matters as how 'life might be on the moon or what would happen if the earth stopped turning'. By contrast, Salviati is characterised in particular by the use of slow, prudent and rigorous reasoning. Calvino argues that the two figures are the two temperamental components of Galileo, the resolute innovator as Michael Sharratt defined him in his biography of the Pisan scientist (*Galileo: Decisive Innovator*, Cambridge: Cambridge University Press, 1994).

On the one hand, immersed in their world, the innovators lingers along the usually beaten path, from conception to commercialisation of an idea. On the opposite side is the innovator who, dissatisfied with the world as it is, seeks excitement in moving quickly, skipping intermediate steps to discover and dash down paths that have never been trodden before.

Speed advocates find that fast innovator achieves better financial results and develop more new products. The alternative version shows that hidden in the folds of fast innovation are costs generated by mistakes and inefficiencies caused by overlooking details.

Mental speed to innovate might then take us back to a saying of Sicilian storytellers, 'lu cuntu non metti tempu' ('time takes no time in a story'), echoed by Calvino in his *Memos*, to remind us that, in a story, one can hurry forward in time, shortening the route of the narrative. However, then one is forced to go back abruptly.

Spin-Off and Spin-In

Business creation through enterprise. In situations of overstaffing due to company crises and restructuring, spin-offs target employees with an entrepreneurial spirit, thus preserving know-how. In the 1980s and early 1990s of the last century, the vision of the enterprise promoting entrepreneurial spirit among employees matured in France. The entrepreneurial bees that swarmed to create new hives revitalised degraded economic organisms.

Defensive spin-offs are contrasted with offensive spin-offs to enter business areas not yet covered or open up unexplored ones in the world of technology and innovative products for markets with high growth potential.

A third type is an academic spin-off, which translates scientific research into entrepreneurial action.

Developing spin-off firms based on university potential is not the sole role of the incubation process. The process can also spin-in creative ideas from local businesses and help to form partnerships for new venture creation with the pool of knowledge-rich scientific and technical personnel and talented students, backed by the incubator infrastructure and its support staff.

Start-Up

A start-up is a company in the early stages of business development. The start-up phase of a company may last years. In Silicon Valley, a cradle of the start-up movement, entrepreneur Steve Blank adopts the dynamic definition of 'temporary organisation designed to search for a repeatable and scalable business model'. The intention is to overgrow as a result of offering something that addresses a particular market gap.

In the first stage of their operations, their entrepreneurial founders financially back start-ups to capitalise on developing a product or service for which they believe there is a demand.

'STEAM'

When industrialisation was advancing at a steady pace, Camillo Olivetti, who in 1908 had founded Ing. Olivetti e C., wrote in an article on "Lo spirito della industria meccanica" ("The spirit of mechanical industry") published in 1937 in the magazine *Tecnica ed Organizzazione*:

> The education of our bourgeoisie has a purely anti-industrial basis. We are still the children of the Latins, who left industrial work to the servants and the freedmen and who held it in very low regard, so much so that they handed down to us the names of the most mediocre proconsuls and of the rhymesters and histriones who delighted in Roman decadence. However, they did not even remind us of those great engineers who built the roads, the aqueducts and the great monuments of the Roman Empire.

In our time, the rise of artificial intelligence and digital transformation gets technical know-how on the ropes, and it can only be brought back to life if it is coupled with knowing how to think, imagine and understand. A combination of the 'four forms of knowledge' that requires familiarity with the arts. The 'STEM' of Know How To Do (see the corresponding entry in Chapter 4) gives way to 'STEAM' (Science, Technology, Engineering, Mathematics and the Arts) which breaks the spell of incomprehension and incommunicability between literati and scientists. It is replaced by mutual attention and dialogue, as advocated by the English scientist and writer Charles Percy Snow (1905–1980) in his book *The Two Cultures and a Second Look* (Cambridge: University Press, 1959). The innovators took over from the incrementalists.

The intertwining and merging of knowledge give rise to new thoughts that lead to discoveries and innovative entrepreneurial activities. As we reported in Part One under the heading 'Ideators: The Revolutionaries of Knowledge in Action', Einstein said that reading the Scottish philosopher David Hume's writings helped him formulate the theory of special relativity. Assimilating the thought of the humanist Pietro Bembo, the technologist Aldus Pius Manutius invented the pocketbook, the one that can be read anywhere and not only in libraries and lecture halls.

Charles Darwin is said to have considered the paintings of plants and landscapes by the botanical artist Marianne North to be excellent examples of his theory of natural selection.

The proximity of art to business was explored and experimented with by artists whose apprenticeship took place in the cradle of craftsmanship. Thus, the futurist Fortunato Depero, whose early experiences were forged working as an apprentice in a marble workshop, came to design graphic symbols and typefaces for industrial products. From his experiments in miniature art, the carpenter Ole Kirk Kristiansen laid the foundations of the Lego Group, the Danish manufacturer of toys (plastic 'bricks'), turning an artistic production into a major industrial success. These are but two examples among many of the intertwining of art, craftsmanship, innovation and business.

In science, the medical industry using virtual reality requires artists and designers who can collaborate with scientists to develop new interactive and immersive models and tools for medical research, training and education, and drug discovery, simulation, and modelling.

Suspended (to Be Drunk) Coffee

The word 'coffee' stimulates innovation. Coffee, then, is (if it ever was) an ancient medicine that many people now like and enjoy drinking. Above all, it is a delightful drink to share with others, to sip during meetings – which gatherings, in the Age of Exploration, can be regarded as the intellectual counterpoint to geographical discoveries.

As a prelude to the economy of sharing, in Naples, solidarity towards others has always been manifested in 'suspended coffee' (that is, 'to be drunk'), a coffee paid for by a customer and made available to poor people.

Here is how Tonino Guerra, an Italian poet, writer and scriptwriter, described an experience in one such coffee house in his book *The Kamasutra Valley*,

> Vittorio invited me into a bar. Somewhat later, two people came in and ordered four coffees: they paid for all of them but drank only two. The other two were left 'suspended', that is, available for those who could not afford to buy a cup of coffee. And, in fact, a minute later, a tramp came in and asked, 'Excuse me, is there a suspended coffee?' Of course, there was, and they gave it to him. There are many examples of these good deeds in Naples.

'Who shares, multiplies', say the Dutch. In Cambridge, England, in the 1970s, entrepreneurs animated a campaign to share their successes in transforming the glorious university city from a community of only togas and students into a vibrant society of high entrepreneurial fertility.

'T3': Technology, Tolerance, Talent

Technology as a kind of social engineering in the service of diversity, Tolerance for the different from us and Talent that produces new ideas: these are the three 'Ts' that will set the pace of economic and social innovation in the years to come. The cadence of the rhythm will depend on the ability to interweave the three 'Ts' in such a way as to forge virtuous social relations and entrepreneurial links between indigenous people and migrants. The prosperity of communities that have harnessed social technology, tolerance and talent shows that it is possible to enrich the source of immigration that provides general well-being and dry up the one that brings economic and social malaise through urban decay.

In a 'T3'-based international ranking, Sweden and Finland took the lead.

Talent

A mixture of creativity, curiosity, empathy, humour and passion. All these are personal qualities that separate man from machine. Moreover, they are permanent qualities, unlike technical skills, which are temporary. Talent also manifests itself in a deep understanding of different cultures and the mastery of several languages.

Innovations in machines allow us to make the best use of our talents and enjoy more free time. Ireland is the most determined country to raise the economic pressure with talent attracted from abroad to create global start-ups. The Japanese government's policy goal is to cultivate 'global talent' to counteract the ageing and declining population.

In his opening speech at the World Economic Forum 2012 in Davos, Klaus Schwab, founder of the Forum, said:

> ...capital is being superseded by creativity and the ability to innovate—and therefore by human talents—as the most important factors of production. If talent is becoming the decisive competitive factor, we can be confident in stating that capitalism is being replaced by 'talentism'. Just as capital replaced manual trades during the process of industrialization, capital is now giving way to human talent.

Not only capital but also labour. The industrial revolution created jobs. However, with the knowledge revolution, creators trained in the gymnasium of creative thinking will be displacing workers.

Tales

Stories of innovation on the borderline between reality and fantasy propel us into the future. Our future is played out in the no-man's land, between the force of gravity of the facts, which keep us firmly on the ground, and the anti-gravity of the imagination, which helps us discover a New World. With our thoughts, we perceive infinite spaces beyond the hedge 'which, from so many parts of the last horizon, the sight excludes', as Giacomo Leopardi's poem *The Infinite* says.

In the vivid expression used by Sara Thornton, Professor of English and Cultural Studies at the Université Paris Diderot, stories are open windows onto the landscape of human economic life. They offer a poignant illustration of the economy in action, of what each individual, not an undifferentiated mass of people, does when encountering one or another circumstance in real life.

Storytelling has the power to open up the scene to interwoven phenomena that cannot be traced back to a single unifying force. To use Isaiah Berlin's metaphor in his essay on Tolstoy's View of History (*The Hedgehog and the Fox: An Essay on Tolstoy's View of History*, London: Weidenfeld & Nicolson, 1953), later taken up by Gary Morson and Morton Schapiro (*Cents and Sensibility: What Economics Can Learn from the Humanities*, Princeton, NJ: University Press, 2017), the path of innovation trodden by the hedgehog who knows only one big and yet elegant thing is different from the path traced by the fox's aptitude for hunting down many small and sometimes clumsy ideas.

Technopolis

As the ultimate expression of the centrality of knowledge, the Technopolis creates and transmits intellectual potential. It breaks down the rigid boundary erected by past industrial civilisation between working time and private life.

The image ideally credited to it, in stark contrast to the panorama dominated by the black smoke of the chimneys, is that of a 'New Arcadia': a pleasant landscape, a sunny valley with a temperate climate, a green zone for a grey matter that attracts the best human resources involved in its innovative companies and institutes of higher education, and research centres.

Miyazaki, a Japanese prefecture with about 1.2 million inhabitants, has been named 'SUN Technopolis' (SUN: Science, Urbanity, Nature). Its image is evocative of the shining city of science, where scholars, researchers and entrepreneurs live together to innovate. There is a long list of technopolitan utopians, starting with the greats of the seventeenth century: Johannes Valentinus Andreae with his *Christianapolis* (1619), Thomas Campanella with the *City of the Sun* (1623), Francis Bacon with the *New Atlantis* (1627), celebrating the cult of creativity, and Samuel Hartlib with *Macaria* (1641).

Titanic Syndrome

1912–2012: 100 years run between the sinking of the *Titanic*, a British liner owned by the White Star Line shipping company, and the other of the *Costa Concordia*, a Costa Crociere cruise ship. Illuminated by Titanic Belfast, the new museum in the Irish city from whose shipyards the icon of the seas emerged, a century seems to have passed in vain, the statue of 'Customer Satisfaction', carved with the chisel of innovation, having fallen ruinously from its pedestal in both cases.

The *Titanic* showed off a whole bunch of innovations in design, technology (from new steel materials to the telegraph), planning, construction, aesthetics and furnishings. Was it ever possible – the shipowner asked himself – to ruin that beautiful fruit with so many lifeboats that took the view of the sea away from the social and cultural elite housed in first class? Despite the ship's titanic tonnage, the boats were reduced to 16. By marginalising the room (safety) and magnifying the form (open space on the horizon) of the innovation, the owner ended up sacrificing 1,523 lives that could otherwise have been saved with many more lifeboats. History has repeated itself with the *Costa Concordia*. Thanks to the bow at Giglio Island, the beautiful sight was a game of relational innovation between the captain and guests on board, ended in tragedy.

Neither the iceberg nor the rocky step in the shallow waters of Giglio Island caused the old and the new giant of the sea to sink. The two disasters were the result of titanic thinking imbued with arrogance. The satisfied customer syndrome can lead to disaster. Moreover, when disaster strikes, public relations innovate by massaging words. The White Star Line press officer pointed out that there had been no collision but allision. As if *Titanic's* collision with a fixed object (but the iceberg had moved, and how) was a natural fate, as opposed to a collision between two ships due to human error. Comparable 'massages of words' were seen with Costa. Like ships, innovations sink once designed not to promote people's well-being but to tickle their thrills. Now with the unsinkable *Titanic* travelling at top speed. Now with the floating city of fun, the *Concordia*, caressing the coast of Giglio.

Transculturation

A term coined by Cuban anthropologist Fernando Ortiz Fernández, transculturation is a network of mutual exchange of overlapping cultural influences.

Trans-Manageriality

There are words that enter the corporate vocabulary when the value of three cultural metaphors expires: the efficiency of markets, individuals' rationality, and the spontaneous movement of the economy towards an optimal state. However well dressed in the clothes of data and statistical models, those metaphors are losing prestige with the ongoing Copernican revolution. The heliocentrism of the entrepreneur is undermining the geocentrism of management. The entrepreneur is the sun that emanates radiation in various forms such as imagination, intuition and inspiration that give rise to entrepreneurial reactions. This is where the word 'trans-manageriality' enters the lexicon.

In contrast to intra-manageriality, which relegates managers to their own cognitive silo, trans-manageriality transcends disciplinary divisions.

The question that remains open is whether a leap can only achieve this radical change of perspective, or whether it is also possible to do so gradually by passing through the stations of cross-manageriality (observing the silo of another manager from the viewpoint of the latter, rather than from one's own), multi-manageriality (managers from different areas of the company working together, each drawing on their own well of knowledge) and inter-manageriality (finding a synthesis between knowledge and methods that distinguish disciplinary silos).

Uncertainty

Immersed in the age of knowledge, we continue to live with uncertainty, which is a state of doubt about the future. We cannot expect to control all the variables at work. The desire of governments and intergovernmental organisations to lower uncertainty by using forecasting models to plan for the future, dwelling on knowledge and understanding events of the past, narrows the horizon for innovation. To broaden this horizon, one must familiarise oneself with the subjective and quixotic world of possibility, not the mathematical and statistical world of probability. 'I cannot calculate the probability that the innovation I have in mind will or will not happen, but however improbable it may be, it will come to fruition and succeed': in the uncertainty that surrounds us, this is the language of the innovator.

University-Industry Cooperation

Back in 1946, William Wickenden, former president of the Case Institute of Technology in Cleveland and a pioneer of university-industry cooperation, argued that the college dormitories were nothing more than a continuation of the guild programme, which assigned the master craftsman not only the task of training his apprentices but also of hosting them in his own home.

In the first decade of the twentieth century, General Electric, AT&T and Westinghouse founded the first research laboratories in American industry on the wave of an idea conceived by the inventor and entrepreneur Thomas Edison. It soon became apparent that industrial research absorbed human resources that the university produced, hence the need for the industry to financially support higher and advanced education. The reference model is the German system of exchange between universities and manufacturers, investigated by American scientists on a mission to the old continent and transferred to the new. For cooperation, a long apprenticeship process begins with research contracts, the integration of university and industrial teams and the increasing involvement of academics in the development of the local communities where universities and industry settle.

In the case of smaller companies, a significant positive effect of cooperation with universities was the avoidance of staff de-skilling due to the rapid development of knowledge applied to the industry – the so-called 'Diebold effect', named after the US entrepreneur John Diebold. A pioneer in the field of automation, Diebold measured the rate of knowledge consumption over an individual's working life as a function of the rate of knowledge growth.

Unlearning

By unlearning, not to get caught in the trap of success, we break traditions and rules that are taken for granted and unchanging, which lead to deepening what we know to improve what we already do.

Incrementalism is the most fearsome innovation killer, says the Massachusetts Institute of Technology in Boston. By unlearning, mistakes are made, even encouraged, but others are avoided. Make mistakes, get ahead, be fast: this is the winning entrepreneurial mindset advocated by management writer Tom Peters (*The Circle of Innovation*, London: Hodder & Stoughton, 1997).

Unreasonableness

To be unreasonable is to question knowledge holders' authority, who point to the past as the guide to the future.

The Unreasonable Institute based in Denver, Colorado, reflects a new Age foretold by Charles Handy (*The Age of Unreason*, London: Hutchinson) in these words,

> We are entering an Age of Unreason, when the future, in so many areas, is there to be shaped, by us and for us; a time when the only prediction that will hold true is that no predictions will hold true; a time, therefore, for bolding imaginings in private life as well as public, for thinking the unlikely and doing the unreasonable.

Urban Beauty

As Aristotle stated, 'A great city should not be confounded with a populous one'. The beauty of the city is an identity forever. Studies carried out in the field of 'Pulchereconomy' (the Economics of Beauty) have shown that an aesthetically beautiful city gives happiness to its residents and strengthens economic activity. The more attractive its face, the more the city has the charisma necessary to show itself so strongly in the negotiations that it leads to remarkable commercial results. Beautiful cities entice innovation, enjoy higher incomes and entice investors.

It is commonly said that youth and beauty flee sooner or later. Nevertheless, a beautiful city is an aesthetic creature that has no age. The time comes into play if it is a matter of safeguarding its beauty, rediscovering and then regenerating it. It is the time for innovation in civic ethics aimed at regenerating the behaviour of individuals in the social community so that the beauty of the city is perceived as a vital project to be carried on incessantly. Urban beauty entrepreneurs burst into the scene as protagonists. Among them, the local administrators – political entrepreneurs who interpret the vision of the city.

It is primarily the responsibility of that specie of entrepreneurs to invest in urban beauty that raises the values of reputation with a strong emotional impact. As it follows from the annual report of the Reputation Institute (https://www.reputationinstitute.com), the consideration a city is held sees on the top step of the podium the attractiveness of the urban environment. An effective local administration and an advanced economy come second and third, respectively. Investing in beauty enhances the characteristics of the city, gives it charisma and strengthens its ability to negotiate with other cities around the world. The multiplier of one euro invested in beauty is potentially high. With the reputation that rises, more tourists, investors, scientific and artistic talents, aspiring and innovative baby entrepreneurs are attracted. The window of opportunity is widening; interpersonal relationships grow in quantity and quality on an international scale; additional income generated, and standards of living raised in the city. By investing in reputation, the reputation will work for the city. Investing in reputations is a red dot on the city's lips, a sign of trust, and it is the trust that moves society and the economy.

It is widely deemed that beauty is subjective, not measurable. That is why it is not among the indicators of smart cities and urban well-being. The School of Life (http://www.theschooloflife.com) based in London and committed to the development of emotional intelligence affirms that the beauty of the city is objective and therefore computable. Several studies have measured the increase in happiness indexes related to living in a beautiful city. The aesthetic character of the city, perceived as a sign of economic vitality, is also an object of measurement. After all, the city is a mental clock whose hours beat at the time of the pendulum that oscillates between investments for the maintenance of its beauty, and the damage caused both by the time that corrodes everything and the monsters that disfigure beauty by smearing building facades and spreading litter everywhere.

Useful and Useless Knowledge

Useful knowledge is the knowledge that changes behaviour. New ways of thinking and acting make acquired knowledge obsolete. The obsolescence leads to such accelerated changes in the status quo that the ability to understand the present and predict the future is greatly weakened.

Benjamin Franklin, the eclectic scientist and one of the founding fathers of the United States, emphasised useful knowledge, i.e. knowledge that can be applied to a specific use. It is the outcome of conversations that occur in collaborative investigations in the course of experiments. The Open Innovation Strategy and Policy Group of the EU (https://ec.europa.eu/digital-single-market/en/open-innovation-strategy-and-policy-group) aims to achieve with experiments the flow of knowledge from its source upstream to the point of exploitation downstream.

It was Abraham Flexner, an American educational theorist, who emphasised the usefulness of (apparently) useless knowledge. He said so in an article entitled 'The Usefulness of Useless Knowledge', which appeared in *Harper's Magazine* in the June-November 1939 issue,

> From a practical point of view, intellectual and spiritual life is, on the surface, a useless form of activity, in which men indulge because they procure for themselves greater satisfactions than are otherwise obtainable. In this paper I shall concern myself with the question of the extent to which the pursuit of these useless satisfactions proves unexpectedly the source from which undreamed-of utility is derived.

In the 1930s, the philosopher Bertrand Russell wrote in his essay *In Praise of Idleness* (London: George Allen & Unwin Ltd, 1935),

> Perhaps the most important advantage of 'useless' knowledge is that it promotes a contemplative habit of mind. There is in the world too much readiness, not only for action without adequate previous reflection, but also for some sort of action on occasions on which wisdom would counsel inaction. People show their bias on this matter in various curious ways. Mephistopheles tells the young student that theory is grey but the tree of life is green, and everyone quotes this as if it were Goethe's opinion, instead of what he supposes the devil would be likely to say to an undergraduate. Hamlet is held up as an awful warning against thought without action, but no one holds up Othello as a warning against action without thought.

Vespa

Wayne Van Dyck, founder of Windfarms, Ltd and several other enterprises, wrote:

The highest art form is really business. It is an extremely creative form and can be more creative than all the things we classically think of as creative. In business, the tools with which you are working are dynamic: capital and people, and markets and ideas. These tools all have lives of their own. So to take those things and to work with them and reorganize them in new and different ways turns out to be a very creative process.

(https://slideplayer.it/slide/523745/)

A striking example of Van Dyck's 'very creative process' is the Vespa, an Italian brand of motor scooter manufactured by Piaggio and patented on 23 April 1946. The designer of the Piaggio Vespa was the aeronautical engineer Corradino D'Ascanio, who leveraged his expertise in aviation to adopt a front suspension inspired by that of an aircraft's landing gear, and devised an engine conceptually derived from the aircraft engine. D'Ascanio's Vespa displays an interaction between art and innovation triggered by the transposition and transformation of existing materials to create objects that respond to practical and economic needs as well as to symbolic and allegorical visions, just as the art critic Gillo Dorfles argued.

Walkman

It is the word for a cult object, rich in meaning. In Fascist Italy, owning a radio was a status symbol. People resorted to listening at full volume to make neighbours who did not own one envious. As a result, the song 'Abbassa la tua radio' ('turn down your radio') was a big hit of the time. However, it was not always possible to ask for the volume to be reduced. In bathing establishments, which became increasingly popular in the 1930s, the use of loudspeakers was the only way to listen to the radio on the beach. Bring your own radio? Impossible. Perhaps someone dreamt of it, but there is no demand for what does not exist.

During the electronic revolution, anticipating the digital era, Akio Morita, the co-founder of Sony, was looking for new ways to listen to music. So, in 1978, a Sony engineer designed a portable audio cassette player. The device, called the Walkman, radically changed listening habits.

Morita admitted that many considered the Walkman to be an innovative wonder. However, he was the one who claimed that all the components to make it available were already on the shelves. Therefore, its success was due to planning and marketing the product.

Wandering Students

Founded in 1088, the *Alma Mater Studiorum*, the University of Bologna, was entrusted with the mission of bringing knowledge and culture out from the monasteries. Mother of the universities of the Second Millennium, it was the favourite destination and centre of gravity for students wandering along the pathways of knowledge.

Contemporary, talented individuals who circulate internationally are the wandering clerics of the twenty-first century. It is they who create and participate in networks that exist without borders on the value-added flow of collaborative advantage, which connects research at its source to downstream commercial exploitation through the creation of companies involved in the new markets for knowledge. This international free flow of talent enables knowledge-intensive, globally conceived start-ups to flourish. These are the people and the enterprises that shape the highly dynamic, emerging knowledge zones populated by new, creative professionals.

Windproof Wall Madness

As Brian and Sangeeta Mayne, founders of Lift International, used to say, when the winds of change blow, some people react by putting up windproof walls instead of building windmills to take advantage of the increased energy available. The wall is the line of defence that will keep innovation from entering our fence.

Too caught up in manipulating structures, maps, models and guidelines, we are condemned to the wall madness, leading to the paralysis of productivity and, thereby, of economic growth and social progress.

Work

There was a time when companies conceptualised as machines did not, like all machines, have a will of their own. They served the intentions of their owner. Employees were, of course, known to be human beings, but their intentions were irrelevant. They were kept at work as long as it was necessary to meet the objectives of the entrepreneurs.

That is no longer the case, nor is the case in the conceptual-managerial form shaped by the second industrial revolution with the joint-stock company as the dominant player instead of the old 'ironmaster'. What is in the process of becoming is the work of the new generations as entrepreneurs-creators who, as Esko Kilpi (Men and machines: on interactive value creation, http://eskokilpi.-blogging.fi.), a visionary explorer of the future of employment, describes them, are in a state of 'interaction between interdependent people. The new mission of economic policy is to allow us to seize and exploit the opportunity to be all creators who participate in a joint and innovative movement of thought with their ideas and intentions.

The gig economy shows another facet of the work mutation, where the gig has lost its original precious meaning of the unique performance of a musician or a group of musicians, mainly playing modern or pop music. The gig is identified with temporary work performed by independent contractors and obtained via online platforms. The most common image is the home delivery of a pizza on a bicycle. Another different image was accredited by academics at Oxford

University, who interviewed 679 online gig workers in South-East Asia and sub-Saharan Africa. As Sarah O'Connor reports in the *Financial Times* of 31 October 2018, many respondents said they found the tasks they were given challenging and varied and enjoyed the freedom the work offered. Lisa Hufford, the author of *Navigating the Talent Shift: How to Build On-Demand Teams That Drive Innovation, Control Costs, and Get Results* (London: Palgrave Macmillan, 2016), offers a third picture. According to Hufford, the gig economy can help start-ups meet their demand for talent at a lower cost and help mature companies grow. For their part, talents would realise that they have many skills required by companies and have many options.

Yin and Yang of Innovative Entrepreneurship

Along the dark path of knowledge, whose name is Yin, the concept of black according to ancient Chinese philosophy, if guided by emotion, imagination and creativity, one is open to all possibilities to the extent of making discoveries. These will first translate into innovations and entrepreneurship, managing to meet the Yang path, full of light, where, supported by culture, strategies and corporate structures will shape new markets.

As recounted by Bernie Carlson ('The Yin and Yang of entrepreneurship', *Forbes*, 17 September 2018), it is from the intersection of the Yin and Yang paths that the discovery in the early 1950s of a new class of materials, pyroceramics, mutates into innovative entrepreneurship by Corning Incorporated, which in 1958 launched a series of successful products under the CorningWare brand.

Chapter 5

Words and Voices: Who's Who

The words in parentheses at the end of each biographical note indicate the relevant entry or entries in the preceding section.

Giovanni Abramo, Technology Research Directory, The National Research Council of Italy.
(Incubator)

Aesop (620 BC–564 BC), an ancient Greek storyteller known for his fables.
(Co-opetition)

Giovanni Aldini, (1762–1834), the scientist traveller along the paths of the first industrial revolution.
(Brain Circulation)

Rama Allen, a director, interactive artist, strategist and futurist.
(Art and Technology)

Prospero Alpino (1553–1616), a physician-botanist. He makes known to the Venetians the medicinal plant of coffee.
(Fictions: The Coffee Red Thread)

Debra Amidon (1946–2016), founder and CEO at ENTOVATION International Ltd. ((Wilmington, Massachusetts) – a global innovation research and consulting network linking 61 countries throughout the world.)
(Laws of Knowledge Dynamics), (Knowledge Map)

Johannes Valentinus Andreae (1586–1654), a German theologian and a prominent member of the Protestant utopian movement which began in Germany.
(Technopolis)

Hannah Arendt (1906–1975), a German-born American political theorist. *Animal Laborans* is the definition given in her essay The Human Condition to man subjected to technology.
(*Homo Faber, Homo Laborans*)

Ideators, 181–212
Copyright © 2022 Piero Formica
Published under exclusive licence by Emerald Publishing Limited
doi:10.1108/978-1-80262-829-620221005

Aristotle (384/383 BC-322 BC) a Greek philosopher and polymath who questioned who, between slowness and rapidity, has the upper hand.
(Inventive Entrepreneurs and Incremental Innovators), (Intrapreneur), (Possibilist), (Urban Beauty)

Richard Arkwright (1732–1792), an English barber, wig-maker. Patented the first automatic spinning frame.
(Knowledge Growth)

Pellegrino Artusi (1820–1911), an Italian businessman and writer, best known as the author of the 1891 cookbook *La scienza in cucina e l'arte di mangiar bene* (*Science in the Kitchen and the Art of Eating Well*).
(Fictions: The Coffee Red Thread)

Athena, a warrior *goddess*, also the *goddess* of reason, of the arts, of literature and philosophy, of commerce and industry.
(Culture)

Saint Augustine (354–430AD), a theologian, philosopher and the bishop of Hippo Regius in Numidia, Roman North Africa.
(Creative Ignorance)

Octavian Augustus (63 BC-14 BC), the promptness of action accompanied by the slowness of reflection.
('Festina lente')

Avicenna (980–1037), the most famous scientist of Islam. In his *Canon of Medicine* brings to light the therapeutic qualities of coffee.
(Fictions: The Coffee Red Thread)

George F. Babbitt, the protagonist of the homonymous novel by Lewis Sinclar, is an archetype of the American middle class life and the social pressure toward conformity.
(Reform of the Heart)

Francis Bacon (1561–1626), an English philosopher and statesman. The father of empiricism.
(Controlled Sloppiness), (Open Innovation), (Technopolis)

Gerald Jerry Baldwin, Gordon Bowker and Zev Siegl, founders Starbucks of Starbucks, in Seattle, in 1971.
(Fictions: The Coffee Red Thread)

Elinor G. Barber, a former research associate in the Provost's Office at Columbia University.
(Serendipity)

James Bard (1815–1897), testimonial of the first industrial revolution with his portraits of steamboats.
(Art and Technology)

Federico Bastiani, an Italian social innovator. He is the originator of the "social streets" movement.
(Social Streets)

William Baumol (1922–2017), an American economist celebrating the revolutionary innovation of the inventive entrepreneur.
(Inventive Entrepreneurs and Incremental Innovators)

Luigi Bazzi (1892–1986), the longest-standing lieutenant of Enzo Ferrari. In the 1930s, he conceived the Alfa Romeo Bimotore.
(Organisational Knowledge)

Pietro Bembo, (1470–1547), an Italian scholar, poet and literary theorist.
(Brain Circulation), ('STEAM')

Bertha Benz (1849–1944), a German automotive pioneer and inventor. She was the business partner and wife of automobile inventor Karl Benz. On 5 August 1888, she was the first person to drive an automobile over a long distance.
(Journey)

Karl Friedrich Benz (1844–1929), a German engine designer and automotive engineer. His Benz Patent Motorcar from 1885 is considered the first practical automobile put into series production.
(Journey)

Isaiah Berlin (1909–1997), a Latvian-born British social and political theorist, philosopher and historian of ideas. He enriched the landscape of innovation with the fox that knows many things and the hedgehog that knows one great thing: a metaphor from a fragment of the Greek poet Archilochus (680 BC–645 BC).
(Tales)

Timothy John Berners-Lee, an English computer scientist best known as the inventor of the World Wide Web.
(Internauts of Social Networks)

Jeff Bezos, an America Internet entrepreneur.
(Drone), (Path Creators)

Phillip Bradley Bird is an American animator, film director, screenwriter, producer and voice actor.
(Black sheep)

Steve Blank, a Silicon Valley entrepreneur who launched the lean start-up movement.
(Start-up)

Jérôme-Adolphe Blanqui (1798–1854), a French economist. His contributions were made especially the history of economic thought.
(Knowledge Growth)

David Bodanis, a writer of bestselling nonfiction books, notably *E = mc2: A Biography of the World's Most Famous Equation.*
(Regard Multiplier)

Jorge Luis Borges (1899–1986), an Argentine short-story writer, who have contributed to philosophical literature and the fantasy genre.
(Ptolemaic Knowledgists)

Jagadish Chandra Bose (1858–1937), a biologist, physicist, botanist and an early writer of science fiction. He pioneered the investigation of radio and microwave optics and made significant contributions to plant science.
(Science and Art)

Satyendra Nath Bose (1894–1974), an Indian mathematician and physicist specialising in theoretical physics. He is best known for his work on quantum mechanics in the early 1920s.
(Science and Art)

Vujadin Boškov (1931–2014), a Serbian footballer and manager.
(Path Dependency)

Sandro Botticelli (c.1445–1510), Florentine painter, one of the greatest exponents of the early Renaissance.
(Renaissance Coworking Space)

Michelangelo Buonarroti (1475–1564), an Italian sculptor and painter. When it came to frescoing the vault of the Sistine Chapel, he made inexperience his strong point.
(Invisible Horizons), (Method of Freedom), (Talent)

Matthew Boulton (1728–1809), an English manufacturer and business partner of Scottish engineer James Watt.
(Lunar Society)

Adam Brandenburger, the Vice Dean for Graduate Education and the J.P. Valles Professor at the Stern School of Business at New York University.
(Coopetition)

Joseph Brodsky (1940–1996), poet, essayist and Nobel Prize winner for Literature.
(Creatives)

John Seely Brown, former Chief Scientist of Xerox Corporation and the director of its Palo Alto Research, is Chief of Confusion, helping people ask the right questions.
(Communities of Knowledge Practice), (Entrepreneurial University)

Filippo Brunelleschi (1377–1446), founding father of Renaissance architecture; designer and executor of engineering masterpieces.
(Art, Business and Innovation)

Jacob Christoph Burckhardt (1818–1897) Historian of art and culture.
(Entreprenaissance)

David Butterfield, a Latin scholar at the University of Cambridge, United Kingdom.
(Latin)

John Cage (1912–1992), an American composer and conceptual innovator.
(Experimental and Conceptual Innovators)

Nicholas Joseph Callan (1799–1864), theologian and scientist who links adjacent ideas: the electromagnetic induction of the physicist and chemist Michael Faraday (1791–1867) and the electromagnet of the physicist William Sturgeon (1783–1850).
(Connected Cities), (Open Innovation)

Italo Calvino (1923–1985), an Italian journalist and writer of short stories and novels.
(Speed)

Tommaso Campanella (1568–1639), an Italian Dominican friar, philosopher, theologian, astrologer and poet. His philosophical work, *The City of the Sun*, is an important early utopian work.
(Technopolis)

Don Campbell, the author and entrepreneur whose best-selling books *The Mozart Effect* and *The Mozart Effect for Children* provocatively argued for music's power to build mental.
(Mozart Effect)

W. Bernard Carlson, a historian of technology. He is Vaughan Professor of Humanities Chair, Engineering and Society Department, University of Virginia.
(Yin and Yang of Innovative Entrepreneurship)

Thomas Carlyle (1795–1881), a philosopher who defined economics as a 'dismal science'.
(Happiness)

Titus Lucretius Caro (c. 99 – c. 55 BC), a <u>Roman poet</u> and <u>philosopher</u>. His only known work is the philosophical poem *De rerum natura*.
(Nature)

Bruto Carpigiani (1903–1945), the father of a generation of technicians and designers who worked in the packaging machinery sector and enabled the development of Bologna's entire industrial sector.
(Know How To Do)

Carlo Cattaneo (1801–1869), an Italian patriot, political thinker, economic theorist and brilliant practical economist who counted intelligence among development factors alongside those traditionally acknowledged: land, labour and capital.
(Intelligence), (Scientific Clairvoyance, Practical Wisdom and Entrepreneurial Creativity)

Paul Cézanne (1839–1906), a French artist and Post-Impressionist painter. He was an unrelenting reviser of his pictorial art, like Charles Darwin in science.
(Experimental and Conceptual Innovators)

Émilie du Châtelet (1706–1749), a French natural philosopher and mathematician.
(Conversation)

Zia Chishti, the Chairman of the Board and CEO of Afiniti.
(Algorithm)

Carlo M. Cipolla (1922–2000), an Italian economic historian. He outlined *The Basic Laws of Human Stupidity*.
(Expert)

John Amos Comenius (1592–1670), educator and reformer of knowledge.
(Conversation)

Confucius (551–479 BC), a Chinese philosopher and politician. Confucius's philosophy continues to remain influential across China and East Asia today.
Martin Cooper (1928), an American engineer. He is a pioneer in the wireless communications industry.
(Imagination)

Martin Cooper, an American engineer. He is a pioneer in the wireless communications industry.
(Imagination)

Benedetta Craveri (1942), is an Italian literary critic, academic and writer.
(Intellectual Salons, the 'Mind Salons')

Francis Harry Compton Crick (1916–2004), a British molecular biologist, biophysicist and neuroscientist. He, James Watson and Rosalind Franklin played crucial roles in deciphering the helical structure of the DNA molecule.
(Conversation)

Marie Salomea Skłodowska Curie (1867–1934), a Polish and naturalised-French physicist and chemist who conducted pioneering research on radioactivity, she was the first person to win the Nobel Prize twice, and the only person to win the Nobel Prize in two scientific fields, physics and chemistry.
(Future Universities)

Nicholas of Cusa (1401–1464), a German philosopher, theologian, jurist, mathematician and astronomer. One of the first German proponents of Renaissance humanism.
(Creative Ignorance)

Francesco Procopio Cutò (1651–1727), the Sicilian entrepreneur of the first Parisian literary café, Le Procope.
(Fictions: The Coffee Red Thread)

Joseph Dambrosio, an American innovation history scholar.
(Recombination)

Erasmus Darwin (1731–1802), an English physician. One of the key thinkers of the Midlands Enlightenment.
(Lunar Society)

Charles Darwin (1809–1882), an English naturalist who solved the puzzle of evolution by travelling across disciplinary boundaries. Darwin glimpsed in the paintings of plants and landscapes by the botanical artist Marianne North (1830–1890) excellent examples of his theory of natural selection.
(Conversation), (Experimental and Conceptual Innovators), ('STEAM')

Corradino D'Ascanio (1891–1981 in Pisa), an Italian aeronautical engineer. D'Ascanio Invented the first modern helicopter prototype and was the designer of the Piaggio Vespa.
(Vespa)

Humphry Davy (1778–1829), a British chemist best known for his experiments in electro-chemistry and his invention of a miner's safety lamp.
(Regard Multiplier)

Leonardo da Vinci (1452–1519), an Italian polymath of the High Renaissance; the universal genius.
(Cultural Consumption), (Digital Craftsmen), (Entreprenaissance), (Renaissance Coworking Space), (Science and Art), (Science and Technology)

Edward de Bono (1933), a British physician, theorist of lateral thinking and proponent of thinking as a subject of school learning.
('Ago Ergo Erigo'), (Creatives)

Bernard Le Bovier de Fontenelle (1657–1757), a French author. He was noted for ability to explain scientific topics during the Age of Enlightenment.
(Fictions: The Coffee Red Thread)

George Charles de Hevesy (1885–1966), a Hungarian radiochemist and Nobel Prize in Chemistry, recognized for his key role in the development of radioactive tracers to study chemical processes such as in the metabolism of animals.

Jean de La Bruyère (1645–1696), a philosopher, moralist and satirist.
(Conversation)

Marie-Madeleine Pioche de La Vergne, comtesse de La Fayette, better known as Madame de La Fayette (1634–1693), a French writer; she authored *La Princesse de Clèves*, France's first historical novel and one of the earliest novels in literature.
(Reform of the Heart)

Pierre Guillet de Monthoux, the director of the Stockholm School of Economics Art Initiative.
(Science and Art)

Catherine de Vivonne, marquise de Rambouillet, known as Madame de Rambouillet (1588–1655), a society hostess and a major figure in the literary history of seventeenth-century France. Her 'Chambre Bleue' at the Hotel de Rambouillet inaugurated the age of conversation in intellectual salons. Other salons followed, including those of Madame de Tencin (1682–1749) and Madame Geoffrin (1699–1777). In Italy, in their Venetian palaces, the salons of Caterina Dolfin Tron (1736–1793), Giustina Renier Michiel (1755–1832), Marina Querini Benzon (1757–1839) and Isabella Teotochi Albrizzi (1760–1836).
(Intellectual Salons, the 'Mind Salons')

Jean Baptiste Le Rond d'Alembert (1717–1783), an encyclopedist, assiduous frequenter of the Parisian salons, centres of the Enlightenment.
(Conversation)

Richard Peter Davenport-Hines, a British historian, literary biographer and expert on the Cambridge economist John Maynard Keynes.
(Experimental Laboratory)

Andrea del Verrocchio (1435–1488), a stimulator of intellectual energies, mentor of artistic talents.
(Renaissance Coworking Space)

Pope Julius II, born Giuliano della Rovere (1443–1513), was head of the Catholic Church and ruler of the Papal States from 1503 to his death in 1513.
(Invisible Horizons)

Michael Saul Dell, an American billionaire businessman and philanthropist. He is the founder of Dell Technologies.
(Disrupter)

Xiaoping Deng (1904–1997), the architect of Modern China.
(Fu Xing)

Fortunato Depero (1892–1960), an Italian futurist painter, writer, sculptor and graphic designer.
('STEAM')

John Dewey (1859–1952), an American philosopher, psychologist and educational reformer. He valued genuine ignorance.
(Creative Ignorance)

Denis Diderot (1713–1784), the entrepreneur of the *Encyclopédie*.
(Conversation), (Fictions: The Coffee Red Thread)

John Diebold (1926–2005), advocate of the combination between technological innovation and strategic planning.
(University-Industry Cooperation)

Darcy DiNucci, a web designer and expert in user experience. DiNucci coined the term *Web 2.0* in 1999 and predicted the influence it would have on public relations.
(Internauts of Social Networks)

Wakt Disney (1901–1966), an American entrepreneur, animator, designer, conceptual innovator.
(Experimental and Conceptual Innovators)

Gillo Dorfles (1910–2018), an Italian art critic who uncovers links between the artist's work and the industrial product.
(Olivetti Lettera 22), (Vespa)

Peter Drucker (1909–2005), management guru, whose writings contributed to the philosophical and practical foundations of the modern business corporation.
(Conversation), (Culture), (Entrepreneurial enterprise), (Future Universities), (Knowledge Workers)

Paul Duguid, an adjunct full professor at the School of Information at the University of California, Berkeley and formerly Professorial Research Fellow at Queen Mary, University of London.
(Entrepreneurial University)

Thomas Edison (1847–1931), the originator of the research laboratory as a place of relentless production of technological innovations.
(Experimental Laboratory), (University-Industry Cooperation)

Luigi Einaudi (1874–1961), an Italian economist and politician, preacher and champion of education freedom. He served as the second president of Italy from 1948 to 1955.
(Method of Freedom)

Albert Einstein (1879–1955), the distinctive multifaceted mind of the twentieth century for whom knowledge is limited to all we now know and understand, whereas imagination embraces the whole world.
(Big Data), (Experimental and Conceptual Innovators), (Imaginative Entrepreneur), (Pure and Applied Research), (Regard Multiplier), (Reimagined and Ludic Schools), ('STEAM')

Lawrence Joseph Ellison, an American business magnate and investor who is a co-founder of Oracle Corporation.
(Disrupter)

Hans Magnus Enzensberger, a German author, poet, translator and editor.
(Creative Ignorance)

Aaron Epstein, co-founder of *Creative Market* to help independent creators around the world make a living doing what they love.
(Creative Markets)

Desiderius Erasmus (1469–1536), a Dutch philosopher and one the greatest scholars of the northern Renaissance, who praised freedom of expression.
(Brain Circulation), (Conversation), ('Festina Lente')

Isabella d'Este (1474–1539), a patroness of the arts and fashion innovator.
(Cultural Consumption)

Gabriele Falciasecca, Chairman of the Scientific Committee of the Consortium Elettra 2000 devoted to the study and to the diffusion of scientific results in the field of health issues related to electromagnetic waves.
(Doubt)

Oriana Fallaci (1929–2006), an Italian journalist, author and political interviewer.
(Speed)

Michael Faraday, (1791–1867), an English scientist who contributed to the study of electromagnetism and electrochemistry.
(Open Innovation)

Battista 'Pinin' Farina (1893–1966), an icon of Made in Italy. The founding father of the renowned Italian school of car design.
(Cooperation)

Enrico Fermi (1901–1954), an Italian physicist and the creator of the world's first nuclear reactor, the Chicago Pile-1. He has been called the architect of the nuclear age. 1938 Nobel Prize in Physics.
(Imagination)

Fernando Ortiz Fernández (1881–1969), a Cuban essayist and anthropologist. Ortiz coined the term 'transculturation', the notion of converging cultures.
(Transculturation)

Enzo Ferrari (1898–1988), the historical founder of the well-known 'prancing horse', a symbol of Italian excellence.
(Cooperation), (Organisational Knowledge)

Paul Feyerabend (1924–1994), an Austrian-born philosopher of science, best known for his theory of epistemological anarchism.
(Knowledge in Action), (Open Innovation), (Reimagined and Ludic Schools)

Richard P. Feynman (1918–1998), Nobel Prize winner for Physics, credited with pioneering the field of quantum computing and introducing the concept of nanotechnology.
(Cargo Cult Science), (Experimental Laboratory), (Path Dependency)

Johann Gottlieb Fichte (1762–1814), one of the first philosophers of the movement known as German idealism. 'Not knowing is an endless journey'.
(Creative Ignorance)

Cyrus West Field (1819–1892), an American businessman and financier who created the Atlantic Telegraph Company and laid the first telegraph cable across the Atlantic Ocean in 1858.
(Passion for Innovating)

Stuart J. Firestein, Chairman of the Department of Biology at Columbia University, Professor of Neuroscience.
(Creative Ignorance)

Alexander Fleming (1881–1955), a Scottish physician and microbiologist, best known for discovering the world's first broadly effective antibiotic substance, which he named penicillin.
(Controlled Sloppiness)

Abraham Flexner (1866–1959), a reformer of higher education and the founder of the Institute for Advanced Study at Princeton.
(Useful and Useless Knowledge)

Henry Ford (1863–1947), an American industrialist, founder of the Ford Motor Company and chief developer of the assembly line technique of mass production. The ingenious innovator who changed lifestyles with the 'Ford T'.
(Communication)

Mark Forsyth (1977), a British writer of entertaining non-fiction who came to prominence with a series of books concerning the meaning and etymology of English words.
(Learning)

Benjamin Franklin (1706–1790), a versatile talent. One of the Founding Fathers of the United States.
(Conversation), (Useful and Useless Knowledge)

Rober Friedel, an American historian of science and technology.
(Discovery and Invention)

Milton Friedman (1912–2006), an American economist and statistician who received the 1976 Nobel Memorial Prize in Economic Sciences for his research on consumption analysis, monetary history and theory and the complexity of stabilization policy.
(Leadership)

Caspar David Friedrich (1744–1840), a German Romantic landscape painter.
(Intrapreneur), (Inventive Entrepreneurs and Incremental Innovators)

Richard Buckminster Fuller (1895–1983), an American architect, systems theorist and inventor who asserted that there are no failed experiments, only experiments with unexpected results.
(Experimental Laboratory)

David Walter Galenson, a professor in the Department of Economics and the College at the University of Chicago, and a Research Associate of the National Bureau of Economic Research.
(Experimental and Conceptual Innovators)

Ferdinando Galiani (1728–1787), an Italian economist; he was actively involved in conversations held in French literary salons, maintaining that markets are conversation.
(Brain Circulation), (Conversation),

Galileo Galilei (1564–1642), an Italian astronomer, physicist and engineer. The father of the scientific method.
(Conversation), (Craftsmen, 'Merchants of Light'), (Speed)

Indira Priyadarshini Gandhi (1917–1984), the first and, to date, only female Prime Minister of India.
(Great Government Versus Big Government), (Speed)

Adi Gaskell, a British innovation writer and consultant who has worked with leading organisations from the private and public sectors.
(Recombination)

William Henry Gates III, an American business magnate, software developer, investor, author and philanthropist. He is the co-founder of Microsoft Corporation.
(Disrupter)

Domenico Ghirlandaio (1448–1494), a Florentine painter, protagonist of the Renaissance at the time of Lorenzo the Magnificent.
(Renaissance Coworking Space)

Giotto di Bondone (c.1267–January 8 1337), an Italian painter and architect from Florence. He is generally thought of as the first in a line of great artists of the Italian Renaissance.
(Method of Freedom)

Johann Wolfgang von Goethe (1749–1832), a fervent advocate of innovation.
('Festina Lente'), (Nature)

Goldmund, a wanderer (a Dionysian endeavour) balanced out by Narcissus, the structured and stable priest-monk (an Apollonian approach), in a novel written by the German-Swiss author Hermann Hesse.
(Leadership)

Gabriella Greison, an Italian physicist, writer, playwright and theatre actress.
(Open Innovation)

Andrew Grove (1936–2016), an engineer and co-founder of Intel Co. He saw in success the seeds of its destruction.
(Disrupter), (Inventive Entrepreneurs and Incremental Innovators), (Scale-up)

Otto von Guericke (1602–1686), a German scientist, inventor and politician, known for his demonstrations on the physics of the vacuum.
(Otto von Guericke, the Vacuum Experiment)

Tonino Guerra (1920–2012) an Italian poet, writer, and screenwriter.
(Suspended – to be Drunk – Coffee)

Lemuel Gulliver, the protagonist of Jonathan Swift's novel *Gulliver's Travels.*
(Experimenter), (Gulliver's Watch)

Johannes Gutenberg (1400–1468), a German inventor, printer, publisher and goldsmith who introduced printing to Europe with his mechanical movable-type printing press.
(Craftsmen, 'Merchants of Light'), (Experimental Laboratory)

Hamlet: in *The Tragedy of Hamlet, Prince of Denmark*, written by William Shakespeare, Hamlet is the Prince of Denmark. Hamlet's hesitation to kill his uncle raises philosophical and ethical questions.
(Useful and Useless Knowledge)

Charles Hampden-Turner, a British management philosopher, and Senior Research Associate at the Judge Business School at the University of Cambridge, United Kingdom.
(Coopetition), (Knowledge Commercialisation), (Knowledge and Information)

Charles Handy, an Irish author and philosopher specialising in organisational behaviour and management.
(Unreasonableness)

John Harrison (1693–1776), a self-educated English carpenter with a passion for the mechanics of clocks, inventor of the marine chronometer.
(Knowledge Growth).

Samuel Hartlib (c 1600–1662), a polymath of German origin. The utopian *A Description of the Famous Kingdome of Macaria* appeared under Hartlib's name, but is now thought to be by Gabriel Plattes (1600–1655), a friend of his.
(Technopolis)

Hermes, an Olympian deity in ancient Greek religion and mythology. Hermes is considered the protector of travellers. He plays different roles while simultaneously travelling in different directions.
(Controlled Sloppiness)

Heinrich Hertz (1857–1894), a physicist. Thanks to his experiments, it was proved the existence of electromagnetic waves.
(Doubt)

Hermann Karl Hesse (1877–1962), a German-Swiss poet, novelist and painter. In his books, Hesse explores an individual's search for authenticity, self-knowledge and spirituality. In 1946, he received the Nobel Prize in Literature.
(Leadership)

Peter Ware Higgs (1929), a British theoretical physicist, Emeritus Professor in the University of Edinburgh and Nobel Prize laureate for his work on the mass of subatomic particles.
(Science and Technology)

Fred Hirsch, an Oxford-educated economist.
(Polychromatic Culture)

Alfred Joseph Hitchcock (1899–1980), an English film director, producer and screenwriter.
(Experimental and Conceptual Innovators)

Johan Huizinga (1872–1945), one of the founders of modern cultural history. His Homo Ludens will improve, through play, one's emotional, educational and working life.
(Homo Ludens)

Lisa Hufford, the founder and CEO of Simplicity Consulting. *Inc.* Magazine has named Lisa Hufford one of the Top 10 Female Entrepreneurs.
(Work)

Friedrich Wilhelm Christian Karl Ferdinand von Humboldt (1767–1835), a Prussian philosopher, linguist, diplomat and founder of the Humboldt University of Berlin.
(Future Universities)

David Hume (1711–1776), a Scottish Enlightenment philosopher, historian, economist and essayist, who is best known today for his highly influential system of philosophical empiricism, skepticism and naturalism. Hume has exercised influence on Albert Einstein's conception of time and his theory of relativity.
(Open Innovation), ('STEAM')

Joichi Ito, a Japanese entrepreneur and venture capitalist.
(Anti-discipline)

Annie Jameson (1840–1920), mother of Marconi, of the Irish entrepreneurial family known since 1780 for its famous whiskey.
(Doubt)

Steve Jobs (1955–2011), the co-founder of Apple Inc., a pioneer of the digital age.
(Art, Business and Innovation), (Art and Technology), (Digital Craftsmen), (Disrupter), (Imagination), (Inventive Entrepreneurs and Incremental Innovators), (Latin)

Frans Johansson, a Swedish-American writer, entrepreneur and public speaker. He is the author of *The Medici Effect*, a book that became the origin for the term 'Medici Effect'.
(Ideation)

Kaldi: a young shepherd of Ethiopian origin.
(Fictions: The Coffee Red Thread)

Nicholas Kaldor (1908–1986), a Cambridge economist in the post-war period. Working at the United Nations Economic Commission for Europe, Kaldor concentrated on demand–supply relationships to the manufacturing sector. (Manufacture)

Stuart Alan Kauffman (1939), an American medical doctor, theoretical biologist and complex systems researcher. He became known through his association with the Santa Fe Institute (a non-profit research institute dedicated to the study of complex systems) and through his work on models in various areas of biology. These included 'autocatalytic sets in origin of life' research. (Collective Autocatalytic System)

John Anderson Kay, a British economist. He was the first dean of Oxford's Said Business School. His interests focus on the relationships between economics and business. (Controlled Sloppiness), (Coordination),

Kevin Kelly, the founding executive editor of *Wired* magazine. (Science and Technology)

Clark Kerr (1911–2003), first chancellor of the University of California. He coined the term 'multiversity' to describe the multiple and parallel academic missions. (Multiversity)

John Maynard Keynes (1883–1946), the economist as saviour with an aversion to old ideas. (Altruism), (Experimental Laboratory), (Imaginative Entrepreneur), (Incrementalist), (Renaissance Start-ups)

Genghis Khan (c. 1167–1227), a Mongolian ruler who joined with the Mongol tribes and started the Mongol Empire. (Silk Roads)

Kublai Khan (1215–1294) was a military ruler, who brought the Mongol Empire to its greatest height. (Silk Roads)

Esko Kilpi, founder and principal in Esko Kilpi Oy, leading research and consultancy which lays the intellectual foundations for Post-Industrial Work. (Work)

Athanasius Kircher (1602–1680), a scientific star of the Baroque age and a traveller in many worlds of knowledge. (Entrepreneurialism)

Noboru Konno, a knowledge ecologist and President Innovation Network Japan. (Open Innovation)

Maya Kosoff, a freelance writer, reporter and editor.
(Reimagined and Ludic Schools)

David Krakauer (1967), an American evolutionary biologist, the President and William H. Miller Professor of Complex Systems at the Santa Fe Institute.
(Intelligence)

Ole Kirk Kristiansen (1891–1958), a Danish carpenter. In 1932, Kristiansen founded the Danish construction toy company The Lego Group.
('STEAM')

Kronos, a cosmogonic deity, analogous to the Hurrian god Kumarbi.
(Flexibility)

Paul Krugman (1953), Nobel Prize winner for Economics for his analysis of trade patterns and location of economic activity.
(Competitiveness and Productivity)

Simon Kuznets (1901–1985), in his works we discover the origins of the Gross National Product.
(Big Data)

Pierre Lafitte (1925–2021), a French scientist and politician, founder of the Sophia-Antipolis technology park, created in 1970 on the French Riviera.
(Science and Technology Parks)

Ulf Larsson, the Senior Curator at Nobel Museum.
(Curiosity), (Journey)

Ervin László (1932), a Hungarian philosopher of science. He is an advocate of the theory of quantum consciousness.

Dorothy Leonard, the William J. Abernathy Professor of Business Administration, Emerita, Harvard Business School.
(Knowledge and Information)

Giacomo Leopardi (1798–1837), an Italian writer, spearhead of Italian literature. He identified doubt as the source of truth.
(Imaginative Entrepreneur), (Tales)

Alan Lerner (1902–1992), an American journalist and educator; a convinced possibilist.
(Possibilist)

Bernard Lewis (1916–2018), a British American historian specialised in Oriental studies.
(Polychromatic Culture)

Sinclair Lewis (1885–1951), an American novelist and playwright. The George F. Babbitt's story, the famous protagonist of his homonymous novel, is a warning to the egoist who rejects the 'reform of the heart' called for in the eighteenth century by Madame de La Fayette.
(Reform of the Heart)

Geoffrey Ernest Richard Lloyd (1933), a historian of Ancient Science and Medicine at the University of Cambridge. He is the Senior Scholar in Residence at the Needham Research Institute in Cambridge, England.
(Controlled Sloppiness)

John Locke (1632–1704), the founder of empiricism and promoter of the Enlightenment.
(Conversation), (Open Innovation)

Salvador Edward Luria (1912–1991), an Italian microbiologist, later a naturalised US citizen. He won the Nobel Prize for the discoveries on the replication mechanism and the genetic structure of viruses. Advocate of controlled sloppiness in research.
(Controlled Sloppiness)

Lynceus, a king of Argos in Greek mythology.
(Coevolution), (Gulliver's Watch)

René Magritte (1898–1967), a Belgian surrealist artist. His *Ignorant Fairy* represents the promise of new knowledge.
(Path Creators)

Mohammed bin Rashid Al Maktoum (1949), the Vice President and Prime Minister of the United Arab Emirates (UAE) and ruler of the Emirate of Dubai.
(Seigniories of the Twenty-first Century)

Thomas Robert Malthus (1766–1834), an English cleric, scholar and influential economist in the fields of political economy and demography.
(Conversation)

Thomas Mann (1875–1955), a German novelist who said of Johann Wolfgang von Goethe, <<the] slowness is inseparable from his genius>>.
('Festina Lente')

Aldus Pius Manutius (1449/1452–1515), an Italian humanist, scholar, educator and the founder of the Aldine Press. His enchiridia, small portable books, revolutionised personal reading and are the predecessor of the modern paperback.
(Brain Circulation), ('STEAM')

Guglielmo Marconi (1874–1937), an Italian inventor and electrical engineer, known for his pioneering work on long-distance radio transmission.
(Doubt)

Barry J. Marshall and Robin Warren, The Nobel Laureates in Physiology or Medicine 2005 'for their discovery of the bacterium *Helicobacter pylori* and its role in gastritis and peptic ulcer disease'.
(Imagination)

Ron Martin, a professor of Economic Geography, Department of Geography, University of Cambridge.
(Path Dependency)

James Clerk Maxwell (1831–1879), a physicist to whom we owe the modern theory of electromagnetism.
(Doubt)

Brian Mayne, an author and leader on the science of positive thinking and goal achievement.
(Windproof Wall Madness)

Sangeeta Mayne, an experiential trainer, mentor and guide.
(Windproof Wall Madness)

John McTaggart (1866–1925), an idealist philosopher.
(Happiness)

Medici, the family also known as the House of Medici, first attained wealth and political power in Florence in the thirteenth century through its success in commerce and banking.
(Ideation)

Gene Meieran, senior Intel Fellow (retired), coined the term knowledgification, the 21st century equivalent of the combination of electricity and mass manufacturing, which transformed the 20th century.
(Beautification and Knowledgification)

Herman Melville (1819–1891), an American novelist. Legend has it that the Starbucks coffee chain was named after the character Starbuck in his novel *Moby Dick*.
(Fictions: The Coffee Red Thread)

Eunika Mercier-Laurent, a Global Innovation Strategist, expert of ENTOVA-TION International since 1996, and Professor of Artificial Intelligence and Knowledge eco-Innovation at the Université de Reims Champagne Ardenne, France.
(Laws of Knowledge Dynamics)

Robert King Merton (1910–2003), an American sociologist who is considered a founding father of modern sociology.
(Serendipity)

Raymond E. Miles, Professor Emeritus and former dean of the Walter A. Haas School of Business, University of California, Berkeley.
(Networks)

John Stuart Mill (1806–1873), an English philosopher and political economist. He was a utilitarian complex thinker.
(Nature)

Minerva, the Roman goddess of wisdom.
(Reimagined and Ludic School)

André Morellet (1727–1819), a French economist and contributor to the *Encyclopédie*. One of the last Enlightenment Age philosophers.
(Intellectual Salons, the 'Mind Salons')

Akio Morita (1921–1999), a physicist, entrepreneur and protagonist of the Japanese economic miracle. He was the co-founder of Sony.
(Scientific Clairvoyance, Practical Wisdom and Entrepreneurial Creativity), (Walkman)

Samuel Morse (1791–1872), an American inventor and painter.
(Art, Business and Innovation)

Gary Saul Morson, the Lawrence B. Dumas Professor of the Arts and Humanities and professor of Slavic languages and literatures at Northwestern University.
(Tales)

Wolfgang Amadeus Mozart (1756–1791), a prodigious composer from his earliest childhood.
(Mozart Effect)

Robert Musil (1880–1942), an Austrian philosophical writer and playwright who warned of the danger of taking the bait like a fish on a hook without seeing the line when the lens of reality is put on.
(Possibilist)

Elon Reeve Musk (1971), a South African-born Canadian-American business magnate, engineer, inventor. He is the founder, CEO, and Chief Engineer at SpaceX; CEO and Product Architect of Tesla, Inc.
(Entreprenaissance), (Reimagined and Ludic Schools)

Azar Nafisi (1948), an Iranian-American writer and professor of English literature.
(Reform of the Heart)

Barry J. Nalebuff (1958), an American businessman, business theorist and writer. He is a Milton Steinbach Professor of Management at Yale School of Management and author who specialises in business strategy and game theory.
(Coopetition)

Narcissus, in Greek mythology, the son of the river god Cephissus and the nymph Liriope. According to myth, his rejection of the love of the nymph Echo or of the young man Ameinias drew upon him the vengeance of the gods and he fell in love with his own reflection in the waters of a spring and pined away.
(Leadership)

Nicholas Negroponte (1943), a Greek American architect. He is the founder and chairman Emeritus of Massachusetts Institute of Technology's Media Lab.
(Anti-discipline)

Jawaharlal Nehru (1889–1964), an Indian independence activist and, subsequently, the first Prime Minister of India.
(Great Government Versus Big Government)

Ben Nelson, the Founder of Minerva Schools, and a visionary with a passion to reinvent higher education.
(Reimagined and Ludic Schools)

Isaac Newton (1643–1727), a father of the modern science.
(Conversation)

Kitarō Nishida (1870–1945), a Japanese philosopher. He was the founder of what has been called the Kyoto School of philosophy. Nishida proposed the concept of 'Ba'.
(Open Innovation)

Marcello Nizzoli (1887–1969), an Italian artist, industrial and graphic designer. He was the chief designer for Olivetti f and was responsible notably for the iconic Lettera 22 portable typewriters.
(Olivetti Lettera 22)

Ikujiro Nonaka (1935), a Japanese organisational theorist, best known for his study of knowledge management. Nonaka adapts the concept of 'Ba' for the purpose of elaborating SECI model of knowledge creation.
(Explicit and Tacit Knowledge), (Open Innovation)

Marianne North (1830–1890), a prolific English Victorian biologist and botanical artist, notable for her plant and landscape paintings.
('STEAM')

Sarah O'Connor, a columnist, reporter and associate editor at the *Financial Times*.
(Work)

Camillo Olivetti (1868–1943), the founder of Ing. C. Olivetti and C, supporter of technical education.
(Coevolution), ('STEAM')

George Orwell, pseudonym of the British journalist Eric Arthur Blair, (1903–1950). The narrator of the society of mass surveillance.
(Cognitive and Emotional Conflict)

Othello: in *The Tragedy of Othello, the Moor of Venice* written by William Shakespeare, Othello is a military commander of Moorish race who was serving as general of the Venetian army in defense of Cyprus against invasion by Ottoman Turks. Othello is an archetype of amorous passion which, misdirected by jealousy, leads to self-destruction.
(Useful and Useless Knowledge)

Jason Owen-Smith, an American sociologist who examines how science, commerce and the law cohere and conflict in contemporary societies and economies.
(Recombination)

Robert Palladino (1932–2016), a calligrapher; inspirer of Steve Jobs.
(Art, Business and Innovation)

Giovanni Papini (1881–1956), an Italian revolutionary educator, with his essay *Chiudiamo le scuole*, Firenze: Vallecchi, 1919.
(Future Universities), (Learning), (Project: A 'Promising Monster')

Louis Pasteur (1822–1895), discoverer of the principles of vaccination.
(Doubt)

Linus Carl Pauling (1901–1994), an American chemist, biochemist, chemical engineer and peace activist. For his scientific work, Pauling was awarded the Nobel Prize in Chemistry in 1954. For his peace activism, he was awarded the Nobel Peace Prize in 1962.
(Conversation)

Alex Sandy Pentland (1951), a computational scientist, Director of the MIT Media Lab Entrepreneurship Program.
(Big Data)

Pietro Perugino (c. 1446–1523), a Renaissance painter of the Urbino school.
(Renaissance Coworking Space)

Thomas J. Peters, an American writer on business management practices.
(Unlearning)

Armen E. Petrosyan, Institute for Business Tver, Russia.
(Imagination)

Pablo Picasso (1881–1973), the archetypal conceptual innovator. He was part of the group of avant-garde artists who conducted experiments in the field of non-Euclidean geometry. Among them: Fernand Léger (1881–1955), Marcel Duchamp (1887–1968), Juan Gris (1887–1927) and Georges Braque (1882–1963). (Experimental and Conceptual Innovators), (Path Creators), (Science and Art)

Plato (424/423–348/347 BC), an Athenian philosopher during the Classical period in Ancient Greece, founder of the Platonist school of thought and the Academy, the first institution of higher learning in the Western world. (Beautification and Knowledgefication)

Jules Henri Poincaré (1854–1912), a French mathematician and scientist. (Regard Multiplier)

Marco Polo (1254–1324), a Venetian merchant, explorer and writer who travelled through Asia along the Silk Road between 1271 and 1295. His travels are recorded in *The Travels of Marco Polo* (also known as *Book of the Marvels of the World* and *Il Milione*, c. 1300). (Silk Roads)

Ignazio Pomini, the founder of Hsl, a Trentino-based company that has been using stereolithographic printing technology since the late 1980s. (Art Business and Innovation)

Pope Benedict XVI, born Joseph Aloisius Ratzinger, a retired prelate of the Catholic Church who served as the head of the Church and the sovereign of the Vatican City State from 2005 until his resignation in 2013. (Latin)

Adam Posen, president of the Peterson Institute for International Economics in Washington. (Great Government Versus Big Government)

Creel Price, Creel, one of Australia's most active and successful Angel Investors with investments in over 80 companies across three continents. (Entreprenaissance)

Joseph Priestley (1733–1804), an English chemist, natural philosopher and liberal political theorist. He has historically been credited with the independently discovery of oxygen in 1774. (Discovery and Invention), (Lunar Society)

Robert Neel Proctor (1954), an American historian of science and Professor of the History of Science at Stanford University. (Learning)

Ovid (Publius Ovidius Naso, 43 BC–17/18 AD), a Roman poet who lived during the reign of Augustus. *The Metamorphoses* is considered his magnum opus. ('Festina Lente'), (Nature)

Leonhard Rauwolf (1535–1596), a German physician. He published one of the first books on coffee.
(Fictions: The Coffee Red Thread)

Ronald Wilson Reagan (1911–2004), an American politician and the 40th president of the United States. His economic policy, referred to as Reaganomics, reduced domestic spending, which was more than offset by increased military spending, creating a net deficit throughout his two terms.
(Great Government Versus Big Government)

Robert Recorde (c. 1512–1558), the controller of the Royal Mint, advocated the applied sciences as a means by which people could have full control over the course of their lives.

Ernest Renan (1823–1892), a French philosopher for whom certainty is the antechamber to fanaticism.
(Imaginative Entrepreneur)

Ferdinand von Richthofen (1833–1905), a German traveller, geographer and scientist. He is noted for coining the terms 'Silk Road' in 1877.
(Silk Roads)

Matthew White Ridley, a British journalist. He is best known for his writings on science, the environment and economics.
(Science and Technology)

Augusto Righi (1850–1920), a physicist and a pioneer in the study of electromagnetism.
(Doubt)

Gianni Rodari (1920–1980), an Italian writer and journalist, most famous for his works of children's literature and his metaphors for cognition.
(Cognition and Conation)

Paul Michael Romer, an American economist at the NYU Stern School of Business, Department of Economics, and School of Law. He is also the co-recipient of the Nobel Memorial Prize in Economic Sciences (shared with William Nordhaus) in 2018 for his contributions to endogenous growth theory.
(Ideation)

Franklin Delano Roosevelt (1882–1945), an American politician who served as the 32nd President of the United States. During the Great Depression, he built the New Deal Coalition.
(Experimental laboratory)

Wilhelm Conrad Röntgen (1845–1923), a German physicist who was a recipient of the first Nobel Prize for Physics, in 1901, for his discovery of X-rays, which heralded the age of modern physics and revolutionised diagnostic medicine. (Discovery and Invention)

Bertrand Russell (1872–1970), a British polymath, exponent of the peace movement and Nobel laureate. (Reimagined and Ludic Schools), (Useful and Useless Knowledge)

Giovanni Francesco Sagredo (1571–1620), a Venetian mathematician and close friend of Galileo. (Craftsmen, 'Merchants of Light'), (Speed)

Jerome David Salinger (1919–2010), the author of *The Catcher in the Rye*, the boy who hated school as it was. (Child)

Filippo Salviati, a scientist and astronomer from a noble Florentine family. He championed Galileo's Copernican ideas. (Speed)

George Santayana (1863–1952), a philosopher, essayist, poet and novelist. (Inventive Entrepreneurs and Incremental Innovators)

AnnaLee Saxenian, Dean of the UC Berkeley School of Information, known for her work on technology clusters and social networks in Silicon Valley. (Brain Circulation)

Morton Schapiro, the president of Northwestern University and a Professor of Economics. (Tales)

Friedrich Schiller (1759–1805), a German playwright, poet and philosopher. Schiller sees in the player the fully human being. (Reimagined and Ludic Schools)

Howard D. Schultz, an American businessman. He served as the chairman and chief executive officer (CEO) of the Starbucks Coffee Company. (Fictions: The Coffee Red Thread)

Ernst Schumacher (1911–1977), the advocate of 'Small is beautiful'.

Klaus Martin Schwab, a German engineer and economist best known as the founder and executive chairman of the World Economic Forum (Talent)

Duns Scotus (c. 1265/66–1308), a Scottish Catholic priest and Franciscan friar, university professor, philosopher and theologian.
(Open Innovation)

Lucius Anneus Seneca (4 BC–65), a philosopher and innovative writer of the *Letters to Lucilius*.
(Happiness)

Robert Sennett, the founding director of the New York Institute for the Humanities.
(Digital Craftsmen)

Ludovico Maria Sforza, also known as Ludovico il Moro (1452–1508), an Italian Renaissance nobleman who ruled as Duke of Milan from 1494. He was famed as a patron of Leonardo da Vinci and presided over the final and most productive stage of the Milanese Renaissance.
(Science and Art)

Steven Shapin, an American historian and sociologist of science. He is the Franklin L. Ford Research Professor of the History of Science at Harvard University.
(Pure and Applied Research)

Ruchir Sharma, head of the Emerging Markets Equity team at Morgan Stanley Investment Management.
(Great Government Versus Big Government)

Michael Sharratt, the author of *Galileo: Decisive Innovator*.
(Speed)

Hu Shih (1891–1962), a poet and philosopher, leader of the 'New Cultural Movement' in China in the 1910s.
(New Cultural Movement)

Hiroshi Shimizu, a life systems researcher, who further developed the concept of 'Ba'.

Prince Shōtoku, also known as Prince Umayado or Prince Kamitsumiya (574–622), a semi-legendary regent and a politician of the Asuka period in Japan who served under Empress Suiko.
(Cognitive and Emotional Conflict)

Siegfried, figure from the heroic literature of the ancient Germanic people.
(Nibelungs)

Tom Siegfried, the former Editor-in-Chief of *Science News* and the author of three books: *The Bit and the Pendulum*, *Strange Matters* and *A Beautiful Math*.
(Anti-discipline)

Igor Sikorski (1889–1972), the engineer who built the first working helicopter, drawing on the future of flight predicted by Jules Verne (1828–1905).
(Imagination)

Herbert Alexander Simon (1916–2001), an American economist, political scientist and cognitive psychologist, best known for the theories of 'bounded rationality' and 'satisficing'.
(Project: A 'Promising Monster')

Adam Smith (1723–1790), a Scottish economist, a moral philosopher, a pioneer of political economy and a key figure during the Scottish Enlightenment, also known as 'The Father of Economics' or 'The Father of Capitalism'.
(Altruism), (Craftsmen, 'Merchants of Light'), (Great Government Versus Big Government), (Manufacture), (Regard Multiplier)

Charles C. Snow, an American professor who has been at Penn State University since 1974. He is a Fellow of the Academy of Management.
(Networks)

Charles Percy Snow (1905–1980), an English novelist and physical chemist. He is best known for *The Two Cultures and a Second Look*, a 1959 lecture in which he laments the gulf between scientists and 'literary intellectuals'.
('STEAM')

Socrates (c. 470–399 BCE), a Greek philosopher from Athens who is credited as one of the founders of Western philosophy. He argued about creative decisions.
(Creative Ignorance)

Rob van der Spek, Head of department advisory services Energy systems at DNV, Netherlands.
(Knowledge and Information)

André Spijkervet, Managing Partner, Inner Ragility, Amsterdam.
(Knowledge and Information)

Tom Standage, a British journalist, author of *The Victorian Internet* and *A History of the World in 6 Glasses*.
(Fictions: The Coffee Red Thread)

Xenia Stanford, President, Stanford Solutions and Editor-in-Chief, KnowMap.
(Knowledge Map)

Neal Town Stephenson, an American writer known for his works of speculative fiction.
(Imagination)

Al (formerly Alan) Stewart, a process artist, facilitator of conversations that matter.
(Conversation)

Peter Sunley, a professor of Geography, Southampton University.
(Path Dependency)

Albert Szent-Györgyi (1893–1986), a Hungarian biochemist who won the Nobel Prize in Physiology or Medicine in 1937. He is credited with first isolating vitamin C.
(Discovery and Invention)

William Sturgeon (1783–1850), an English physicist and inventor who made the first electromagnets.
(Open Innovation)

Shunryu Suzuki (1904–1971), author of *Zen Mind, Beginner's Mind.*
(Expert)

Karl-Erik Sveiby, one of the founding fathers of Knowledge Management.
(Knowledge and Information)

Jonathan Swift (1667–1745), an Anglo-Irish satirist, essayist, political pamphleteer. Forerunner of crowdfunding.
(Crowdfunding e Crowdsourcing), (Gulliver's watch)

Publius Cornelius Tacitus (c. AD 56–c. 120), a Roman historian and politician.
(Incrementalist)

Nassim Nicholas Taleb, a Lebanese-American essayist, scholar, mathematical statistician.
(Fragilista)

Hirotaka Takeuchi, a Professor of Management Practice in the Strategy Unit at Harvard Business School, known for influencing business practices worldwide.
(Explicit and Tacit Knowledge)

Nassim Nicholas Taleb, a Lebanese-American essayist, scholar, mathematical statistician.

Shotaro Tani, a Nikkei staff writer.
(Reimagined and Ludic Schools)

George Tansley (1871–1955), a botanist and pioneer of ecology. He is credited with introducing the term 'ecosystem'.
(Ecosystem)

Tiziano Terzani (1938–2004) was an Italian journalist and writer, best known for his extensive knowledge of twentieth-century East Asia.
(Reimagined and Ludic Schools)

Margaret Hilda Thatcher (1925–2013), a British stateswoman who served as Prime Minister of the United Kingdom. She implemented policies that became known as Thatcherism, a belief in free markets and a small state.
(Great Government Versus Big Government).

Sara Margaret Thornton, a Professor of English and Cultural Studies at the Université Paris Diderot.
(Tales)

Lev Nikolayevich Tolstoy (1828–1910), a Russian writer, best known for the novels *War and Peace* and *Anna Karenina*.
(Coopetition), (Tales)

Arnold Toynbee (1852–1883), a British economic historian to whom the expression 'Industrial Revolution' is attributed.
(Knowledge Growth)

Alfonsus Trompenaars, a Dutch organisational theorist.
(Coopetition), (Knowledge and Information)

Anne Robert Jacques Turgot (1727–1781), a French economist and statesman; an early advocate for economic liberalism.
(Happiness)

Joseph Mallord William Turner (1775–1851), an English Romantic painter, printmaker and watercolourist.
(Inventive Entrepreneurs and Incremental Innovators)

Steve Tyler, an American songwriter and musician.
(Cooperation)

Laura D'Andrea Tyson (1947), an American economist and former Chair of the US President's Council of Economic Advisers during the Clinton Administration.
(Competitiveness and Productivity)

Lao Tzu, an ancient Chinese philosopher. He is the founder of philosophical Taoism and a deity in religious Taoism and traditional Chinese religions.
(Open Innovation)

Jennifer Sheila Uglow, a British biographer, historian, critic and publisher.
(Science and Art)

Luigi Valeriani (1758–1828), an Italian economist; scholar of the organisation of technical education.
(Brain Circulation)

Wayne Van Dyck, an investment banker and venture capitalist. He was the founder/CEO of the first utility wind energy developer, Windfarms Ltd.
(Vespa)

Christina Van Houten, the founder of Women at Work. Based in Boston
(Open Innovation)

Giorgio Vasari (1511–1574), an Italian multifaceted scholar, forerunner of art history and criticism.
(Science and Art)

Thorstein Bunde Veblen (1857–1929), an American economist and sociologist. A well-known critic of capitalism.

Johannes Vermeer (1632–1675), a Dutch Baroque Period painter. *The Geographer*, one of his evocative paintings, suggests a path creator.
(Path Creators)

Jules Verne (1828–1905), a French writer. He is one of the most important authors of children's stories and thanks to his scientific novels is considered, together with H. G. Wells, the father of modern science fiction.
(Imagination)

Virgil, Publius Vergilius Maro (70 BC. 19 BC), an ancient Roman poet of the Augustan period.
(Open Innovation)

Voltaire, pseudonym of François-Marie Arouet Le June (1694–1778), an encyclopaedist of the Age of Enlightenment, also known as the 'Age of Voltaire'.
(Conversation), (Fictions: The Coffee Red Thread)

Graham Wallas (1858–1932), an English social psychologist and educationalist; co-founder of the London School of Economics and forerunner of the creativity theory.
(Creative Thinking)

Horace Walpole (1717–1797), an English man of letters and Whig politician.
(Serendipity)

James Watson, an American molecular biologist, geneticist and zoologist. In 1953, he co-authored with Francis Crick the academic paper proposing the double helix structure of the DNA molecule.

James Watt (1736–1819), a Scottish mechanical engineer and chemist who improved on Thomas Newcomen's 1712 Newcomen steam engine with his Watt steam engine in 1776, a source of useable economic power.
(Knowledge Growth), (Lunar Society)

Josiah Wedgwood (1730–1795), an English entrepreneur famous for the ceramics that bear his name.
(Lunar Society)

Horace Wells (1815–1848), an American dentist who pioneered the use of anesthesia in dentistry.
(Discovery and Invention)

Étienne Charles Wenger, an educational theorist and practitioner, best known for his work in the field of communities of practice.
(Communities of Knowledge Practice)

William Wickenden (1882–1947), the third president of Case School of Applied Science. He oversaw the name change transition of Case School of Applied Science to Case Institute of Technology.
(University-Industry Cooperation)

Robin McLaurin Williams (1951–2014), one of the best comedians of all time.
(Ideation)

Edward Osborne Wilson, an American biologist; founder of the socio-biology research programme.
(Anti-discipline)

David Sloan Wilson, an American evolutionary biologist.
(Altruism)

Stephen Gary Wozniak, an American electronics engineer, computer programmer, philanthropist and technology entrepreneur. In 1976, he co-founded Apple Inc.
(Disrupter)

Ronald Wright, a Canadian author who has written books of travel, history and fiction.
(Conservative and Innovative Leaders)

Jinping Xi, the paramount leader of China, the most prominent political leader in China, since 2012.
(Fu Xing)

Lee Kuan Yew (1923–2015), a Singaporean statesman and lawyer who served as Prime Minister of Singapore from 1959 to 1990.
(Seigniories of the Twenty-first Century)

Muhammad Yunus (1940), Nobel Peace Prize for founding the Grameen Bank and pioneering the concepts of microcredit and microfinance.
(Crowdfunding e Crowdsourcing)

Zeno of Elea (c. 495 BC–430 BC), a pre-Socratic Greek philosopher of Magna Graecia, inventor of dialectic (according to Aristotle).
(Inventive Entrepreneurs and Incremental Innovators)

Stefan Zweig (1881–1942), an Austrian novelist, playwright, journalist and biographer.
(Passion for Innovating)

The protagonists of the quest for quality in the order in which they appear in the text:
William Edwards Deming (1900–1993)
Joseph M. Juran (1904–2008)
Armand V. Feigenbaum (1920–2014)
Kaoru Ishikawa (1915–1989)
Genichi Taguchi (1924–2012)
Shineo Shingō (1909–1990)
Philip B. Crosby (1926–2001)
Tom Peters
Claus Møller
(Quality)

Afterword

Ideation and Exploring and Mapping the Unknown

Alan Barrell

It is the year 2021 and I am in enforced isolation in Cambridge, UK. The enforcer, my government is effectively under orders from a virus – COVID-19. An unseen, microscopic entity – some say not quite a living thing – which has devastated our wonderful knowledge filled world. Globally, we are in retreat from an organism so basic, compared with ourselves that there is no way to compare. Everything we know collectively has been of no avail. And yet – for the future hope has sprung – not from what we knew or had capability to do – but through a collective admission – that perhaps if we explored the realms of what we do not know – or even do not know the extent of what we might not know – we might save us from ourselves. The means whereby vaccines have been developed so fast to counter the COVID-19 pandemic owe much to a species of entrepreneurial thinking that admits to the value of ignorance as a possible starting point. What a wonderfully coincidental surprise to receive today, information about new thoughts from my mentor about Creative Ignorance, Professor Piero Formica. I am looking forward to the time when with the engagement of students from around the world we may see stimulated the writing and publication of a collection of pieces focussed on the title 'MAPS OF THE UNKOWN – Creative Ignorance in the Quest for a Better World'. In the meantime we can enjoy a feast of forward-looking narrative and re-imagination on the subject of those who venture into unexplored territories of the mind and 'IDEATE' – what a wonderful new word. Ideation – 'Creation in the mind'.

Piero Formica, resident now in Bologna, but of international renown and, amongst other things, Founder of the International Entrepreneurship Academy, challenges us in the words just read, to stir ourselves from any incipient lethargy of mind and journey with him along pathways new, as he did with earlier writings such as *Stories of Innovation for the Millennial Generation.* Today Piero's student and academic followers are many and some, from Nigeria, India, the Gulf Countries, Estonia, Sweden, and Italy are joining forces to push further the boundaries of his outrageous propositions about Creative Ignorance. Outrageous is here used as a complimentary descriptive. Like disruptive, it conjures in the minds of some, negative concerns and anxiety. But outrage and disruption have been essential in moving the mountains of conventional wisdom that so often have been barriers to progress and enlightenment. It was once believed the world was flat and imprisonment or death could result from expressing a contrary view – even if the thinker such as Galileo – should be the perpetrator. Brilliant physician William Harvey, in the seventeenth century, delayed writing about his work on the human circulatory system – life-changing new knowledge – for fear of persecution. Indeed, long after he described and proved his theories – those wedded to the mistaken earlier beliefs that we had two circulatory mechanisms – not one – argued for his insanity and some threatened to end his life. We could find many more examples.

It is exciting and heartening that a movement is now abroad vocal and gaining momentum – inspired by Piero's thought provoking and philosophical prose. Path creators who are Ideators change the world. Often at great pains to themselves whilst on the journey. Ignaz Philippe Semmelweis was driven mad in the nineteenth century, years after proving that the terrible toll of deaths in Viennese hospitals from childbed fever could be all but eliminated if those clever doctors would just wash their hands in between examining the unfortunate mothers recently delivered of healthy babies. His reward for his work and discoveries was to become a derided outcast – eventually driven to insanity. His tragedy which proved one of the greatest realisations in medical science – the definition of sepsis and infectious disease – exemplifies unfortunately the reward awaiting many who may be described as 'the creative ignorant'. Ideators must face challenge and derision. They offer disturbing and troubling thoughts and directions which militate against the comfortable and the ordinary.

Entrepreneurs are Ideators and they have changed the world. I despair that the term is so narrowly applied. Often apportioned to those who start companies and make fortunes (or fail to). Entrepreneurial thinking to Piero – and to others amongst us is so much more. Quoting from earlier words of wisdom I have read from Piero and others – I feel much more able to identify with entrepreneurs as those who 'By choosing the journey along the road less travelled, path creators make huge changes in their personal lives and in the industries that they disrupt by their ideas'.

It is immensely encouraging to look forward, having seen so far, only review copies of some of the work recently generated by Piero and his students and associates in addition to this current work. I have been given glimpses of re-imaginings and new pathways to be mapped and explored as a result of this movement inspired by thoughts outrageous and disruptive. The COVID-19 pandemic is not something any of us would wish upon any world or age. But it has shaken conventional wisdom and behaviour and forced new thinking and the admission of relative ignorance. It will lead to drastic changes in behaviour as well as thinking. When risk becomes a norm, most of us undergo change – knowing or unknowing. To have a collection of next generation thinkers from a variety of cultural backgrounds – leading our thoughts on Creative Ignorance and the discipline of Ideation, is exciting – and to explore with younger minds 'the unknown unknowns' might be revelatory. Not only do we have the 'wisdom of ages' in these present thoughts and words of Piero Formica, but the promise of next-generation followers inspired to commit imagination to expressions in words we can all share.

In my own experience, as an octogenarian, and one very close to medicine and medical practice and research and the healthcare industry, it has been exhilarating to see mindsets and approaches changed in the quest for life-saving solutions to desperate and dire human suffering and circumstances. Regulatory mechanisms and reservations have been overcome by openness to innovation and acceptance that the unthinkable may in extremis be thought and acted upon. Such a pity it takes the fear of more deaths to enable the immense potential of the human brain to be exercised with constructive abandon. But I see it happening around me today. Which is not to say that ignorance is all, nor that a lack of organised thinking is obsolete or to be abandoned. I believe that Ideation and the recognition of the value of Creative Ignorance can live alongside the wise observations of such as Jules Verne – who emphasised the importance of timing when he wrote '*There is nothing in the whole world more powerful than an idea whose time has come*'. Creative Ignorance can be the generator of such ideas – without which action may not take place at any time. I can also reconcile my belief in the importance of the well-trained mind and mental processes to be important alongside the need for Ideation – and the proposition of another great and different French thinker, scientist, Louis Pasteur – who emphasised that '*Chance favours the prepared mind*'. The words of an Ideator indeed.

As 2021 proceeds to sweep away the trauma and sadness of 2020 it is encouraging to be able to look forward to the surprises I expect to be awaiting us in future publications. The great early explorers produced maps to chart their journeys and to enable others to follow where the path creators had preceded. I love the concept of capture of word maps describing prospective new territories. 'Maps of the Unknown' would be a great topic and title for publications exploring these exciting unexplored territories. And all of this in a quest for a Better World. My hope is that we will all be challenged by the provocative and open-minded expressions I anticipate will be presented to us in such exciting publications. For the present we have a great deal to think about having been stimulated by '*Ideators: Their Words and Voices*'.

Index